Content 10x

More Content, Less Time
Maximum Results

Amy Woods

Published by Content 10x Media 2019
ISBN: 978-1-9161811-1-3

For Charlie & Jake

Foreword

I first met Amy in February 2017 when she attended a 1-day mastermind that I was running in London. At the time she was completely unknown to me - she'd reached out by email with a new business idea which had piqued my interest. So, we added another seat at the table to allow this super-keen lady to attend.

Amy turned up with the idea for a content repurposing business that she'd named Content 10x, seeking validation of the concept. In her 1-hour hot seat she impressed me and the other attendees with her preparation, sharp delivery and zest to bring her content repurposing business to life. I remember feeling excited for her, as she seemed to have not only identified a genuine problem that existed, but more importantly a solution to that problem. She left with the positive validation she needed to bring the concept to life.

Fast forward two years and she has become a globally recognized authority on content repurposing and is asked to speak on stages around the world on the topic.

Her knowledge of content repurposing is second to none, and the business that she has established goes way beyond just being helpful. Amy has so much to share on the topic of content repurposing. She's seen it all, done it all, walks the walk, talks the talk, and now she has quite literally written the book!

So why read this book?

Content marketing is the only marketing left that actually works. There, I said it! As a serial entrepreneur, speaker, author and business coach, I've worked with thousands of people who are creating content to grow their business. I myself am a podcaster, vlogger and blogger, and as a thought leader who helps entrepreneurs become the go-to leader in their industry, creating highly valuable, original content is the driving force behind almost everything I do as the founder of youpreneur.com on a daily basis.

What I love about this book is that it's a fluff-free, detail packed and action focused guide to reaching more people online with your content. It's the kind of book that you read, you implement, and you get results.

As you devour page after page, you'll see that Amy brings to the table an uncanny knack of helping others to break their problems down, and then implement solutions in simple and strategic ways. She takes many of the problems associated with content marketing and repurposing, and shows you exactly how you can overcome them, step by step, tool by tool.

Since that initial meeting in 2017, Amy has been a member of my Youpreneur community, as well as my inner circle 'Round Table' mastermind, so I've worked with her closely and got to know her very well. I've even become a Content 10x client myself!

I truly believe that this book will be a game-changer for many.

If you're in the business of creating content - whether you're a podcaster, blogger, vlogger, you run a membership, put on live events - whatever content you create, you need to read this book. Doing so will help you to never again fail to achieve the full value from your content.

Chris Ducker

Founder - Youpreneur.com

August 2019

Contents

PART 4: Making Content Repurposing Manageable With Systems & Processes

PART 5: Next Steps & Resources

IMPLEMENT WHAT YOU LEARN IN THE BOOK TODAY!

The Content 10x Toolkit equips you with templates, tools, videos, processes, swipe files and more...so that you can repurpose your content, reach more people, and grow your business

Head to **www.content10x.com/toolkit** to find out more

PART 1

An Introduction To Content Repurposing

CHAPTER 1

What is content repurposing?

Imagine a world where Spiderman had never evolved beyond Stan Lee's comic books. Without the blockbuster movies, childhood TV shows, computer games, toys, merchandise or book, think how many people would have missed out on getting to know their hero 'Spidey'.

What if Walt Disney had stuck with cartoon animations? Without Disneyland, The Disney Channel and Disney Stores, millions of children would have missed out on his magical stories.

And how about Victor Hugo's Les Misérables? Without the stage show and TV and film adaptations of this 19th century French novel, few would know this powerful tale of redemption and loss.

Had these iconic stories not been repurposed into multiple formats, millions of people would be completely unaware of their existence.

And it's exactly the same with your content.

If you are only sharing your content in one format, e.g. as a podcast episode, blog post or YouTube video, thousands - millions even - of people could be missing out on your message.

Most content creators recognize that to reach their intended audience they need to be present on multiple platforms. It's very easy to get lost deciding where to begin, or become inconsistent when you run out of time, leaving you stressed and exasperated.

It's time for this to stop.

With the right mindset, systems and processes (plus some ninja tricks) you can maximize the potential of every piece of content you create.

This process is known as content repurposing and will allow you to connect with a bigger audience than you ever thought possible.

If this sounds good, then buckle up and get ready to learn how to harness the power of content repurposing.

Let's start with the content

When I tell my friends and family that I'm an expert in content repurposing, that I run a creative agency that creates and manages content, they often don't quite understand what that means: "What do you mean by content?" and "what sort of content?"

So, before we set off on our journey to discover how to repurpose content like a pro, it's worth pausing for a moment, not just to define what content *repurposing* is, but also what *content* is too.

In marketing terms, 'content' is simply a message or information, packaged up in a particular format, to reach its intended audience.

Content marketing is a form of marketing that is focused on sharing information and messages. It's about adding value and it's about storytelling. Content marketing is more about your audience than it is about you. By sharing content with your audience that will benefit them you're also subtly stimulating an interest in you and your products or services. Content marketing is a long game but ultimately it's about developing a relationship with your audience. Content marketing builds trust and that's what converts a browser to a lead, and ultimately to a customer.

Content comes in many forms and can vary wildly in terms of usefulness, relevance and quality!

Blog posts, eBooks, YouTube videos, vlogs, social media posts, articles, white papers, press releases, published books, livestreams, webinars, seminars, live events, online events, infographics, presentations. All of these can be classed as "content"; because they're all communicating a message to an intended audience.

Now we're agreed on what content it is, it's time to consider content repurposing.

Content repurposing is about getting the maximum return from every single piece of content you create. Content repurposing can take many forms, and there are lots of different and creative ways that you can repurpose your content, but every content creator must repurpose.

For example, you might record a video, turn the audio into a podcast, use a number of short clips to create audio/video trailers, then turn the transcript of your video into a blog post and so on.

Repurposing is not just about reaching more people - part of its power is that it gives you the opportunity to communicate with people in the way that they *want* to be communicated with, in the places where they already hang out. It enhances your chances of connecting with your audience. When you establish a connection you're more likely to convert leads to sales.

But for many people, content repurposing can feel like a chore. If it feels like something you should do more of or don't do enough, please feel reassured you are not alone.

For some reason content repurposing seems to be the one thing that almost every content creator knows that they *should* do more of, but they simply don't. In fact, instead of repurposing their existing content, many simply keep creating more and more new content. And yes, you should be doing this, but you don't always have to reinvent the wheel.

The desire to produce more new content reminds me of an early digital marketing course I took, a few years back. It pushed the idea of writing a blog post and emailing your subscribers every day. When digital marketing was in its infancy this might have been an approach that delivered results, but today with content over-saturation, I am firmly of the view that developing a handful of high-quality ideas each month and socializing these properly will win over a volume strategy nine times out of ten.

When you repurpose your content you put rocket fuel on it. It's a content marketing strategy that simply shouldn't be ignored because the majority of the hard work has already been done. You owe it to yourself, your content and your audience to repurpose.

Content repurposing is not 'copy and paste'

Let's dispel another myth. Content repurposing is not limited to copying and pasting the same content in a bid to republish that content in different places. You *can* do this, and it's often not a bad idea, but repurposing goes so much further than republishing.

It's about being imaginative and creative with the content that you have already created so that it can be used in different ways.

Many types of content can be repurposed. Often when we talk about content repurposing we talk about repurposing a blog post, a podcast episode or video but it doesn't stop there.

Perhaps you have written a substantial post on LinkedIn, recorded a Facebook Live video or created oodles of membership site content? All of these types of content can be repurposed into different formats and for different uses.

In other words, content that can be repurposed can be anything that you create and share in order to inform, educate and/or entertain others. In part 2 of this book I share lots of ideas, tips, and tricks for repurposing all forms of content. The key thing is that you continue to add value to your audience.

Repurposing is not just a content thing

Imagine if J.K. Rowling had stopped with the Harry Potter books. There would be no Harry Potter films, theme park, merchandise or spin off books and films.

When you think about what repurposing is, it's taking something that has already been created and then working out ways to maximize the value and the potential. You want to ensure that all of the hard work that went into creating it doesn't go to waste – the more unconstrained your thinking is, the better, as we'll see later in the book.

I'm currently watching *The Walking Dead*, which started as a comic book and was later repurposed into a TV series.

Architects are continually repurposing buildings. For example, repurposing a power station into an art gallery (Tate Modern, London) or repurposing old disused warehouses into a rave venue or fabulous apartments. So much good can come out of repurposing!

It's critical to embrace the idea that your repurposed content may have more impact than the original

Many people assume that nothing will ever be as good as that first/original piece of content. It becomes a flagship piece of content, and nothing can knock it down from its pedestal, right? Wrong!

When you repurpose your content, your repurposed content should not be seen as the 'seconds' of the original content, it should stand alone as valuable content.

There may even be occasions where your repurposed content proves to be more effective and impactful than the original piece of content it was repurposed from. That's okay!

In fact, instead of thinking that the original piece of content is where you have expressed your thoughts and opinions in the best light, consider this ... What if that original piece of content is *not* your finest hour? What if your finest hour is yet to come in the way that you repurpose your content?

Let me share a few real-life examples of where *great* things have come from repurposed content because the people who created it were able to see beyond the original content, to create something even more exceptional.

Dom Pérignon - Wine into champagne

Dom Pérignon was a French Benedictine monk from the 17th century. He is known for pioneering a variety of winemaking techniques and it was his forward thinking that led him to look beyond the existing wine they produced to see its real potential.

So the story goes, the problem with the wine was the fact that it was quite bubbly. The bubbles were a sign of poor-quality and something that winemakers didn't want to see. Instead of getting rid of the spoiled batch of wine and starting over again, Dom Pérignon experimented with different blending techniques, and thus champagne was born!

This is a perfect example of someone who was able to see beyond the original to discover something even more precious.

In the same way, we can shift our mindset and start to consider the possibility that our original piece of content may be repurposed into spectacular, wonderful, 'bubbly' new content!

Stephen King - Novel into movie

Have you ever heard of Stephen King's book, *Different Seasons*? If you're a fan of the famous horror writer, chances are you have it on your bookshelf or Kindle library but if you're not that familiar with his work, you've probably never heard of it.

Different Seasons is a collection of short stories and although it's not as popular as say, *The Shining*, it yielded two very well-known movies: *The Shawshank Redemption* and *Stand By Me.*

Shawshank Redemption is based on *Rita Hayworth and Shawshank Redemption*, the first novella in *Different Seasons* while *Stand By Me* is based on the third story, *The Body.*

This is another prime example of content that has been repurposed into something much bigger and more successful than the original piece of content. Both of those films are fantastic - in my opinion. I have watched them more times than I can remember!

Pareto Principle - The 80/20 rule

Another excellent example of repurposed content that took on a life of its own is the Pareto Principle, otherwise known as the 80/20 Rule.

An Italian economist called Vilfredo Pareto published the paper, *Cours d'economie politique* in 1896, based on the fact that 20% of the population owned around 80% of the land in Italy.

This is where the 80/20 rule originated, but how many of us have actually read the original paper? I'm betting not many! And yet, you've probably still heard of the 80/20 rule. You might have even said "80/20" in some way, shape or form in your life perhaps?! How did this happen?

Well, the original writer did a lot of lectures and public speaking and other people listened to his idea and spread the word. Throughout the years, the Pareto Principle has gained further exposure and worldwide recognition thanks to word of mouth.

People took Pareto's original paper and theory and repurposed it into something much greater. Nowadays, we talk about the 80/20 rule in business, marketing and management without any real link to the original paper that Pareto wrote, all the way back in 1896.

Pareto's paper wasn't what gave him international acclaim, but rather the first stepping stone that his content took towards greatness.

Pareto's story is the perfect example of the power of socializing our ideas (aka. repurposing!). Repurposing and repackaging an original message and adding even more value to it with the new form of content.

Always look for ways to add more value

With everything you create, you should always try to add value by expanding one piece of content into a new piece and then adding even more value to your original idea or concept.

You should also look at opportunities to add more impact and a little edge - I dare you to try! Take your blog post or podcast to a live audience on Facebook or Instagram for example. Or, take it to a live Twitter chat. Invite people with opposing viewpoints to you. Bring in a little bit of a debate.

There are so many different ways that you can repurpose your original message and that's what it's all about. Not so much repurposing content but rather repackaging a message.

You have a message that you have communicated in one way. How can you communicate that same message in different ways to reach and connect with more people? Sometimes the first piece of content you create is just the beginning, with something even more fantastic to come!

CHAPTER 2

Connecting with your audience

It's important to remember that different people are going to connect with you in different ways. This means that if you create just one original piece of content to communicate your message, such as a video, a podcast episode, a live talk, or a blog post, you limit your content's potential to connect with a large group of people.

Repurposing and repackaging your original piece of content can help you to connect with a broader audience.

Our brains work differently

Have you ever had someone try to teach you something and you just don't get it. Finally, they draw it out visually and you have your 'ah-ha' moment?

Or maybe you've read and re-read (and re-read!) something and you just can't understand it, but once you've talked it through with someone out loud, it starts to make sense?

That's because how easy or how difficult we find it to grasp information can often depend on our preferred learning style.

Learning styles are highly relevant to the world of content creation

We all learn things in different ways because our brains are wired differently. Each of us tend to have one preferred way of learning over another, and that can vary depending on the situation too.

For example, when I'm trying to learn something physical like a new exercise in the gym, I need to watch someone else doing it. In a situation like this just telling me what to do or asking me to read the instructions would not work very well.

In contrast, if I'm learning to cook something from a new recipe, I much prefer to read and re-read exactly what to do and learn the recipe in that way. On this occasion, I consume the information better if written down as opposed to if I watch someone doing a demonstration.

I can think of other examples where for me, my preferred learning style varies depending on what I'm learning but we're also all very different as human beings. My preferred learning style for one particular circumstance can be very different to yours.

For example, when I was on a skiing holiday in France last year, one of the hotel staff members told me that he was learning to snowboard. I naturally assumed that, like me, he'd be up on the slopes being taught by an instructor. However, he informed me that he was teaching himself. How was he doing this? By watching YouTube videos!

Yes, trusty old YouTube. He was watching 'how to snowboard' videos back at the hotel in the evening, and then going and applying what he'd learnt on the slopes the next day. I could never have done this. When I learnt how to ski I needed someone right in front of me showing me, allowing me to try and copy what they were doing.

How is this relevant to your content?

At the heart of any content strategy, what most of us are trying to do is add value to our audience. We can enhance just how much value we add by making it easy for our audience to consume our content.

Repurposing your content can play a key role in helping you to convey your message in a way that suits the multitude of learning styles that will be present in your audience. Varying your approach gives you a better chance of creating content learning styles that suit more people.

If you create content in a non-preferred learning style for someone it doesn't mean that they *won't* consume your content or understand it, they just need to work a bit harder. For example, someone who prefers to learn by listening will have to work a little harder to understand your message if the only content you create is a written blog. However, if you have a podcast or even just an audio file on your website, you're making it easier for that person to connect with your message.

What are the learning styles you need to cater for?

When I researched the learning styles I found multiple schools of thought on just how many styles there are. However, most commonly they're categorized into the following seven learning styles:

- **Visual** - learning from pictures, images, charts, photos, slideshows and animations
- **Aural** - these learners prefer sound; music, podcasts and audiobooks
- **Verbal** - people in this category will enjoy discussion. Online this can come from Facebook Lives, webinars, live Q&A sessions and groups

- **Physical** - this is a difficult one for online content as it normally means touch, being hands-on etc. but this can be somewhat aided online via, for example, a detailed (maybe printable) step-by-step guide that brings things to life or gamification

- **Logical** - these learners enjoy data, so we can try to provide charts, structured blogs and infographics to attract them

- **Social/interpersonal** - people who like to learn in groups so it's possible to appeal to them with forums, group Skype calls, face-to-face events etc.

- **Solitary** - this subset like to learn alone so are more likely to sign-up for online courses and online membership sites

What role does content repurposing play?

You're probably wondering how on Earth you can please all of these different kinds of learners?!? Well, the answer is it's not easy (and fortunately, not necessary all of the time) but content repurposing can really help.

When we talk about content repurposing we often talk about being in more than one place to find and reach new audiences. Content repurposing can also be about finding different ways to communicate the same message.

Essentially, we could say that it helps us to accommodate different learning styles

When you create your content, try to always have in mind which learning style the content that you're creating is best suited for. Then, when you are looking for ways to repurpose your content, try and consider what *different* learning styles you could cater to.

As an example, my podcast is perfectly suited for aural

learners. I also write a blog post about the same topic, and I create images/graphics, and very often I'll create a short video too. Through repurposing my podcast, my content lends itself well to visual learners and in many cases the logical learners too.

Next time you create a piece of content and you want to repurpose it, stop! Think about the learning style that your original content best lends itself to, then think about a new learning style that you'd like to reach. By doing this, you're making your content easier to consume for more people.

If someone is able to consume your message with minimal effort, they will pay more attention. They'll learn. They'll remember. They'll love it. They'll share it. And they may become a customer - and that is an absolute win-win for everyone!

To see this in action, read the section on repurposing Live video in chapter seven.

CHAPTER 3

Repurposing content & the impact on your business

Content marketing is essential for many businesses. Creating free content for your audience that will inform, educate or entertain them will help you build trust and really connect with your audience. Done well, content marketing really pays off.

By way of example, let's imagine you're looking for an architect to help draw up plans for an extension on your house. You find two local architects after searching on Google.

Architect number one has a very simple website, it's more like an online brochure. There's contact information and a short explanation of who he is, a couple of testimonials and a contact page. That's it. Could be worth a phone call?

Architect number two has all the usual features that you would expect from a website - and so much more! He has a blog with article after article about working with architects, how to plan for home extensions, advice on challenges you will face and so on. He has a few downloadable guides and super useful checklists, and he has videos from his YouTube channel where he's sharing examples of the projects that he's worked on.

Who are you more likely to call? Who do you already feel like you can trust to do a good job? Who do you feel like you know before you've even met them? Architect number two of course!

Whilst content marketing can often feel like more of a long game, that's actually a benefit and not a drawback – think of it as investing in an asset. Your content is always online, always searchable and you never know when it's going to pay off ten-fold. The reality is, you *can* ignore content marketing, but always be aware that your competitors may not!

Still not convinced? Here are the stats from one study on content marketing versus traditional marketing:[1]

- 70% of consumers would rather get to know a company through articles than advertisements.
- 85% of B2B buyers believe that companies should share useful information through social media.
- 90% of people say that informative or instructional videos are helpful in the purchasing process.
- 33% of people on the internet find digital displays ads "completely intolerable"
- 54% of people won't click on banner ads because they don't trust them.

Five reasons why you should repurpose your content

You're probably already sold on the concept of content marketing, if nothing other than by virtue of the fact you're reading this book! You value the importance of creating great content.

I hope I've made a good case that creating great content isn't enough. You need to have a strategy for managing your content. Content repurposing simply *must* feature within your

1 https://landerapp.com/blog/content-vs-traditional-marketing/

overall content strategy. And that's where this book comes in.

Five reasons why you must repurpose your content:

1. Increase your audience reach

Content repurposing puts your content in front of new and different audiences. If you only ever create podcast episodes then how do you reach people who never listen to podcasts? Currently seven out of ten Americans don't regularly or ever listen to podcasts (Edison Research 2019).

If you only ever create written content, how do you reach people who hate to read? If you only ever put content on your own website, how do you reach people who are never going to just stumble upon your website?

The fact is, you are going to increase your audience reach if you repurpose your content into different formats and publish it in different locations. Increasing your audience reach = more conversations with people.

Conversations ultimately lead to conversions

2. It helps you get found by the search engines

Never underestimate the importance of SEO (search engine optimization). When we want to know anything new these days what is the first thing we do? We head to a search engine!

The term SEO can strike fear into many of us. It can be a confusing and overwhelming topic, but don't worry, you don't need a Ph.D. in SEO-ology (or a huge pot of cash and the services of a SEO consultant) to be able to understand the basics and help your content get found!

In basic terms, SEO focuses on your webpages' "organic" rankings on popular search engines such as Google. You can't buy these rankings. The placements are earned through using SEO effectively and this makes a big difference when it comes to people finding your content. It is important to remember that only a web page will rank on Google. Your website as a whole will never rank.

There are three main factors that affect SEO and why a web page will rank:

i. Authority (Links)

Your webpage must have sufficient credibility within the search engine to be considered a useful page on your chosen topic. This credibility is built up as other sites and pages link to your page. As more people link to your web page, Google gains trust in your content.

Content repurposing can improve SEO through increasing your outreach, attracting mentions from other content creators and improving your chances of outside sources linking to your page. Content repurposing helps you gain the authority that search engines look for.

ii. Relevance (key phrases)

For a search engine to register your content it must recognize that it is relevant to your chosen topic. The use of appropriate key phrases throughout the copy of your webpage - including titles, headings, sub-headings and text - will optimize the page and allow it to rank.

Keyword research is an important part of SEO and you should consider which key words and phrases are most relevant to your page, which ones you want to rank for and how much competition you are facing.

iii. User interaction signals

User interaction signals can be positive or negative.

Positive:

A person is online (let's call them Gary), searching your key phrase and he clicks on your webpage. Yay! Gary is impressed with the page, there are some great graphics and a video to watch, so he stays a while. This increases the average session duration for your page. Google associates Gary's longer dwell time (another SEO in-the-know term) with your key phrase and web page and pushes your quality content further up the ranks.

Negative:

Another person is online (let's call them Shirley), searching your key phrase and she clicks on someone else's page. Boo! But Shirley is not impressed. The article looks like an essay and she bores her quickly, so Shirley quickly leaves the page to continue her search. Google registers the short dwell time and marks the page as lower quality content, lessening the chance of it ranking in search.

While it's impossible to please everyone, content repurposing can improve SEO by adding great visual content to your web page that will attract visitors and keep them on your page longer.

That is why at my agency, Content 10x, we always aim to create blog posts and web pages that provide a multimedia experience. When different types of content can be consumed, people can find their preferred learning style and dig deep into that content. You don't lose people so fast and if your content is good (it still has to be good content!), they stay.

Have the best page for your topic

For your blog posts and articles to rank on Google you want to show that you have the best page on the internet for your chosen topic. You must satisfy your visitors' needs and that means producing high quality content.

Articles that do well on search:

- How-to posts that answer questions

- Step-by-step guides
- Best practice pieces

For repurposing your written content to improve SEO, consider creating your blog post's evil twin, the 'How-not to' article.

This alternative version of your original piece is great for pitching to bloggers, trade publications and other websites where they accept guest posts - especially because these sites often won't accept content that has been published elsewhere.

When an outside source prints your article, they should include a link to your page, either in the body of text or in your bio, and this will build authority and improve your chances of ranking in search.

It's important to note that you will not (repeat: *will not*) be penalized by Google if you post the exact same content on multiple platforms. It is fine to copy and paste your content to websites such as Medium and LinkedIn but be wary of overdoing it.

SEO vs social media

Someone recently said to me that SEO is dead, that it takes too much time and effort to rank on Google and it's easier and faster to advertise on social media. The thing is, paid ads on social media are fast but temporary. They disappear as soon as you stop paying. Organic growth through ranking might be slow, but it's durable.

With website visitors from search you know nothing about *who* they are but you know exactly *what* they are thinking. With website visitors from social media you know a lot about who they are, but you have no idea what they're thinking.

The answer lies in content repurposing

To understand why, consider this: What works well on search? Long, detailed, in-depth articles. What works well on social? Collaborative, striking visual content and engaging posts.

With content repurposing you can have the best of both worlds. Great visual content that performs well on social can be repurposed it into a long form blog post that will perform well in search - and vice versa.

The real connection between content repurposing and SEO is that content repurposing can make a webpage more visible.

It is extremely difficult for a web page to rank if it's sitting alone out there like an island. Content repurposing can - through links, mentions off-site, outreach to influencers and blogger relations - build hubs of interconnected content, not solo islands.

If you make a piece of content, repurpose it to build more credibility, relevance and authority.

3. The 'Rule of Seven'

There is an old marketing concept called the "Rule of Seven" which states that people need to see something seven times before they really take notice and take action. The number seven isn't really the thing to focus on here. Instead, focus on the point being made. People don't tend to buy the first time they meet you or hear your message. Rather, people respond to consistent messaging and repetition and over time this leads to familiarity and trust.

The "Rule of Seven" was developed in the 1930s, at a time when it wasn't quite so easy to reach people as it is today. But whilst it's easier to reach people, it's a noisy world out there and it can be difficult to get noticed. That's why it's even more important to get your message in front of people as much as possible. Content repurposing can really help you out here.

For example, imagine that you are running an event and trying to sell tickets for it. A potential new customer we'll call Jenny lands on your website. Jenny landed on your website because she searched for a particular term and your ultra-helpful blog post came top of the search results. Go SEO! She really likes what she sees about your event and she makes a mental note to come back soon and buy a ticket from you.

Her mental note isn't good enough though because it pretty much got wiped out of her brain the moment she went onto Facebook and started looking at funny cat videos!

Low and behold though, you repurposed the blog post into some engaging social media posts too. Later that evening Jenny sees a post from you on Facebook and she remembers how much she enjoyed your blog post.

The following day Jenny is on Twitter and she sees some Tweets from you that are super-useful and build on from the blog post that she previously loved.

A few days later Jenny is looking for a new podcast to listen to in her industry and blow me down, there you are again with what looks like a great podcast.

The next time Jenny is on Instagram she sees a post by you about your event and she's sold!

All of the content that Jenny consumed was repurposed content from the one blog post but with that repurposed content, you kept yourself front of mind and eventually she purchased a ticket.

4. Touch all of the senses

In chapter three we explore in more detail how people learn in different ways. Some people read, some people watch and some people listen. In fact, there are seven different learning styles and this is why repurposing your content into different formats is important.

You want your content to really connect with your audience. Only through building a true connection will you be able to gain trust. And through trust you will turn prospects into leads into sales.

5. Gain authority & credibility

If you repurpose your content, you're basically finding new and creative ways to communicate the same message. The more you talk about something, the more you get 'known' for that particular topic.

Reiterating your advice, points and ideas in many different ways allows you to demonstrate your knowledge and expertise and helps you to build your authority.

If you think about it, if someone says something once then maybe people will remember but maybe they won't. If someone says something a few times, people may start to take notice. If someone says something repeatedly, in different formats and in different places, always consistently communicating the same clear and concise message, people will remember. You become 'known' for talking about that particular topic or concept.

If you repurpose your content effectively, by continually adding value to your audience, you can generate more leads, more traffic, and more shares of your content and you can reach more people.

My philosophy is that you should focus on quality far more than quantity. Meaning, you should produce less and then re-purpose, promote and share more.

So, when you spend a lot of time creating a really good piece of content, do not let the 'publish' button be the end. That's just the start of the journey to more and more great content.

You can repurpose both old content and new content. Look back into your archives for evergreen content and content that's performing really well. Follow the suggestions in this book to repurpose that content and bring it back to life again. You can also create a repurposing plan for all the new content that you create.

Whatever you do, don't let repurposing opportunities pass you by on your journey to build that all important authority and credibility!

CHAPTER 4

How to read this book

Unlike the works of literature that you devour before bed-time...or were forced to read in school (depending on your reading preferences!), this isn't intended as a book to sit and read from cover to cover.

By all means do read it from cover to cover if you choose, but my hope is that you come to see this book as a your content repurposing bible, always by your side to guide you and help you as you discover ways of making your content go further.

Now that you understand *why* content repurposing is so valuable - both for you and your audience, it's time to choose the path that best suits your needs right now. Think of it like one of those "Choose Your Own Adventure" stories you read as a kid.

If you have a specific piece of content and you're ready to repurpose, Part Two of this book is for you.

We look at repurposing the following:

- Podcasts
- Videos

- Live videos
- Blogs
- Membership site content
- Live events
- Webinars
- Emails
- Transcripts
- Social media
- Books & eBooks
- Plus so much more!

As you start to repurpose your content, or as you start to plan ahead for when you become a repurposing machine, Part Three, with its focus on approach and strategy is for you.

Part Four helps you put systems in place to make your content repurposing not just more manageable, but also more effective and even fun!

So, by all means read the book from cover to cover, or find what you need to learn, when you need to learn it, and consider the book to always have you content repurposing back!

Finally, it's worth noting that the digital world moves fast. For example, the social media platforms are always updating their features and evolving. Everything in this book is correct at the time of writing, to the best of my knowledge, but please do be mindful that things change. For example, even between writing the first draft of the manuscript and reviewing the edited second version, I had to rewrite a number of sections and that's just how it goes. That said, regardless of the whimsical nature of digital platforms, the theories, principles and overall guidance are all rock solid. Okay, let's jump in ...

PART 2

What You Can Repurpose & How

CHAPTER 5

Podcasts

The podcast industry has been on an exciting upward trajectory for many years now. Some would consider podcasts to be a mainstream medium these days. According to Edison Research in 2019[2], 51% of the total US population over the age of 12 have listened to a podcast, and 32% said they had listened to one in the past month. The average podcast listener listens to seven a week. If you're a podcaster that's pretty cool, right?!

You only have to look at an event like Podcast Movement, the biggest annual podcasting event, to see this growth. It started in 2013 with just a few hundred people and by 2018 it had over 2000 attendees - and it expects to grow and grow!

I have my own podcast, The Content 10x Podcast, which I started in October 2017 and I've been putting out regular weekly episodes ever since.

At Content 10x, our Podcast 10x repurposing service is one of our most popular offerings, and with more and more people tuning into podcasts each week, it's no surprise that so many

2 https://www.edisonresearch.com/wp-content/uploads/2019/03/Infinite-Dial-2019-PDF-1.pdf

podcasters want to expand their outreach. If you don't have a podcast yet but you want to start one, The Content 10x Toolkit provides a step-by-step guide on exactly how to launch a podcast - taking you through the exact same process that we work through with our clients who are launching podcasts for the first time.

I know from first-hand experience that whilst podcasts are awesome, creating and running a podcast is no walk in the park. It can be time consuming, and with that in mind you need to make sure that you maximize the value from your podcasting efforts.

But how do you ensure that as many people as possible listen to your podcast, and how do you reach the people who aren't podcast listeners?

49% of the US population have not listened to a podcast. These statistics are based on the US population, one of the leading countries when it comes to podcasting, so that figure will likely be lower for many other countries right now.

The answer is to repurpose your podcast episodes into many different formats for many different locations

Let me share with you some of the ways that you can repurpose podcast episodes by taking you through what we do with The Content 10x Podcast and some of the variations we provide for our clients. This will give you lots of ideas for what you could do with your own podcast episode.

Begin with an audio file

So, first thing's first. If you want to repurpose a podcast episode, you need an audio file - so get recording! This aspect can be as simple or as complicated as you want it to be. Some people simply hit record using free, built-in software on their computer or phone, and that's it.

Others invest in microphones, mixers and all sorts of sound equipment and software. If you're don't have a podcast yet and you're deciding how to start, it's up to you but personally, I kept it simple. I purchased a Blue Yeti microphone and I record using Audacity on my Mac. Guest interviews are recorded on Skype's built in recorder.

You will also need a podcast host, for example Captivate. This is the location online where you upload your audio file, together with information about the episode. The host then transmits your episode to many of the apps that you want it to play from via an RSS feed. E.g. Apple Podcasts, Spotify, iHeart-Radio, Stitcher.

Write show notes - turning audio into written content

In my opinion, you can't have a podcast without show notes. They're like strawberries and cream at Wimbledon. They have to go together!

One reason is because it's important to provide your audience with an idea of what the episode is all about. In exactly the same way that Netflix provide descriptions of what their shows are about, and books have a summary explaining the premise of the book, usually on the back cover. You can't expect people to listen based on the title alone!

But that's not the only reason why I think show notes are essential. They're also important because they improve your SEO, your ability to get your podcast found by the search engines (SEO = search engine optimization).

Improve SEO

You might think that if you have a podcast, SEO doesn't apply to you, but it can be invaluable in growing your audience and increasing your downloads.

Never underestimate the importance of SEO. When we want to know anything new these days what is the first thing we do?

We head to a search engine! The Podcast Consumer 2019, a report from Edison Research and Triton Digital, found that of the people who said they occasionally listen to podcasts, 73% said they find them via searching the internet.

Whilst podcasts are fantastic, a key challenge they face is discoverability. Which is a buzz-word used a lot in podcasting, and basically means 'being found by people who you want to be found by'.

Both Google and Apple have been working on ways to improve podcast SEO, which in 2019 has included the introduction technologies that transcribe podcast audio using AI (artificial intelligence...bots). This happens in the back end of their apps (i.e. these transcriptions are not for the public to see) in order to crawl the transcript, understand the content, and rank in search results. Pretty clever and pretty cool right?!

Whilst this is a good step forward, you don't want to just publish your podcast through your host's website, like Captivate, because you're missing out on the opportunity for this content to help your website rank on Google - very important if you're growing a business.

So, we've established it's important to put your show notes into the episode description with your host to feed to the apps that your podcast is on, that's not *all* you should do.

You want to also publish your podcast on your own website. If you don't have a website, create one especially for your podcast.

On your website you can embed a podcast player on an individual web page with a keyword focused title header and show notes for each episode. Repurposing your podcast into a text-based article will allow you to apply the same SEO rules to your copy as you would for any article or blog post and this will improve your chances of people finding you via Google.

For a search engine to register your content it must recognize that it is relevant to your chosen topic. The use of appropriate key phrases throughout the copy of your webpage, including titles, headings, sub-headings and text, will optimize the page and allow it to rank.

You can decide whether you want to write short show notes, a long form blog post, or both.

Short show notes would usually be in the form or an introduction to the episode, a bullet-pointed summary of the discussion, and a conclusion with important links and mentions and a call to action (if appropriate). The benefit of short show notes is that these days we're all a nation of skim readers. Short show notes can very quickly give people just enough information to judge whether the episode is for them. You may want to consider adding time-stamps as well, which would give people the opportunity to jump to exactly the part of the show that they want to listen to.

The downside of short show notes is that you're not as likely to rank on Google and other search engines. You won't get the opportunity to include your keyword/key phrase many times. You would struggle to rank in search engines if your post is under 500 words.

The posts that Google and the other search engines prefer are longer. The longer the post the better your chances of a search engine ranking. Over 1000 words is good, over 2000 words is far better.

As I've already mentioned, you can do both. Go ahead and write show notes that are short, simple and will really help people who have already landed on your website or found you in a podcast app. They will be able to quickly get the gist of your podcast episode and hopefully be tempted enough to give it a listen.

Meanwhile, you could also write a long-form blog post. All the better if your blog post is stand-alone and evergreen.

If you're not familiar with this marketing term, think about an evergreen blog post in the same way you think about an evergreen tree that has leaves and foliage all year round. It's the same concept. It's a blog post that will remain relevant and stand the test of time - plus it's brilliant for SEO!

Writing a long-form evergreen blog post is not always a simple task. I find it's possible whenever solo shows are recorded. However, with guest interviews it's not always as straightforward because the topic is not always as focused, but it is still possible (and we do it all the time for our clients at Content 10x).

Make sure your blog post is always based on some of the key points made during the discussion on the podcast.

Writing an article gives people who prefer to read rather than listen the opportunity to get to know you via an alternative form of content.

You can publish your post on your website and other places on the internet such as Medium and LinkedIn. Turn to chapter 8 to read more about blog syndication.

For example, a unique service we offer one particular client is publishing her content on high-authority websites and professional publications. She is a top influencer in the medical industry so posting her material on places like this helps cement her authority as an expert in her industry.

You'll find different show notes templates, with SEO checklists, are in The Content 10x Toolkit.

Create social media posts

When it comes to repurposing podcast episodes, we always create engaging social media posts that will grab people's attention, increase awareness and drive traffic to the podcast episode. There are many ways you can do this.

If you have written a blog post then why not take extracts from it to post on social media? When choosing excerpts from the blog post always ensure you choose shareable content that provides value to your audience.

Some great examples of extracts that work well on social media are things that make people laugh or something that will pique their interest and curiosity. It's really a case of trying to induce an emotional response. You can select a key point that you made during the episode or choose a fantastic quote from a special guest.

Start planning posts for your social media channels and try to mix it up to add some diversity. For example, try publishing short posts, long posts, posts with links, posts without links or posts with questions. The primary goal with your posts is to drive engagement and get people to stop scrolling on their newsfeed, read your post and take action! You want thumb-stopping content.

Design images for social media

I recommend creating images to accompany your social media posts. Stand-out images and graphics will always help to attract more people to your post and listeners to your podcast.

The main objective with the images that you create is to make them as eye-catching as possible. There is a lot of visual content out there for your audience to choose from, so give them a reason to spend time with yours.

You can create images using **www.canva.com.** It's a great tool and one my team use extensively for creating simple images.

We rarely post anything without an image or video. It's just smart marketing!

Read chapter 14: Social Media, for more on this.

Repurpose images for your blog post

If you're creating a few great images for your social media channels, why not repurpose those images and use them in your blog post too?

Adding images to your written articles will bring color to them, break up the text and make them look good. Also, it increases the time that a person spends on your page, a vital statistic in the SEO rankings.

According to research by Hubspot,[3] when people hear information they usually don't remember more than 10% of what they hear but if you add a few images into the mix, people are likely to retain at least 65% of the information three days later!

Create video teasers/audiograms for your podcast

Short animated teaser videos, often called audiograms, are easy for an audience to digest. Audiograms are short audio files that have been converted into a video file.

They are created by pairing together a section of audio with an image. When you hit play on the file you hear the audio snippet, which is usually taken from a podcast episode. Quite often, hitting play also triggers an animation of a moving audio wave.

You can create some really awesome designs, with very engaging moving audio waves, that make the audiogram really pop out when shared on social media.

We create audiograms that are around 15 to 30 seconds long, and they're created in square format for easy sharing on Facebook, Instagram and Twitter. We also create a teaser in vertical form for Instagram or Facebook Stories.

Creating audiograms offers a perfect way to share audio content on social media.

I imagine you'll be pleased to hear that you don't need to

---

3 https://blog.hubspot.com/marketing/visual-content-marketing-strategy

be a programmer to learn how to create audiograms. There are tools and software that are very easy to use.

I'll let you into a secret ... when I started my business, Content 10x, I told my first ever client that I could create audiograms, "Yep, absolutely no problem, I can do that". Only to find that it wasn't as easy as I first thought. It took me quite a while to find the perfect tool that did what I wanted it to do.

Today, my two faves are Wavve and Headliner, because they've got a ton of great features and, at the time of writing, they both have free to use options as well as 'pro' paid plansPersonally Wavve is my favorite and what we use at Content 10x. There is a video tutorial on audiograms in The Content 10x Toolkit.

I think audiograms are great on social media, especially Instagram, because they catch people's eyes and get them to stop scrolling long enough to have a listen. And that's exactly what you want them to do!

In case you need more convincing about the benefits of using audiograms, here are some statistics from experiments carried out by the *New York Public Radio WNYC:*[4]

- The average engagement for an audiogram posted on Twitter is 8x higher than a non-audiogram tweet!
- On Facebook, posts with audiograms outperformed those with photos and links by up to 83%!

Create video content for your podcast

There are so many benefits to having a podcast but one area where you can lose out, as I've discussed already, is not being found by the search engines.

I've talked about repurposing your podcast episodes into show notes and long-form evergreen blog posts, but did you

4 https://medium.com/@WNYC/socialaudio-e648e8a5f2e9

know that if you repurpose your podcast episodes into video format and put your video onto YouTube you are onto an SEO winner?!

YouTube is the second largest search engine in the world, second only to Google. Then there is the added bonus that Google own YouTube! This means that YouTube videos often appear within the organic search results of Google itself.

Another reason why repurposing your podcast into video format is a great idea is social media. Social video content has exploded in the past few years. According to Brandwatch in 2019[5], over 100 million hours of videos are watched on Facebook every day.

Facebook loves video content and people who are posting quality videos get some Facebook love by way of enhanced organic reach. It's not just the organic reach, but also the engagement. Video content gets more likes, shares, and comments.

As well as putting your video onto YouTube and social media, don't forget your website as well.

Adding video content onto your website creates a multimedia experience for your visitors. They can consume the content on your website in the way that best suits them. Also, adding a video to your podcast is known to keep your visitors on your page for longer, which yet again, helps with SEO.

According to Cisco,[6] online videos will account for more than 80% of all consumer internet traffic by 2021. It's important to get in on the action but, since I'm all about repurposing your content, I think if you have a podcast then there's no need to reinvent the wheel when it comes to creating videos. Instead, repurpose your podcast into video content.

Here are five ways to repurpose your podcast into video:

---

5 **https://www.brandwatch.com/blog/facebook-statistics/**

6 https://techblog.comsoc.org/2017/06/10/cisco-increased-use-of-web-video-to-be-82-of-all-internet-traffic-by-2021/

1. Video yourself whilst recording your podcast episode

If you video record yourself whilst recording your podcast episode you can succeed in increasing the engagement factor for your audience. It gives them the opportunity to get to know you and you get some brownie points when it comes to enhancing your 'know, like and trust' credibility.

You don't need fancy equipment to do this, you can just use the camera on your smartphone. For me, my iPhone camera is far better than any camera I've ever bought and it's brilliant for video recording.

You need to think about creating a space but again, it doesn't need to be anything fancy. It just needs to be somewhere that you feel comfortable putting on camera and, as you would for any podcast episode, you will need to consider the sound.

You may have seen Gary Vaynerchuk doing this for his Ask GaryVee show. He records his podcast episodes and video at the same time. In fact, this is a pretty common thing to do. Lots of people video themselves recording a podcast episode.

A benefit of this is that it creates a one-take situation. If you're video recording and podcast recording at the same time then you're more likely to go with the flow right through to the end. Whereas if you are recording audio only, it's far more tempting to do take two, take three, or take four. Or maybe that's just me?!

I recognize that this option is not for everyone. Not everyone wants to put themselves on camera, but if you're comfortable doing it (or willing to give it a go) then it really is a really great way of having both video and podcast from one piece of content/recording.

2. Video record your guest interview

This option is for those of you who invite guests onto your

show for interviews. If the interviews are conducted remotely via a call e.g. using software like Skype or Zoom, don't just record the audio. Record the screen and/or video as well.

That way you will be provided with an audio recording of your podcast plus a video recording that you can post to YouTube, your website and social media.

If you conduct your podcast interviews over Skype then there are a couple of ways that you can do this. If you have a Mac then you can download a recording tool that will record the audio and video of your Skype call. I use eCamm. There are other similar tools out there. Skype also has a built-in call recorder. I've personally started to use that for my own podcast and it's been working out really well. If you have a Microsoft PC, you can use Skype with software called Pamela to record calls.

If you use Zoom instead of Skype then Zoom will also allow you to record your screen as well as the audio. There are other call recording software options in addition to Skype and Zoom.

Quite often you can play around with how the video will look, for example, split screen options. This can look really good. This will bring your video to life for your audience, and for those people who don't listen to podcasts, it gives them a chance to see your interview.

If you have a popular guest and you put this video onto YouTube and social media there is a high chance that it will get found by more people, which is what we all want, isn't it?

3. Present whilst recording your screen and using your webcam

An option that puts you on video without making you center of attention is to present to your screen whilst using your webcam. This will put your webcam recording i.e. you in front of your webcam, into a small section of the screen. People will see you and they will see you talking, but they will also see your screen.

On your screen you could have slides, images, anything that is appropriate. If you create slides or images then think about repurposing them. They could be shared as social media images for example.

This can be really engaging. You are on camera so people are getting to know you but you're not the focal point and you can create engaging content to capture the attention of video viewers.

If you do this, one thing that you must be careful of is leaving out your podcast audience. You must remember that you are creating a podcast episode and your podcast listeners are not looking at your screen so don't refer to it in such a way that it's annoying or neglects your podcast listeners.

In terms of how you do this, there are various screen recording software options out there. Probably the most popular are Camtasia for Microsoft PC and Screenflow or Screencastomatic for Mac.

The next two ways that you can create video from a podcast don't require you to be on camera at all and you can still repurpose your podcast into a video.

4. Create a video from your audio file and add images

Take the audio from your podcast, create images and then pair the audio and images together to create a video.

You can do this for the whole podcast episode. You could create one static image (this could be your podcast artwork) or you could create many images where the image changes as the context of the podcast changes (like talking to slides). You can create this kind of video by using video editing software. At Content 10x we use iMovie and Final Cut Pro on Mac.

You could create a video for your full podcast episode. Or, something that we do at Content 10x for ourselves and our clients, is create a slimmed-down, shorter video which we call a trailer. This is good for YouTube and social media. Typically, we produce trailers that are around 2.5 to 4 minutes long.

Think of it like a movie trailer. We take out the interesting bits and showcase them to people. This video gives people a sneak peek and plants the seed of curiosity in their minds. Once they see your trailer, they can't help but click to listen to the rest of the podcast episode!

We also burn captions onto the videos because when people scroll through their Facebook newsfeed, a lot of them tend to watch videos in silent mode. With captions people can view your videos in silence and read the subtitles. The Content 10x Toolkit includes a tutorial on creating video trailers like these.

5. Upload your podcast episode to YouTube or Facebook

Lastly, number five is to take the whole audio file from your podcast episode and put that on YouTube or Facebook (or elsewhere). Some podcast audio hosts, for example Libsyn, allow you to set this up automatically.

How it works is that every time you release your podcast, in the same way that they might release it to a podcast player on your website or to Apple Podcasts, it automatically gets published on YouTube for you too. The audio file is published, along with artwork if you have any.

There are other ways that you can do this in an automated fashion if your podcast host doesn't provide this as an option. For example, a software called Repurpose.io will do something similar whereby it will automatically post your podcast audio to YouTube, Facebook and other places as you wish.

Whilst I question whether people really want long videos (e.g. 1-hour podcast episodes) that are really just audio with an image, I also appreciate that not everyone has time or budget to create videos and this at the very least gets your podcast onto a different platform. It's better than no action at all.

Email marketing

If your email marketing routine is looking a bit dull, why not use your latest podcast episode as an excuse to reach out to your subscribers and drive more traffic to your podcast?

It's important to keep in touch with your subscribers and add value to the emails that you send. Make them aware that you've just released a new podcast episode. Let them know what it's about and encourage them to check it out.

If you've already written a blog post or show notes then you've already converted your podcast episode into written format. Going one step further and writing an email won't seem too much of a hurdle to overcome.

If your podcast show is also available via video format, put that in the email subject line and let your readers know. According to Hubspot, simply having the word "video" in your email will increase open rates by 19% and click-through rates by 65%!

You can't assume that your email subscribers are aware of the content you are putting out onto different platforms so you're actually helping them by letting them know. As long as you're not emailing them every single day I think they'll be okay with it!

Provide a content upgrade

A content upgrade is something of additional value that you can provide to your audience in exchange for their email. In Europe that would be handled in a fully GDPR compliant way of course. This can be anything from a checklist to a planner or swipe file. I talk more about content upgrades in chapter sixteen.

It's okay to get creative and think outside the box when it comes to your content upgrades. Think about what your consumers would like to receive from you and then give it to them.

The beauty of a content upgrade, as opposed to a more typical lead magnet on your website or landing page, is that it is directly relevant to the podcast episode. It's supposed to be, quite literally, an upgrade on what you have already discussed. If people listened to your podcast episode and they liked it and are interested in the topic then it's almost a no-brainer to get the free upgrade. Be sure to ask for their email address when providing the upgrade, ensuring any new audience members get added to your email list.

Go Live on Facebook, Instagram or YouTube

Another method for enticing more people to listen to your podcast is going live on Facebook, Instagram or YouTube and talking about your latest podcast episode. At the time of writing this book, LinkedIn live video is being rolled out too. You can talk about a few key points from the episode and start a discussion with your live audience to generate excitement and interest in your podcast.

Going live turns your content into an experience. You provide people with the opportunity to interact with you. They can ask you questions and you can further demonstrate your knowledge and expertise. Creating live experiences also enhances your ability to connect with your audience and for them to connect with each other too. This is how communities often start to form.

Instagram Stories

If you have an audience on Instagram and you are on it too, don't neglect Instagram Stories. They are a great way to generate interest in your podcast, and you might also get a few new followers too! Let people know about your podcast and start posting to the platform on a weekly basis.

I love Instagram Stories. You can use them to create regular vlog content - short and sweet 15 second updates about your day. What better news to share than to let everyone know about your latest podcast episode? I talk more about this in chapter 14, Social media.

In conclusion

Podcasts are a great form of content but they can be difficult to grow because they struggle with discoverability. This makes repurposing essential. I don't want you to pour your heart and soul into your podcast, create astonishingly good episodes, and then fail to squeeze the value from them.

Whilst lots of ideas have been shared in this chapter on how to repurpose your podcast, I'm not suggesting you take all of these ideas and do it all of it straight away. Unless you have a lot of available time, a big team, or a budget to hire help (like my creative agency, Content 10x) that's crazy talk!

To get started, I suggest that you pick a few and try to incorporate them into your marketing routine. Pick what you can be consistent with. Take small steps towards new processes for your podcast and watch those download numbers increase!

A resource that will help you tremendously with podcast repurposing is The Content 10x Toolkit - it's packed full of templates, video tutorials and more!

PODCAST REPURPOSING CASE STUDY 1

Dr. Anissa Holmes - Delivering WOW

Effective content repurposing helped propel Anissa from successful dentist to a globally recognized leader in her industry.

Effective content repurposing helped propel Anissa from successful dentist to a globally recognized leader in her industry

Dr. Anissa Holmes is a dentist but she's certainly no ordinary dentist. Anissa has a successful dental practice in Kingston, Jamaica, but she decided that she wanted more as she considered what her legacy would be. She wanted to help other dentists build successful practices, to transform lives, and make a huge positive impact on the dental industry as a whole.

When Anissa published her first book, Delivering WOW, she quickly realized her audience was not big enough to have the impact she desired - she had an audience problem! To build her audience she launched a podcast. When I first met and started working with Anissa, her podcast was growing steadily, but she was doing everything herself. Given her busy schedule, having time to record and publish the podcast was an accomplishment. However, Anissa wanted to grow faster and it was clear that opportunities to repurpose were being missed.

We worked with Anissa to repurpose her podcast into a blog post for her website. We also turned the podcast content into a weekly email for her subscribers. We generated social media content from every episode for her profiles on all platforms. The social media content consists of graphics, videos and audiograms. We were also able to turn her podcast episodes into short podcast video trailers for YouTube and Facebook. Additionally, we published her podcast and blog not only on all main podcast apps, but also on a professional dental industry subscriber-only site too.

The result: after only a month of effectively repurposing and marketing Anissa's podcast her listeners increased by over

60%. It didn't take long for this to increase almost 10-fold and she gained listeners in over 100 countries. Her Facebook Group grew way beyond 10k members, as more and more people started to join her membership community.

Today, Anissa no longer has an 'audience problem'! She is one of the most well-known names in the dental industry having been featured in top dental publications, spoken on world stages, and has been featured as one of the Top 25 Women in Dentistry. She is changing lives every single day.

PODCAST REPURPOSING CASE STUDY 2

Mike Richards - The Treasury Recruitment Company

Mike became a trailblazer in his industry by establishing a successful podcast and leveraging the power of repurposing.

Mike became a trailblazer in his industry by establishing a successful podcast and leveraging the power of repurposing

Mike Richards is the CEO of The Treasury Recruitment Company, and, thanks to a very smart decision that he made in September 2018, he's also the host of The Treasury Career Corner podcast!

When I first met Mike he was looking for the perfect way to grow his personal brand and position himself front and center in the treasury industry as the leading authority on recruitment. His business was established in 2002 and whilst his company become the recruitment partner of choice with many large corporate clients, Mike was aware that content marketing was something that they were not doing enough of and they were not consistent in. He wanted to change that

We guided Mike through the process of setting up and launching a weekly podcast, where Mike interviews treasury professionals from around the globe about their career. This represented a bold decision to do something different and stand out from his competitors - it was also the first podcast of its kind within his specialist area of recruitment.

Repurposing was part of our strategy from day one. Unsurprisingly, many of Mike's audience were not already podcast listeners or even familiar with podcasts at all. His audience were mainly on LinkedIn, so repurposing podcast content onto LinkedIn was essential.

We work with Mike to repurpose his podcast into engaging visual content, audiograms/video teasers, short video trailers, and written show notes on his website, LinkedIn and Twitter.

We ensured his podcast was available on all main podcast apps and a podcast video trailer goes out onto YouTube and LinkedIn. His podcast also features in his newsletter to his subscribers. We've also made the most of video content and repurposed that into podcast episodes, including video footage from events.

Through repurposing, content never dries up on the social media platforms and fresh new content gets posted each week onto his website (good for SEO).

It's fair to say that The Treasury Career Corner has been a huge hit. This one-of-a-kind podcast created a buzz in the industry - all of a sudden Mike was 'everywhere', talking to industry leaders, and still is! Mike's grown a large audience of avid listeners. As download numbers have grown, so too has Mike's personal brand. Interest and awareness in Mike's business also grew - he found even if people didn't listen to the podcast, they certainly knew about it and this has helped build his authority.

A huge business advantage arising from his podcast has been Mike's ability to sit down and interview his dream clients who, in turn, through the power of relationship building (and Mike's charm), have become his clients.

CHAPTER 6

Videos

It's finally happened. Mainstream companies are beginning to understand what many of us have known for a long time: Online content is big enough to shape the world. Specifically, video content.

A study conducted by Cisco predicted that by 2021, 82% of content consumed online will be video. Don't skip over this ...

82% of content consumed online is going to be video!

Only time will tell if this prediction is right (and if you're reading this in 2022, the verdict will be in!).

The Importance of Online Video Reflected in the Music Industry

In the UK, like most countries, the Official Charts Company publishes a rank order of music by popularity every week. They recently changed the way they compile the numbers for the charts. They now include online video views. They've finally acknowledged the extent of music consumption on YouTube and other video platforms.

They aren't going to count a video view as though it were a sale - which would massively favor artists who have a good online presence. Instead, at the time of writing this book, they're going to treat 600 free views as equivalent to a sale. For music viewed through YouTube's new subscription service, which removes ads from the experience, 100 views will be classed as a sale. That's because the ad revenue from 600 views and the percentage of a subscription payment that 100 views represents, on average, are roughly equivalent to the sale of a single.

This is huge! It's proof that enough people are consuming music video content online that you can't only go by traditional sales to get an accurate measure of the musical tastes in the country and the popularity of any song or artist.

Actually, online video has been widely used for a long time, and since incumbent organizations like this have proven themselves pretty slow when it comes to getting onboard with the online revolution, I guess you can discount the charts from the last decade or so!

Then we have the big audio platforms deciding audio isn't enough. Even Spotify doesn't think they can ignore the opportunity in video anymore. Both Spotify and Apple Music have added video to their content offerings. Soon we'll have people going to platforms that have been audio-only since forever in order to consume video!

Add that to the waves of people going to YouTube to consume music. It's no surprise that online video is being taken a lot more seriously now than it ever was before.

Improve SEO with video content

As well as the fact that people just love video content online, there are SEO benefits of producing video content too. We will often publish on platforms such as YouTube and Vimeo. These sites tend to have their own search engines but by putting out regular video content that gains traction and engagement, these videos can also be found on Google search, especially since Google owns YouTube.

The more people who see your videos, the more likely they are to want to follow a link to your content, especially if you have a call to action to your webpage in your video description. Video content is a great way to really get your content to rank. Social streaming sites *love* video and their algorithms push this type of content right to the top.

The repurposing potential for video content

When it comes to repurposing content, I believe that the easiest way to do that is to start with video. The repurposing potential is almost limitless when the starting point, the content that sparks it all off, is video.

This is a good thing, because it's not always easy to create video content. There's often far more involved than say, writing a blog or recording a podcast. Podcasts require a fair amount of technical set-up too, but with video you're also thinking about the camera and other equipment, your location, the visual appeal, your hair, your make-up. The list goes on!

How much time we put into our video content can vary of course. Often it depends on whether it's a highly-produced video as opposed to a more raw, vlog-style video. That said, even the raw vlog-style videos can still take quite some time to edit.

Nonetheless, when you've spent hours pouring yourself into your video, it may well be that the prospect of then repurposing your video seems like a whole load more time you'd rather not invest. You might consider not bothering.

The fact is, you need to repurpose precisely *because* your video was a lot of work. If you don't, you're letting some of that hard work go to waste, when instead you could multiply it.

Okay, let's look at some of the ways that you can repurpose your video content:

Publish your video to other online locations

The first thing to do, before we start talking about repurposing into different formats, is simply to look at the potential to publish your video onto other platforms.

If you've recorded your video directly on a social media platform, for example, Facebook or Instagram, it's simple enough to extract the video file. Whichever your preferred platform to record your video for, make sure it ends up on YouTube. Having your content on Google's protégé-platform will increase the likelihood of appearing in the search engine. Yes, they play favorites!

Many YouTubers believe the platform gives them a boost when they put out content more than once a week. The effect may come from their audiences being more engaged with their content due to their consistency and frequency but hey, whatever the root cause, it's a good thing! So if you can get your edited live videos onto YouTube following a regular, consistent publishing schedule you'll likely start to gain some traction.

Also, embed your video onto your website, too. Whether it's in a blog post or another page, it's good to have all your cornerstone content visible on your own property. Having a video on a webpage increases the time that a visitor spends on your webpage which, as you've heard me mention enough times already by now, is good for SEO.

Repurpose your video into a podcast

Podcasts, as a form of audio-distribution technology, are as revolutionary as the printing press when it democratized the written word. The beautiful thing about the spoken word is that people can listen to it while they do other things such as driving, cooking, doing housework, or exercising.

All those hours when you don't need 100% of your focus is called "found time", or time that audio technology has suddenly made available for learning and personal growth.

Make it easy for your audience to fill their found time with your lovely voice by publishing the audio of your video as a podcast. After-all, if you're creating video content already, then the audio is right there for you to repurpose.

Turning your video into a podcast episode is a great way to reach an entirely new audience. 51% of the US adult population have listened to a podcast episode and that figure is growing.[7] A lot of people who listen to podcasts may not find you on Facebook, or YouTube, or your website but they will find you on Apple Podcasts, Spotify, or their favorite podcast app.

Repurposing videos to podcast episodes when you already have a podcast

If you already have a podcast, then everything is set-up for you. Presumably you have a podcast host, you're live on Apple Podcasts and various podcast apps. For example, Spotify, iHeartRadio, Stitcher and so on. And you either produce your episodes yourself, or have someone to do that for you.

If you want to repurpose your videos into podcast episodes it can be as simple as saving and converting your video file to an audio file. If you are editing your video in video editing software, for example iMovie or Camtasia, you can render the file as an .mp3 or .wav which will provide you with the audio file that you're after. Then you simply carry out the usual podcast editing that you would do for any podcast episode that you produce.

Alternatively, Quicktime Player, which comes as default on all Macs, has the option to export the audio from a video file. Click File > Export > Audio Only. This is a nice and easy way to

7 https://www.edisonresearch.com/the-podcast-consumer-2019/

record and extract audio.

To avoid using video editing software, if you want to convert a video file straight to audio there are apps that you can use. For example, on Mac there is an app from the App Store called To MP3 Converter Free that will convert single files for you.

There are some websites that will offer to convert video to audio files for you for free. These sites can be found via a Google search but be careful as 'free' often means being forced into downloading a plugin or providing certain information in order to proceed.

Once you have an audio file, since you're already a seasoned podcaster, treat it like any other podcast episode and follow your usual publishing process.

Repurposing videos to podcast episodes when you don't already have a podcast

I get a lot of questions from people who want to repurpose video content into podcast episodes but they don't already have an established podcast.

Starting a podcast for the first time can seem intimidating. There are quite a number of steps involved in launching a podcast. But don't worry. It's easier than it seems. If you already produce digital content of some kind you probably have all the technical knowledge you need to get your podcast set up. If you have access to The Content 10x Toolkit we have a guide that takes you through the steps to set up a podcast.

The key things that you'll need to do are:

1. Decide on your podcast details

Decide on your title, subtitle and description. Use keywords related to your niche in each section. Think about both what your target audience might type into the search bar when looking for new podcasts and what they would be attracted to when they're browsing.

If you're stuck, go to Apples Podcasts or similar and see what title other people in your niche have given their podcasts. How can you stand out from them while remaining relevant and interesting to your potential audience?

TOP TIP: Don't be tempted to 'keyword stuff' your podcast title and author field. Apple have taken a big exception to this and will remove your podcast from Apple Podcasts with no warning.

For example, if my podcast title was 'The Content 10x Podcast: Content Repurposing and Content Marketing' this would be frowned upon. They may remove me from Apple Podcasts until I changed the title to 'The Content 10x Podcast'.

Similarly, if my author field was 'Amy Woods: Content Repurposing Expert, Entrepreneur & Coach', they would expect this field to be simply 'Amy Woods' and I'd likely get penalized.

This isn't an issue for new podcasters, it can happen to anyone. A client of mine who has been podcasting for over three years, with a very successful podcast (over three million downloads) got removed from Apple Podcasts with no warning because they took exception to his podcast name that had been perfectly fine for three years previously. Yes, frustrating! But you have to play the game if you want to be on these big (free) platforms.

2. Create your artwork

Any podcast needs a square cover photo or "artwork" in order to show up properly. It's a lot like an album cover in the music store.Your artwork will need to be approved by Apple Podcasts/Apple Podcasts but their criteria is not very strict. It only needs to be "PG" rated and readable. Having said that, it's important to get it right. This will be the first thing people see when they're browsing the podcast marketplace. It'll be an easy job for any competent freelance designer, but if you'd like to do it yourself you can tinker with a number of free design templates on Canva.

No matter how you create your artwork, the most important thing is to make sure it's easy to read even as a small thumbnail. Think of ways you can stand out from the other podcasts in your niche, too. Many of your potential listeners will first see your podcast nestled in amongst a bunch of others as they browse.

You'll need to follow these technical specifications:

- Pixel Size: a minimum of 1,400 by 1,400 pixels, and a maximum of 3,000 by 3,000
- Format: either in .jpg or .png format
- Color: RBG color scheme

3. Create your intro & outro

It's not essential to have an intro and/or outro but some say it adds a certain level of professionalism to your show. It's up to you. Others say it wastes valuable time!

You can find voiceover freelancers easily on Fiverr and there are a number of directories online of royalty free music. Throw out a Google search and you'll find yourself spoilt for choice.

Personally, I found it a little overwhelming when I tried creating my own intro. In the end I decided to save time and use a done-for-you podcast intro service called Music Radio Creative. They took all the stress out of the process, so I'd recommend them to anyone else who's struggling with this step.

4. Get decent sound recording equipment

As an audio-only medium, sound quality is obviously crucial in podcasting. Since you will be recording videos, consider investing in a discreet lapel mic. Most podcasters who focus on audio only use a large mic with a stand, but the lapel mic is perfect for recording in video as well since you don't need to worry about how far the microphone is from your mouth the whole time you're on camera.

You may decide not to get a lapel mic and to go for a more standard podcasting microphone. There are lots of options, it could get overwhelming. Here are two to consider:

- **Audio-Technica ATR2100** - This is one of the most commonly used microphones for recording. It offers a great, natural sound, and is very easy to use. Simple USB output so it connects to a computer very easily.
- **Blue Yeti** - Very similar to the ATR2100 in both sound quality and ease of use. The Yeti has a slight edge in that it has a range of recording patterns which you can select.

I use the Blue Yeti for my podcast episodes but when I'm repurposing video to podcast I usually use a lapel mic.

If you are strapped for cash, you might be able to get away with using the microphone built into your earphones. Record a few seconds of speaking using that microphone and listen back. Ask yourself, would it bother you if you found a podcast that sounded like that? If not, go right ahead because it would be a shame to let the tech hold you back.

5. Host your podcast

Just as your website needs hosting, so does your podcast. The hosting process creates an RSS feed, the same as a blog. This RSS feed is also called the feed URL or feed address. Once you supply this feed URL onto a given podcast platform, all future episodes you upload to your host will be automatically be syndicated. Easy!

There are many different podcast hosts to choose from. Rather like choosing a website host. The price can range from $5 to $25+ per month. Price plans vary depending on factors such as how much data you use per month, the level of support offered, features such as access to analytics and integration with 3rd parties like the social media platforms.

Libsyn are one of the largest, established podcast hosts. My friends at Rebel Base Media have launched a podcast hosting platform called Captivate which is extremely simple to use and boasts the best analytics on the market. I highly recommend checking it out.

Once you sign up with your host they walk you through the rest of the process. It shouldn't take more than 10-15 minutes to get set-up if you already have your artwork and podcast details to hand.

Every time you have a new podcast episode to publish, you simply upload your podcast audio plus some show notes (title and brief description) to your host.

6. Record your first episode

Even though your overall plan is to repurpose your videos to podcast episodes, I recommend your first episode be a simple introduction/trailer rather than an ordinary episode. Imagine if someone were to find your podcast and they are wondering what it's all about, they could go straight to your trailer, often labeled episode 0, and in a couple of minutes they'd find out the answer to their questions.

Include things like:

- Who you are
- What your podcast is about and why anyone should care
- Who it's meant for
- What to expect (such as duration and frequency)

I recommend recording a 2-5 minute trailer. It'll be long enough to register as a download, but short enough to do the job of piquing interest in your show. A short trailer is the perfect episode to send people to if they show interest in your podcast. It's a lot to ask people, especially non-podcast listeners, to listen to a full-length episode straight away, but a trailer is easily digestible. Always be sure to tell people it's free too, not everyone knows that podcasts are free, the term 'subscribe' can sound like something you pay for.

Your host needs at least one episode to register you with the directories. It doesn't need to be anything amazing but remember it may be the first episode people listen to when they find you.

If you are recording audio only, rather than making a video and taking the audio from it, then you will want to use voice recording software or an app. Audacity is a good option. It's free to use and there are plenty of tutorials on YouTube that show you how to use it. Another alternative if you're on a Mac is Garage Band. It comes as standard and includes a nice, easy 'export to Apple Podcasts' option.

7. Submit your first episode

After uploading the audio to your host, follow their instructions to get your feed onto any podcast platforms where you want to appear.

Apple Podcasts is a must, but there are many other places e.g. Spotify, iHeartRadio, Stitcher, Google Play Music, Acast, to name a few popular ones.

You may even want to consider publishing your audio on Amazon Alexa Flash Briefing. It's a new platform, but one I can see growing substantially in the future, and the early adopters are going to benefit the most from its growth. It's perhaps not the easiest process to follow but certainly something to consider and likely the process will become easier and easier as the platform grows.

If you've followed these steps then congratulations, you have a podcast show of your own!

When you record videos that you would like to turn into a podcast episode, all you need to do is extract the audio (you may want to do some audio editing) then you upload to your host.

A few things to consider when repurposing video to podcast:

- Think about the terminology that you use in your video if you know it's going to become a podcast episode. For example, try not to say 'in this video'. It's more universal to say 'in this episode'.

- You want to consider how visually dependent your videos are. If you do need to show your video viewers certain things on camera then that's okay, but they are the parts that you will likely want to edit out of your podcast episode. For example, where you are showing something and saying "look at this...", podcast listeners will get no value from hearing that. In that case, think about keeping those parts of the video very stand-alone so the edit out will be simple enough to do.

- If you're savvy enough, and you have the time, you might add a few pauses, then add-in additional vocal commentary to your audio file to fill the listeners in on anything they would need the visuals to understand.

- If you don't want to edit anything out, then at the start of your video introduce the fact that the audio is also going to be used for a podcast episode, welcome your podcast listeners and explain that the audio is from a video so they understand.

- Consider the background noise more so than you might usually for a video. When there is video content you can often get away with less than perfect audio, but when the audio is stripped from the video and the audio is all that you have left, you'll be surprised just how important it becomes! I know first-hand, having recorded myself recently on video. I was going to strip the audio for my podcast but when I listened back, you could hear lots of background noise. There were birds tweeting, the sound of an aeroplane thundered in through the window ... all in all, the audio was not great. It wasn't due to anything other than environmental circumstances that I couldn't control and whilst the video was okay, the audio wasn't. Such is life! All of this can depend on your brand and your sensibilities of course. Some brands might work with "rough-and-ready" content that has no polish. For me, however, the audio just wasn't good enough for us in that situation.

Repurpose your video into little video babies!

Short video clips are popular. People love them, and so do the online platforms. When I say short video clips, I mean taking an interesting and/or entertaining clip from one of your longer videos, say a 30 second clip, and sharing it. If you are on Instagram in particular, you'll have seen plenty of short video clips being shared on the platform which are often clips taken from a longer video.

Once you edit clips for one platform, it's easy to adjust them for the other major platforms too. You just need to follow their criteria for maximum length and aspect ratio.

So, how do you make all these clips?

If you're a Mac user you can make simple, no-frills clips by trimming the video with your built-in QuickTime Player. You can use iMovie to make other changes like adding an intro sequence, putting your video into a frame, adding music, etc.If you'd like more feature-rich editing software without investing up front, try the free HitFilm. If you're willing to invest then perhaps try Camtasia (Mac or PC), Adobe Premier (Mac or PC), or Final Cut Pro. This is what my team and I currently use, but, at the time of writing, it's Mac only.

Six tips for repurposing video content for social media

1. Think about the purpose of your clip

If you've taken a 30-second clip from a larger video to share on social media, you need to think about the ultimate purpose of that clip. What do I mean by this?

Well, each clip needs a purpose, otherwise it's just pointless. You need to think about the action you want people to take when they see your content and choose a clip that will help invoke that action.

Well, each clip needs a purpose, otherwise it's just pointless. You need to think about the action you want people to take when they see your content and choose a clip that will help invoke that action.

For example, if you're repurposing video content for social media with the purpose of getting people to engage with your post, choose a clip that's going to encourage them to leave feedback. Ask your audience a question that they can't resist. Make it interesting, and you're sure to get some engagement.

If you want people to watch the full video i.e. go to your website or YouTube etc to watch the video the clip comes from, you need to choose a clip that leaves them wanting more. For example, instead of sharing all five of your top tips in the teaser clip, share one and let them know that there's more waiting for them in the source video.

Think about what the primary purpose of the video clip is and try to choose one that helps fulfill that purpose. You could even have ten clips from the same video, and each clip can have a different goal.

You may not require any action to be taken as such, but you must to ensure that your idea or insight conveyed clearly.

2. Think about how your video looks without sound

How many times have you scrolled through Facebook with the sound turned off? Perhaps you have a secret browse through your social media channels at work, and you've put your smartphone on silent mode?

We've all done this, which is why you need to think about how your video clip will look without any sound. When repurposing video content for social media you should think about adding captions.

According to Facebook, 85% of their videos are watched without sound so if you add captions to your video, people are more likely to stop scrolling through their feed to pay attention to your video.

Some social media platforms (such as Facebook) can auto-generate captions for your video, but they aren't always accurate. I recommend sending your video clip to www.rev.com and letting them do the legwork. They create captions that you can add directly onto your video clip, or you can upload into Facebook, YouTube, LinkedIn etc and then enable them to show captions. This allows you to post the video on social media and whether viewers watch with or without sound, they still receive value.

3. Think about the duration of the video clip

Repurposing video content for social media in a way that will grab people's attention often depends on the duration of your video clip. Each platform has different maximum video durations that they accept, which is something you need to think about when repurposing video content for social media.

Sites such as Facebook and YouTube let you post longer videos while an Instagram video post has a maximum video length of 60 seconds. Videos posted on Instagram Stories must be 15 seconds or less. Twitter has a video length limit of up to 240 seconds. We now have IGTV (Instagram TV) allowing 10 minute videos for the majority of people, and up to an hour for verified accounts.

Reminder: All of the above durations are correct at the time of writing but platforms do change these things rather often so be sure to check!

Another consideration: Just because you *can* post a longer video on a particular platform, doesn't mean you *should*. HubSpot discovered the "ideal length" that videos should be if you want to get engagement on social media.

Here's a quick overview of their findings:

Facebook - 1 minute

Instagram - 30 seconds

Twitter - 45 seconds

YouTube - 2 minutes

4. Think about the aspect ratio of your clip

The aspect ratio of your video clip is something that you need to address when repurposing video content for social media. When you film a video for YouTube, you usually have a standard horizontal aspect ratio. But when you bring this onto social media, you'll often need to change it into a square or vertical aspect ratio.

If you don't change the aspect ratio, you might find that the published version has been altered. The video may have been stretched out or is zoomed in too much, both of which can look ugly!

So, if you want to edit the aspect ratio of your video clips, use video editing software such as Camtasia, Final Cut Pro, Filmora or Adobe Premiere or a site like https://crop.video

Posting your horizontal videos in portrait form - for IGTV and Instagram/Facebook Stories

I often get asked the question "how can you repurpose your horizontal videos onto Instagram Stories or IGTV?".

Instagram Stories and IGTV both feature vertical videos (as does Snapchat and Facebook Stories).

Given its focus on catering to the modern-day smartphone user, IGTV is a dream platform if you want to share and consume long form, vertical videos.

When IGTV first launched it was very bold in only accepting vertical video format. This was met with mixed reactions.

Many people were saying who on earth wants to watch long-form vertical videos?! But my view was that Instagram were onto something. We all consume a lot of content on mobile devices. Video content is consumed more than any other form of content. Watching horizontal videos, on our vertical, mobile devices is not always ideal. IGTV - a vertical 'TV' platform, made complete sense.

Other objections that people had were based on not being able to easily repurpose videos for YouTube onto IGTV.

Did you know that mobile video will account for 78% of total mobile data traffic by 2021? What's more, younger audiences are spending more time with their favorite amateur creators rather than watching professionally produced shows.[8]

Nowadays, we're spending less time watching online videos on our desktops and more time binge-watching them on our smartphones.[9] Vertical video has gone mainstream. And it's all thanks to mobile apps such as Instagram and Snapchat.

But why have vertical videos become so popular?

Well, most of us keep our phones locked on portrait orientation. And who can blame us? Nobody likes it when you're scrolling through your newsfeed and the screen decides to flip horizontally - it's so annoying! As a result, we've become accustomed to consuming videos in portrait mode when we're on our phones.

Another reason why vertical video has become so popular is the fact that it's super accessible. Not everyone can shoot films in 4K resolution, but even the biggest technophobes out there can film a quick video with their smartphone - and people tend to hold phones vertically when they do this!

---

8 https://business.instagram.com/a/IGTV

9 https://mashable.com/2017/12/28/vertical-video-mainstream-year

Instagram have said that they believe vertical videos to be more immersive and native. They are good for individuals trying to build a connection with their audience.

All this being said, in mid-2019, less than a year before IGTV launched, they lifted their vertical video format only feature! They made it possible for you to upload and view horizontal videos. They stated that some types of videos e.g. sports videos and videos where there are multiple people in the frame, are often best viewed in landscape mode and they don't want to limit the viewers experience.

So IGTV has moved away from its unique feature of being vertical only, but it still favors vertical and prioritizes vertical video format. However, if a video was uploaded in landscape format then viewers can opt to watch it in landscape format and then turn their phone to view.

On the one hand, it's good that IGTV accepts horizontal video format now because people can repurpose their YouTube videos onto the platform. On the other hand, it could be a negative thing because...people can repurpose their YouTube videos onto the platform! There is a worry that IGTV will become flooded with duplicate content from YouTube and there will be less native content.

k it's fair to say that IGTV is still figuring itself out. All that I have written here is true at the time of typing, things may have moved on further by the time you are reading this!

Whilst IGTV does allow horizontal video upload now, videos can only be 10 minutes long (for most accounts). Instagram Stories is still vertical video format only, as is Facebook Stories and Snapchat.

Just because these apps prioritize vertical videos, doesn't mean you can't post your horizontal videos onto these apps.

How do you repurpose your horizontal videos into portrait format? Maybe you have an entire back catalogue of horizontal videos that you want to repurpose onto IGTV, Instagram/Facebook Stories or Snapchat. Or maybe, you have plans to make lots of horizontal videos in the future and you want to post them onto YouTube *and* IGTV (in vertical format so people don't have to elect to turn the screen).

Don't worry, it's not too complicated. All you need is video editing software and some basic image editing skills.

For a long time, vertical videos were a sign of low-quality production, especially when they appear with two large black bars to the left and right because someone held their phone the wrong way around when video recording! But not anymore.

If you want to post a landscape video on Instagram, IGTV or Snapchat (without cropping out content), here's what you need to do:

A. Edit the aspect ratio

The first step is to download video editing software such as Final Cut Pro or Filmora (to name just two!). There are plenty of video editing software options out there so do some research and find one that suits your needs (and is within your budget!).

Next, launch the software and create a new project.

When prompted to choose an aspect ratio for your new project, search for a pre-set option for Instagram Stories. If it's nowhere to be seen, choose the custom resolution option.

Edit the aspect ratio to 9:16 with a resolution of 1920 x 1080.

Now you should see a blank vertical canvas on your screen.

B. Upload your horizontal video

Now that you have the perfect blank canvas, it's time to add your video.

You can crop your video to fit the length and width of the

vertical canvas. But most of us (including me) would rather not cut or trim our videos.

Instead, I recommend placing your landscape video onto the canvas in a centered position.

Take your time and get the position of your video just right. You want to retain its original horizontal aspects without accidentally trimming off the edge!

C. Create a design for the top and bottom spaces of your video

You've put your video onto a vertical canvas, and it looks great, except for the two blank spaces on the top and bottom of your video.

Unfortunately, you can't get rid of them. But you can turn them into a fantastic branding opportunity.

All you need to do is create an image or graphic design that will go above and below (or around) your horizontal video.

You can create this image using software like Photoshop, PicMonkey, or Canva. When you create a new image, look for a pre-set canvas ratio for Instagram Stories. If there is none, create your canvas using the same dimensions as above (1920 x 1080).

Now you've got your blank canvas it's time to get creative!

You can use any color or image you like, just make sure it doesn't take away focus from the video.

You could use your businesses branded colors, your logo or some text to add some more value to your video.

For example, if you want people to sign up to something (such as an online training course or workshop), you can add the information in the space above or below the video. Alternatively, you could add a powerful quote or a branded image.

Once you're happy with how it looks, download the final version. The graphics you create can also be re-used for future videos and for repurposing onto social media, so don't be afraid to get creative and include some shameless self-promotion where you can!

D. Embed the image into your video

You've got your video and your image, but how do you combine the two?

All you have to do is return to your video editing software, where your video is ready and waiting.

Next, add the image you created as additional media and bring it into the canvas as a second layer. The important thing here is to make sure the video is brought to the front, and the image is set to the back to avoid any overlapping.

It may take a few tries to get the positioning of the image just right. Once you're happy with how it looks, it's time to extract the video as an MP4 video file.

And there you have it. You've successfully converted your horizontal video into a vertical video you can put on IGTV, Instagram/Facebook Stories and Snapchat.

Now, there is a question of whether you should repurpose your horizontal/landscape videos for Instagram, or whether you should only create native content. After all, and I've said this before, just because you can do something doesn't always mean that you should!

Only you know your audience and what they will respond well to. As with any platform a good idea to test, test, test. See what works and what doesn't work.

I do think it's a good idea to create native content for platforms, but I also think that exploring repurposing opportunities when it makes sense

There is a video tutorial on how to do this in the Content 10x Toolkit

5. Think about branding your videos

As already mentioned above, you can add extra impact to your videos by adding text, color, images, titles or captions. You do this by creating a template that includes a space for captions, your business logo or the title of the video etc.

Use image editing software like Photoshop to create a branded template for your video. You can also use a website like Canva which is my favorite! It's easy to use and gives you the freedom to get creative with your template without making the process unnecessarily complicated.

Once you've created your template, save it as a transparent file and place it over your video as an image using video editing software (a few examples mentioned above). It instantly makes your videos look more professional and made for the platform. We show you how to do this in The Content 10x Toolkit.

6. Create GIFs from your videos

Everyone loves GIFs! If you've been keeping up with my blog you'll notice that I include lots of fun GIFs throughout my content.

If your video includes a funny moment you can transform it into a hilarious GIF to share on social media. Not a lot of people realize that they can create their own GIFs. Nope, not all GIFs are funny scenes from Friends! Who knows, your GIF could even go viral!

Creating your own GIF is a great way to make all the time you spent creating a video go further by repurposing video content for social media in a way that grabs people's attention and makes them want more.

Let me just clarify what I mean by a GIF. Getting all techie, GIF stands for Graphics Interchange Format and is a short looping animation. GIFs are a halfway point between an image and a video, using no sound and therefore less memory.

GIFs are currently undergoing a resurgence, but have

actually been around for quite some time, so long in fact they may even be considered retro. They are usually included to add humor, fun or emotion, and can add a little more impact an image alone.

So, how do you create your own GIF?

There are a few different ways. If you have it you can use Adobe After Effects program (paid) but perhaps a whole lot easier is to use free online tools too such as Giphy.com or EzGif.com.

Ezgif.com has a bit more functionality. For example, it allows you to create a transparent GIF, which works well on an image background or embedded into a website rather than if it were on a plain white background.

TOP TIP: You can apply for a brand channel on Giphy.com. This means that other people can find your GIFs and use them, as long as you make them public. This enables your followers to promote you via GIFs. These GIFs show in search on Facebook, Twitter, Messenger, Slack and WhatsApp to name a few places. And the great news is that, at the time or writing at least, it's free!

My good friends and content marketing heroes, Andrew and Pete from Andrewandpete.com create a lot of GIFs and in fact were on The Content 10x Podcast to talk about this very subject. In the past week alone my team and I have randomly had Andrew and Pete's GIFs come up in our searches for GIFs on Slack about ten times, which I always find hilarious because you don't expect your friends to pop up in GIF searches!

Making GIFs from images

You may be surprised to learn that you don't have to have a video to create your GIF from. You can also create a GIF from images too.

If you are new to GIFs it is fairly simple to use a handful of images and only change minor details, like perhaps add an arrow, to create an effective GIF.

Uses of GIFs

- **GIF games**

When Andrew and Pete came onto my podcast to talk about GIFs, they shared how they created a really fun game from a GIF that they made on Giphy with images. Their GIF had been created from a number of images of different speakers at the huge annual conference, Social Media Marketing World. It was a very fast paced GIF (the images of the speakers changed faster than the blink of an eye). When shared on Twitter, if someone touched the GIF it stopped. The game was to encourage people who were attending Social Media Marketing World to touch the GIF and whoever they landed on, to go take a selfie with that speaker!

Can you think of a similar fun GIF game that you could create for your business?

- **GIFs as a call to action**

Any call to action will be maximized if you use a GIF. It will give an edge over just providing a link in an email or an image in a blog post.

Say for example you want people to provide you with a review. Why not create a GIF asking them to, and embed the GIF in your email? If they click it, it takes them straight to where they need to write the review.

Or, for example, you can use GIFs in your emails. Let's say you want someone to click on something in your email, why not create a GIF with a play button or 'click me' call to action. This might get more attention than text alone.

- **GIFs as a short instructional guide**

Simple instructions can be communicated in GIFs, such as the classic 'add us to your mailing list' in your welcome emails, as long as it can be done in under 10 seconds. Instruction can often sound boring or time consuming, but watching something in 5-10 seconds is more likely to get attention and the person is then more likely to take action. So, when you're thinking of adding a short video, could you go a step further and add a short, fun GIF?

If you want to get started with GIFs, why not head straight over to Giphy, set up a brand channel to get ahead of most others (for free), grab a video and follow the instructions. It's easier than you think!

Repurpose your video into an article

Lots of people out there still want to read. Shock horror! Reading is *not* a thing of the past, not at all!

While many people find it easier to absorb visual or verbal information as opposed to written, it can be a lot faster to read and easier to find the specific sections you're most interested in.

In fact, there are many people who would take an article over a video any day!

Sometimes it's not even a case of preference, you may be in a situation where watching a video is out of the question. E.g. you're at work or you're in a library or another quiet place. In this situation, having something to read is perfect.

Not to mention the fact that having written content to accompany your video really helps with SEO. Read more about SEO in chapter one.

There are a few different options for repurposing your video content into written content:

A. Show notes: A summary of the video, potentially with timestamps if you want to help people hop to the section that appeals to them the most. Show notes are a synopsis of the video

B. Blog Post: Write a blog post based on the content in your video. Think about what your core message is and write a blog post about the topic of the video. You might consider getting your video transcribed first and *then* write your post

C. Transcription: A straight transcription of your video is an option. You can use services to create the transcription for you. Read chapter 13 for more on transcriptions. Transcriptions are not great for SEO compared to a well written post. The SEO bots can get confused by transcriptions because we don't necessarily speak how we write and this can make transcriptions a bit less logical for a bot to crawl.

D. Evergreen Article: A little different from the standard blog post repurpose, the evergreen article doesn't reference the video at all. Simply take the ideas from the video and expand them into an entirely separate, stand-alone piece of content that could go into any location. E.g. Onto a third-party site as a guest post on someone else's blog. This is called article syndication and can be great for growing your audience.

TOP TIP: Post the article to your own site at least one week before syndicating it elsewhere. That way, Google will index your site as the original source.

Very importantly, do some keyword research and aim to write a keyword focused blog post/article. This will help with your SEO. Think about the terms that your audience may use to search on Google or other search engines to find an article just like yours. Use keyword tools like Keywords Everywhere and Google Adwords in order to find your perfect keywords.

Repurpose your video into visual content

In this busy age we now live in, people have shorter attention spans than ever before. It's often the visual content that catches our eye more than anything else. Remember when I talked about the learning styles in chapter three? Well visual learners are those who are much more likely to be scrolling Instagram or feasting on Pinterest versus reading a blog post or watching a Facebook Live video.

Repurposing your video content into visuals can be a prolific way to produce new content in terms of the sheer number of potential pieces. Just think of all the quotable lines, questions from the audience, or even slides from your presentation if you had them, that you could repurpose into a great looking graphic. How many do you think you could get? Five? Ten? Twenty? More?

As long as each quote or question is a real "golden nugget", I don't see any problem with making as many as you can, since they're so versatile to use.

My favorite online software for this kind of graphic design is Canva. They couldn't make it easier for a non-designer to produce great visual content! There are a lot of platform specific templates you can work from. Additionally, because you have the video as your source content, it can be nice to take still images from your video and then create some social visuals from the stills.

Once you have your stack of graphics, schedule them to post on Facebook, Twitter, Instagram, Pinterest, and anywhere else that you're using that you think will be appropriate for your audience and the platform.

You can also sprinkle your graphics into your blog post if you write one. Adding graphics to blog posts brings them to life, suits the skim-readers, and can even help with SEO because the added graphics may just mean that a visitor stays on your page longer which reduces your bounce rate, something all websites are measured on. Reminder: Bounce rate is the time that someone arrives then leaves your site. They 'bounce' off your site.

Repurpose your video into a content upgrade lead magnet and grow your email list

A content upgrade is something additional you give your audience. It's directly related to the piece of content, and is usually given in exchange for an email address. A content upgrade may be a checklist, a template, a 'swipe file', a quick guide, a blueprint, a plan. The list is endless.

Back in 2016, SEO expert Brian Dean reported a 785% increase in opt-ins[10] after deploying content upgrades in his posts.

Your results are unlikely to be quite as high (but you never know!) since people have become a little more used to seeing content upgrades around. But rest assured, they will always have a higher conversion rate than generalized lead magnets for the simple reason that the value they provide is specific, clear, and believable. It's directly related to the content, and if they liked the content and found they got value from it, why would they not want the upgrade?

For example, if your video is about the '10 Best French Red Wines for Winter', you could offer your viewers a list of the 10 wines to be downloaded, with extra information about where to buy them, a price guide and what food to pair them with.

7. Repurpose your video into email

I'm amazed by how many of my clients create regular content but say that they don't regularly email their email subscribers. Even if they're posting everywhere else, they open up their email service provider and feel like they don't have anything to say!

One of the joys of repurposing is it can completely dismantle writer's block. You don't need to come up with anything new, you did that when you created your original piece of content. Perhaps we assume our email subscribers have all seen our video already. Trust me, they're not all following you that closely. We may want them to, *they* may want to, but life gets in the way! And even those who have already seen it won't begrudge you mentioning it to your list.

Your email doesn't have to be all about your video. You don't need to mention the video at all. Your email could standalone as a completely separate piece of content but what you have done here is repurposed the time and effort that you put

10 https://backlinko.com/increase-conversions

into planning and preparing your video and put that straight into the content of your email. You can either expand on the main point in your email with a link to your video or turn it into an entire series of emails, such as an educational course or a time-bound challenge.

Take the example of the '10 Best French Red Wines for Winter', you could email your subscribers and let them know about the video. Or, you could send a daily email for 10 days, each email expanding on one of the selected wines. Invite your email subscribers to report to you if they tried the wine and what they thought of it.

You can go one step further and create email challenges and courses that benefit your existing subscribers, but are also perfectly designed to grow your email list too. The whole idea is to entice people to provide you with their email address in order to receive your French Red Wines Challenge, for example.

8. Create and publish your slides

Did you make slides for your video? If the answer is yes then, for this example, good! If the answer is no then, could you? Could you take the key points from your video, or by now your repurposed blog post, and create a set of slides?

If you have slides, here's what you can do with them:

Log into LinkedIn Slideshare and post them there. You may want to make some enhancements and changes to them to make them engaging when they standalone, or you might be happy with them just as they are.

There are other document sharing sites that you could post your slides to aside from Slideshare. For example, scribd.com.

In conclusion

Video is the most versatile and popular content format around! There's no question it's having a massive impact online. As technology makes it increasingly easy to both record and disseminate video, it's becoming more and more clear that it is the format that people most want to consume.

With video you will always have audio too (unless you're filming Charlie Chaplin style silent movies!), plus so much more can be created. It's a content repurposer's dream!

If content is king, video is the crown.

VIDEO REPURPOSING CASE STUDY

Jay Baer - Convince & Convert

Jay has truly leveraged the power of repurposing for his 'talk triggers' content - proving that when you have great messages to share, repurposing allows you to amplify your ideas and delight both old and new audiences.

Jay Baer is a Hall of Fame speaker and emcee, a New York Times best-selling author of six books and the founder of five, multi-million dollar companies including digital strategy consulting firm Convince & Convert. Furthermore, he's the world's most inspirational marketing, customer experience, and customer service keynote speaker.

When providing an example of super smart and strategic repurposing, it doesn't get much better than Jay's talk triggers content.

My Content 10x team helped Jay and his team with video repurposing but it didn't begin there. It all started with Jay's research, which led to a book and a keynote talk, which led to a weekly video show...which was repurposed into a weekly podcast, blog post, video and visual content for all social media platforms. Epic repurposing.

I first met Jay at Chris Ducker's Youpreneur Summit in November 2018. Jay delivered the closing keynote titled *Talk Triggers: Turn Your Customers Into Volunteer Marketers.*

In Jay's inspirational keynote, he taught the audience that

the best way to grow any business is for your customers to grow it for you. How? Create an unforgettable experience that your customers share called a talk trigger. His talk included dozens of examples from his research.

Wow, all of that research for a talk? Well no, because Jay also has his book that he co-authored with Daniel Lemin - Talk Triggers: The Complete Guide to Creating Customers with Word of Mouth. The book contains proprietary research and more than 30 case studies. The case studies and research findings went into the book AND the keynote. Smart.

But it didn't stop there...

We worked with Jay and his team to launch The Talk Triggers Show. A video show and podcast, where in every episode Jay shares a fascinating story of word of mouth marketing. Where do the stories come from - the research for the book, of course.

A video AND a podcast you say? Yes, but the video is repurposed into each podcast episode - Jay does not need to record both separately.

The video and podcast content are then repurposed into lots of short video teasers and graphics for social media platforms. All of the content is published on Jay's website too providing weekly, fresh content for his site. Plus, via repurposing his talk triggers stories are being communicated on YouTube, all the podcast apps (including Apple Podcasts, Google Podcasts and Spotify), Instagram, Facebook, Twitter and LinkedIn.

Anyone would think Jay knows a thing or two about spreading a message!

All of this content gives watchers/listeners a choice of how they access Jay's ideas. And it all stemmed from Jay's research, and through successive repurposing rounds, has greatly increased his audience and reach. Clearly, Jay knows a thing or two about spreading a message!

CHAPTER 7

Live videos

In chapter six I covered many of the ways that you can repurpose video content. Now, let's take a look at *live* video content.

Live video streaming has become very popular in the past five years or so and it's no surprise. You can go live on various platforms including Facebook (the most popular platform for going-live), Instagram, YouTube, Twitter (via Periscope) and the newest live video kid on the block, LinkedIn.

With live video you create an experience

The internet and social media revolutionized the way information is consumed, in part because it allowed readers and viewers to get involved. Even before social media, you could still comment on articles and get conversations going in message forums but creating live experiences was somewhat more challenging.

Live content takes "audience engagement" to a whole new level. Facebook have announced that they see 10 times more engagement on their Facebook Live videos than their regular videos.[11]

Creating podcast episodes, articles, or pre-recorded videos are all great things to do but there's still a bit of separation between you and your audience. People can leave comments but they know there's likely to be a delay before you respond, if you ever do - not that I'm accusing *you* of not responding, but we've all been there when our comments have gone without a response.

In a live situation, however, they're right there with you and with all the other like-minded people who showed up to hear what you have to say. There's a little bit of suspense because anything could happen, anything could go wrong even. People are drawn to this!

I'll let you into a little secret, I barely watch any of the soap-operas on television anymore, I'm too busy running Content 10x and my family, but on the very rare occasion that I do tune in it's usually because they are doing a special 'live episode'. There is something inside me that just wants to watch so that I can spot something go not quite to plan! The live element can be very intriguing.

Live content can turn an audience into a community

Live experiences have the potential, almost by definition, to be more engaging than any other form of content. This is why content creators, audiences and the platforms themselves love live video. Mark Zuckerberg has stated on more than one occasion that he sees live video as the future of Facebook.

Four reasons why you should consider live video:

1. People get access to you

Sometimes access to you is all people want. Even if they

11 https://www.wired.com/2016/04/facebook-really-really-wants-broadcast-watch-live-video/

know it's not one-on-one and they might get crowded out by other attendees, people greatly appreciate that you are opening yourself up to the community in a live setting. You're not hiding away in secret somewhere!

2. Your audience becomes a community

Bringing your audience together by creating a live experience gives them better access not only to you but to each other and turns a passive audience into an active community. Community is powerful. Seth Godin has thought a lot about where our world is going, and he's noticed that the most valuable currency has shifted from efficiency to connection. Those that bring people together, that build tribes, will thrive in the new economy. You can build your tribe very effectively when you start to offer live experiences.

3. You boost your credibility

This is really important. There are many people jumping onto "educational marketing" and content marketing who, quite frankly, lack depth to their knowledge. And people are getting wise to that.

If you put yourself forward in a live format such as a Q&A however, you're making yourself vulnerable to your knowledge being tested by your audience. By answering questions live you're proving that you're the real deal.

Don't worry too much, by the way, about knowing everything before you get started. Even times when you don't know the answer to a question, being honest about that allows you to demonstrate humility and confidence. People may just love you that little bit more for being honest about the things you don't know. Plus, it also gives you a great springboard to create a new piece of content that serves your community while ensuring that you'll never be stumped by the same question again.

4. You can repurpose it like mad!

I've already taken you through the many different ways that

you can repurpose video content in the previous chapter. All of the repurposing opportunities discussed there can be applied to your live video content too, by the very nature of the fact that it's video content. You simply went one step further and created the live 'experience' first!

Some people consider live video to be a nice, quick and simple method of creating content but in actual fact, it can be really quite time consuming. In fact, I'm going to say that most people who consistently create live video as their core content put lots of time and effort into the whole production. From researching their topic to creating engaging slides (potentially), and collating questions from attendees in advance. If they're doing it right they will be promoting their live video to make sure people turn up (on social media, to their email subscribers and so forth). They will turn up early and get the tech set up just right.

Yes, for some people it's simply a case of grab their phone and hit 'go-live' but for many it's much more than that. Either way, I'm a firm believer that once you have completed your live video, that really is just the starting point of creating awesome content.

Do you want to reach people who missed your live video? After all, that's the risk with live video. You'll never find a time that suits everyone? Do you want to reach the people who just don't like live videos and never watch them? Do you want to reach the people who simply don't hang out on the platform you went live on?

If your answer is "yes" then you need to repurpose your live video.

It may seem like a ton more work to repurpose your video but you don't want to let all your hard work in creating the video in the first place go to waste. You want to maximize the value from all of your content. You owe it to your content, and to yourself! Firstly though, let me provide some tips for planning your live video, especially when you intend to go on and repurpose it. As I always like to say, repurposing starts at the planning phase.

How to plan your live video before you go live

Whilst a big part of the fun with live video is the spontaneity, it's always a good idea to have a plan before you go live, especially if you are going to repurpose your live video. There are things you can do with the format of your video that will really help with repurposing.

I spoke to my good friend, Ian Anderson Gray, an expert in live video and in helping people feel confident when they live stream. Here are his tips:

- **Check your tech beforehand:** Go live to yourself and check all is running okay. You can do this in Facebook by selecting your audience as 'only me'. Also, check your internet speed. You are looking for upload speed not download speed, and you need at least 4mbps or you may encounter issues. Use speedtest.net to check.
- **Get your energy levels up:** You might want to consider doing some voice exercises. This helps to make sure that your live audience are greeted by someone who is going to capture and keep their attention!
- **Start confidently and with purpose:** It's good to bear in mind that the people who will watch your live video from the very beginning are actually your replay viewers. It's your viewers in the future, those who watch the replay, who are going to see your (once-live) video from the very start because live viewers aren't usually there at the very beginning, they tend to sporadically over the first 5-10 minutes. With this in mind, make sure that you start with purpose.
- **Welcome your replay viewers first:** Announce what you're going to be talking about and introduce yourself. It doesn't matter if no one is there live, you are talking to replay viewers and that is good.

- **Then, welcome your live viewers:** Have a look, see who is watching you live and say "hello". Don't spend too long on this, but it's nice to acknowledge your live viewers. You can do this step in one discreet block of time so that it can be edited out later. Let your viewers know that you are going to move onto the main content, encourage them to make comments and ask questions but you won't respond until the end or the middle. If you take questions on the go this will distract you and may not create the best experience for a non-live audience. It's also a pain when you repurpose your video and you want to edit out some of the live interaction!
- **Commence your topic/presentation/main content:** This is the main section that you can use for repurposing later. Keep it focused. As mentioned above, leave questions and comments for later. As a tip, when deciding what content to cover, you could select a blog post that you have written, summarize it into the main points, and use those main points as the plan for your live video
- **After you have delivered your main content, get interactive with your viewers:** Make the most of the live aspect of the video and add lots of value by interacting with your viewers and answer questions. You could potentially create short separate videos from the Q&A sections where you create a video on a question and answer for social sharing, your website or membership site. It's important to get interactive because that's the whole point of live video, right?!

As already mentioned, many of the ways that you can repurpose video content, discussed in chapter six, apply to live video too, but there are some extra considerations.

Download your video file & 3rd party tools

Firstly, when you have completed your live video, you need to ensure that you extract a copy of the video file if you want to do any video editing, audio extraction etc. There are various ways to do this and it really depends on what platform you went live on or if you used any live-streaming software/apps.

For example, if you went live directly in Facebook, whether you recorded a Facebook Live video from your profile or your page, you firstly need to ensure you save the video at the end. You are also asked if you want to post it or delete it. You want to post it. Then, go to your videos. You will see your video there and when you go into it you will see three little dots to the top right-hand side. Clicking on that will give you download options. There are various browser plugins that will also allow you to download videos from your Facebook page or profile.

TOP TIP: When you are downloading your video file, check that you're happy with the title/information related to the video on Facebook. You can add tags and a custom thumbnail.

Disclaimer: Facebook change things *all* the time, so whilst what I have said above is correct at the time of writing, if you find that it's not quite right, just Google how to download your Facebook Live videos.

If you went live on YouTube then you should be able to download your video from Creator Studio/Video Manager.

Instagram lets you download your video directly to your phone after you have gone live. Just remember to click 'save video' *before* you share the video to your profile.

On Twitter, your live videos will automatically be posted as a Tweet when you go live. You can also save your live video right to your device's camera roll at the end of your live video by tapping save to camera roll.

For Apple lovers like me, if you record the video from your iPhone, you can easily send the video file to your Mac via AirDrop et voila!

Tools for live video

There are various third-party tools that you can use to

enhance your live video experience. It's important to not try to overcomplicate things or you may just give up because the tech gets too much.

That said, third-party tools can be really good. They give you, as the host, lots of additional features and a much higher quality video than the video generated for you by the social media platforms. Plus, the attendees to your livestream will notice the additional features and enjoy a more professional, live video experience.

It's not essential to use these tools, but if you want to step your live video experiences up a notch then a few to consider are:

- **BeLive** - BeLive supports Facebook and Twitch and gives 20 minutes broadcast, twice a week for free then starts at $20 per month. It includes options for solo, interview and talk show mode and allows you to add your logo and brand colors. Viewers comments are shown live on the screen. Screen-sharing and photo sharing are also available.

- **eCamm Live** - Desktop - Mac only

  This is great software and it's under $30. You record your live video from within eCamm, which you integrate with Facebook, so that it streams your recording to Facebook Live. You can save your video in full HD and it displays the comments. It's really good but it's only on desktop and only on Mac at the moment.

- **Switcher Studio** - Mac only

  Starts at $29 per month. You can do all sorts of great things with your live video, like create multiple cameras on iPads and iPhone with your iOS devices, add graphics and effects, multiple camera angles and more.

- **OBS Studio** (free) - Mac and PC

  There is a bit more of a learning curve when using OBS

Studio compared to eCamm Live, but there is so much that you can do, and it's free! You record your video in OBS Studio, stream to Facebook Live, and you can then save the video in full HD (great for repurposing). Plus you can do lots of funky things like bring in guests, switch scenes, add webcams.

- **Wirecast** ($249 - $699) - Mac and PC

  Wirecast offer a 30 day free trial to give you the opportunity to experiment with the software before committing to buy. With Wirecast you can post your stream on multiple Facebook pages at the same time. Plus access to over 500,000 unique media assets directly in Wirecast. The Stock Media Library has videos, music, lower thirds, backgrounds and more.

- **Vmix** (up to $1200) - Mac and PC

  vMix is live video production software that allows you to produce, stream and record in HD, SD and even 4K. You can live stream to your favorite streaming providers including Facebook Live, YouTube, Twitch and Ustream. A 60 day free trial is available.

N.B. All of the above is correct at the time of writing. All of the tools/software providers could change features, prices etc. at any time!

There are plenty of other live-streaming tools, apps and software. It's worth considering using one, and if you are going to repurpose your video, if only to get the higher quality video after the broadcast.

But as I mentioned earlier, don't let the tech get in the way. If you try to get all techie and sophisticated it's an easy way to get overwhelmed and ultimately stop creating your live videos.

So, you've gone live. You've downloaded your live video. Let's look at how you can repurpose this fantastic content!

Post your video to YouTube, your website & other

locations

Now that you have a downloaded video file of your live recording, why not go and publish it on other sites too?

To edit or not to edit

You can simply upload your video file, as it is with no editing, onto YouTube, Vimeo, IGTV, your website, into your membership site or whichever location you think appropriate.

Or, what I recommend, is to edit you video *before* you upload it elsewhere. At the very least, I think it's a good idea to edit out parts of the video that are not interesting for a replay, non-live viewer to watch. For example, if there's a bit of 'filler' time at the start when you're waiting for people to join the video or there may be some interaction back and forward with live viewers and time where you will be reminding people to ask you questions. All of this is not exactly valuable viewing for non-live viewers.

My take on this is that whilst you can make it clear to the replay viewers that the video was a live-stream, so they know what is going on, we live at a time when our attention spans are at an all-time low. Having sections of your video that don't add much value and in fact, could result in a viewer deciding not to watch your video. Some minor editing could really improve your retention rate.

Minor editing would be watching back and snipping out those significant live elements so, for example, a 30-minute livestream may end up being edited to 20 to 25 minutes.

Or, you could really go to town with your video editing and edit down a 30-minute livestream into a less than 10-minute video. This is exactly what we tend to do at Content 10x, my content repurposing creative agency. When we work with clients who have livestreams as their core content, we like to edit their video to be 100% value packed and short.

You can edit your video using video editing software like iMovie, Camtasia, Filmora, Final Cut Pro or HitFilm, to name but a few. Whether you decide to edit your video or not, have a think about the various online locations that you could post your video to.

Finally, because you are editing a live video, and we all know one of the risks of going-live is anything can happen, you might end up editing out bloopers. My recommendation is to have a separate file where you store up all of your best bloopers. Bloopers can be good for repurposing!

Let's face it, there's a reason why people love TV shows like 'It'll Be Alright on the Night' and 'Auntie's Bloomers' and it's because we love to see things go wrong! Your bloopers could be really funny and ideal for sharing on social media.

In fact, repurposing bloopers and mistakes into a funny and shareable video can be a good way to connect in a different way with your audience.

The main reason to share bloopers is of course because they are funny and they entertain people. But not only that, sharing bloopers can show you as a good-spirited person.

Sharing bloopers has many benefits:

- It allows you to show your audience you are not one of 'those types' who takes themselves too seriously.
- People generally put up a façade on social media and in their content, once every so often, it is nice to see a raw, funny side of people.
- Your mis-haps show your audience that you and your content are authentic.

Bloopers and mistakes can provide an element of escapism from perfection and a celebration of the flaws that we share. If you can get creative and think of funny or smart ways to reuse bloopers, it could drive viewers to the source content while adding an element of fun to your content. It's also a good way to subtly increase your know, like trust factor.

If I've sold you on the idea of editing out and saving your bloopers then, here are three super smart ways to start repurposing bloopers:

1. Edit them into the end of one of your videos

You could edit the blooper into the end of a video. We see this all the time with movies at the theater where if you stick around when the film is over you can see outtakes added on to the end.

2. Create a compilation of your bloopers

If you collect a whole lot of bloopers, you can edit them all together, create a blooper show reel and share that as one standalone piece of entertaining content on YouTube, Facebook and Instagram. This could be pretty hilarious!

3. Share clips on social media to promote new content

You can edit your bloopers into single files which can then be shared on Facebook, Twitter or Instagram. You can let people know in advance what the outtake is while at the same time, promoting a new upcoming video in a fun and engaging way.

My point being when editing your video, don't ever trash your mishaps because, in time, these mishaps could be useful

YouTube

YouTube is the second most popular search engine after Google plus it's owned by Google, so Google return a lot of YouTube content in their search results. As such, it's great to post your video to YouTube but first, be sure to do some keyword research. It will help you get found much more easily if you spend a bit of time working out a good, SEO-friendly keyword/key phrase for your title, description, and tags.

There are tools that can help you with keyword research for YouTube. Some are free and some are paid. These include TubeBuddy and Morningframe. You can do plenty of research on YouTube itself and don't forget to look at what your competitors are doing.

Your website

Another place you may want to put your video is your website. Once you have uploaded your video onto YouTube you can stream the video to be viewed on your website. If you don't want to stream it from YouTube, you could upload your video to Vimeo or Wistia, and stream to your website from there.

You want to have the video file itself hosted somewhere other than your website, because video files on your website would be quite large and would potentially slow your website down. Creating a blog post about your video topic and having the video within the blog post can work really well.

Membership site or online course

If you have a membership site or an online course, your catalogue of live videos could work really well being served up as membership or course content.

With membership sites, when it comes to providing content for your paying members, you're always looking to add value and to make sure paying members get that bit more than others who simply consume your free content. This could be an opportunity to offer up only your highly edited version of the video to your membership.

It's also about *where* you provide this content. For example, if there are various 'roadmaps' that you take your members on depending on what they want to learn, then knowing exactly where to place this video to help them on their journey can be highly valuable. You're not expecting them to hunt down the right content for themselves. Instead, you're dishing up the perfect content to them on a plate!

Create short 'teaser videos' for social media

I already talked about how you can choose to edit your video before sharing it elsewhere. How about not just editing your video, but more so, extracting short, snack-able sections of the video for sharing on social media?

I explore this in chapter six, where I talk about repurposing your video into little video babies. The same principles apply here because it really makes no difference whether you're working with a pre-recorded video or a once-live video, except your live video may have more bloopers!

People love to consume video content on the social media platforms, and you don't always have to create videos from scratch. Repurpose your longer videos.

Be sure to pay attention to the criteria for maximum length of the video clip and the aspect ratio. Square video clips being the preference on Facebook, Instagram and Twitter posts, whereas it's vertical/portrait videos for Instagram Stories, Facebook Stories, IGTV and Snapchat.

Go ahead and read the *Repurpose your video into little video babies* section in chapter six where I talk about the whole process of selecting and creating these short video snippets in more detail.

Repurpose your live video to a podcast episode

If you have a podcast already, or you're thinking of starting one, then it may just be the case that you can use your live video as your core content and then repurpose the video into a podcast episode by extracting the audio.

At Content 10x, when we work with people who go-live on a weekly basis, we almost always repurpose their live videos to podcast episodes.

The truth of the matter is, not everyone watches live video, not everyone can make your live videos, not everyone likes to watch video at all, and some people just LOVE, love, love to listen to podcasts.

Podcasts have the beauty of being something that we can consume when we are doing something else that doesn't take up much brain capacity. You can drive and listen to a podcast. You can walk your dog or go for a run and listen to a podcast. You can cook your meals and listen to podcasts. They really do have an advantage that most other forms of content do not.

I talk about this in *Repurpose your video into a podcast* section in chapter six and I cover exactly how to repurpose video content into podcast episodes. All of the principles and points made there are relevant here too.

The key differentiator when talking about live videos specifically is that, even more so than pre-recorded videos, you're going to want to consider editing the content before repurposing. For example, I mentioned earlier that the video replay viewers may not want to watch lots of live interaction. It could even be, dare I say it, just plain irritating!

If sitting through live interaction during a replay video might be irritating, how much more so if you have audio only? For example, time spent at the start waiting for people to join, you asking people to 'type questions in the comments field below' and so on.

If you decide to edit your video and already have a version that keeps to the main, value-add aspects of your delivery, it may well be that all you need to do is extract the audio from the edited video and you will have a great piece of audio to use as a podcast episode.

If you want to go a step further and do some more editing of your audio file, or if you decide to leave the video as it is and only edit the audio, then you need audio editing software. You can use Audacity which is free on Mac and Windows. When I first got started, I personally used Audacity and whilst I wouldn't say that it's the most intuitive the first time you use it, there are plenty of tutorials on YouTube that show you what to do.

If you want to edit your audio, clean up the sound, and add in intros and outros then consider Alitu. It's a paid option but it's an extremely simple and user-friendly way to edit your episodes together yourself without needing to have advanced audio editing skills and without lots of fancy tools! I'm good friends with Alitu creator Colin Gray, aka The Podcast Host, and given his vast knowledge of what it takes to edit and produce a good sounding podcast you can guarantee Alitu is going to lead the way as an all in one audio editing tool. It 'tames the tech' and integrates with major podcast hosts too.

I mentioned in chapter six about the need to be aware of your surroundings and your audio when recording your video, particularly if you know you are going onto repurpose into a podcast episode. Really do consider this when you are recording a livestream.

As fun as it may seem to go-live spontaneously at that (noisy) event that you're at or whilst you're waiting for a plane in the (noisy) departure hall at the airport and that may well create a great visual experience for your video viewers, it's likely to create a very poor audio experience for your podcast listeners.

If you're first and foremost focused on creating a great experience for your video viewers then that's okay, but there may well be simple steps that you can take to ensure that the audio pulled from the video is still going to be easy on the ear too.

It may be small things like moving to a far quieter place to record your video, stepping away from the noise and just being more aware of your surroundings. Plus, do make sure that you use a decent microphone.

For example, a couple of days ago I was recording a video in what seemed to be a fairly quiet section of the coffee shop I was in. Except, I didn't realize that I was sat right by the blender that they use to blend ice for the ice smoothies. Is there anything noisier (or more irritating) than the sound of a huge blender, pulverizing a smoothie? I'm sure there is but at the time it sounded like the loudest noise on earth!

My point being, do give your surroundings and sound quality some consideration when going live on video.

Repurpose your live video into visual content

I discussed in chapter six how you can repurpose your video content into visual content. The same principles generally apply for live video as they do for video. This is all about how you can create visual content for the social media platforms, and elsewhere. For example, graphics and images to be shared on Instagram, Facebook, Twitter and Pinterest.

You can take still images from your live video and share them with engaging copy on social media platforms. Ask people questions about the topic covered in your live video. Share what was discussed.

You could edit your still images and add some words to them. Add quotes, tips and key points made during the video. You can do this using a site like Canva. It's simple and easy to use.

Or, rather than use still images from your video, you could create branded quote graphics. You can source free, royalty-free photos from sites like pexels.com, pixabay.com, unsplash.com and many similar sites and have some fun creating graphics with those photos.

Try creating graphics *with* photos and *without* photos. Always ensure that they are 'on-brand' for you and your business. Include your logo, your URL and use your brand colors where possible.

Repurpose your live video into written content

I really recommend doing a write-up of your live video. And no, I don't mean a write up that goes along the lines of... "At first there were no viewers to my live video, then two minutes in I was joined by my Mum..."

Rather, I mean a write-up of the core topic that you discussed: What did you teach people, show people, help people with? If you made notes before you went live, and really planned out your live video, then it may well be that all you need to do is turn your notes into an article.

Or you might consider creating a transcript of your live video. Use software like Otter.ai, a service like Rev.com, or hire a transcriptionist. See chapter 13: Transcripts for more information on this. You could offer the transcript only or, better still, use the transcript as a starting point for writing an article. Transcriptions are not great for SEO compared to a well written post because the SEO bots can get confused by transcriptions. We don't necessarily speak how we would write and this can make transcriptions a bit less logical to a bot and therefore hard to crawl.

Your article could go on your website as a blog post. Bonus points if you also include your video and graphics as and maybe even your repurposed podcast episode?!? Give your blog visitors a multimedia experience!

Very importantly, do some keyword research and aim to write a keyword focused blog post/article. This will help you with your SEO. Think about the terms that your audience may use to search for an article just like yours, and use keyword tools like Keywords Everywhere and Google Adwords in order to find your perfect keywords.

In chapter six on repurposing videos, I talk more about the SEO benefits of having a written article to accompany your video.

Once you have a write-up of your topic, you then have the words that you can use for social media copy for all of the social media videos and visuals that we already discussed in this chapter! After all, it's great to create a teaser video to share on social, an edited-down video for YouTube, or lots of great looking graphics for Instagram but each needs to be accompanied by engaging copy. If you have written a blog post/article about your topic then you have the starting point at least for crafting your engaging social copy.

Repurpose your live video into a content upgrade/ lead magnet

We talk about content upgrades/lead magnets in chapter 16 but in case you haven't got there yet (I don't expect you to read the book in section by section order) then, to clarify, a content upgrade is something additional that you provide your audience with, which is directly related to the piece of content. It's usually offered in exchange for an email address. A content upgrade may be a checklist, a template, a 'swipe file', a quick guide, a blueprint or a plan, to provide just a few examples.

Content upgrades tend to have a higher conversion rate than generalized lead magnets for the simple reason that the value they provide is narrow, clear, and believable. It's directly related to the content, and if they liked the content and got value from it, why would they not want the upgrade?

When your original content is live video, I would say that it's always a good idea to have created your content upgrade in advance, so that you can offer it as a free giveaway during the live video. At multiple times during the video you can provide the URL for the freebie (make it really simple) and encourage people to sign-up for it.

For example, let's say your live video was on the topic of why it's so important to incorporate protein into every meal that you eat. Your freebie could be a PDF guide, *7 Super Tasty & Easy to Prepare High Protein Meals.*

In this case it's not so much that the content upgrade is repurposed from your live video. Instead, you create the content upgrade whilst you are planning out your live video content.

If you don't create your content upgrade in advance, there is still the opportunity *after* your live video to create one. You did all the planning and preparation to bring your live video together, you may well have gone onto to get it transcribed, written up a blog post, maybe even created visual content. Review the core topic and content you have created and see what you could offer of value to your audience in exchange for an email address.

It may well be that creating your content upgrade/lead magnet after your live video was the best thing to do, because the live Q&A that you held with your audience helped you really understand just what they wanted the most help with.

For example, building on my illustration above, perhaps in your Q&A you discovered that people are generally okay with preparing protein rich meal for lunch and evening meals, but what they really struggle with more so than anything else, is a protein rich meal for breakfast. Your live video gave you this really useful feedback so you go on to create *7 Easy to Prepare High Protein Breakfast Recipes.*

Remember, it's not just about getting that all important email address to grow your email subscriber list. It's also about adding value and delighting those who are already in your audience and for whom you already have an email address. It's about always keeping your audience front of mind and always adding value.

Repurpose your live video into an email

We've been talking about how to get more new email subscribers but we mustn't neglect our current subscribers when it comes to creating a content strategy for our live videos.

How often do you think to yourself that perhaps you're not keeping in touch with your subscribers as much as you should? But how often do you worry that you don't want to 'spam' them and that you must only send them emails that are valuable?

These are both valid concerns, good concerns. They show that you're a decent person and marketer! The good news is that the time, thought and effort that you put into creating your live video can be repurposed into an email too.

At the very least, you can email your subscribers to let

them know all about the topic and the key takeaways or lessons learned. You can link to all of the various (repurposed) content relating to the topic, thank those that attended your recent live video, and remind those that didn't of the details of your live videos. For example, do you go live at the same time, every week, on the same platform? Remind people. They may not know and, whilst you are doing so, remind them of the benefits of joining you live.

Your email doesn't need to be focused on the fact that you did a live video on the topic. Keep in mind that we're not necessarily repurposing your live video, we're repurposing your thoughts and ideas that went into the live video. Your email could standalone completely and not even mention your live video.

Repurpose your slides/presentation materials

Did you make slides for your live video to present to? If the answer is yes, then good! As mentioned in chapter six, it's possible to repurpose the slides that you created.

If you didn't have any slides, is this something that you could create afterwards? Especially if you have been a busy repurposing bee then by now you may have visuals and a blog post. Between the written content and visual content, can you create a slide deck?

If you have slides there are a few things you can do with them. This ranges from posting to LinkedIn, Slideshare, and other document sharing sites, e.g. Scribd.com.

If you ever get asked to deliver a webinar, masterclass or an in-person presentation on the same topic, you will be able to use the slides there too. This makes them extremely useful. They can be used again, and again, and again.

In conclusion

As we discussed previously in chapter six, video is the most versatile form or content for repurposing.

Live video is no exception and, in fact, live video gives you everything. You have all of the video repurposing benefits of a pre-recorded video (albeit you may need to do more editing afterwards) plus you have provided your audience with a live experience and direct access to you.

There's no question that the social media platforms love live video, and so you get an added boost when it comes to reaching your audience when you take the plunge and go live.

When we work with clients at my content repurposing agency, Content 10x, we love it when their source content is live video. The repurposing opportunities are always endless.

If content is king, and video is the crown, then live video is the crown with extra sparkles!

LIVE VIDEO CASE STUDY

Tara Walsh - The Lashpreneur

The power of a consistent content repurposing strategy to build authority and a loyal audience within your niche.

Tara Walsh is the founder and CEO of The Lashpreneur. She helps lash business owners to start, build and grow a thriving lash business through her private online membership, The Lashpreneur Society (providing online coaching, mentorship, training and access to a like-minded community).

Tara's mission is extremely clear. She knows exactly who she wants to help...not small business owners, not business owners in the health and beauty industry, but very specifically eye lash artists who want to run their own successful lash businesses. This is about as niche as it gets, right?

Content marketing is essential as this is the vehicle through which new audience members can find her, fall in love with her, gain trust in her as the person who can help them, and join her private membership. You can't achieve this through a Facebook ad.

When we first started working with Tara she was creating great content but was frustrated that she wasn't extracting all the value out of her content. She knew there was potential to create a system whereby the quality content from her Facebook Live video could be extracted and multiplied into lots of new content. She also had a podcast called Lessons of a Lashpreneur, but it was on Soundcloud only and not published consistently.

Cue ... Facebook Live weekly repurposing. Tara turns up for her audience on a Facebook Live every week - same time, same place, and her audience look forward to this and tune in just like they would their favorite TV show.

But what about people either not on Facebook or just not able to watch the video?

We started working with Tara to repurpose her weekly Facebook Live videos into episodes for her Lessons of a Lashpreneur podcast. This immediately brought about weekly consistency, which is essential in podcasting. Plus, we also ensured that the podcast was on all major podcasting apps.

The result has been phenomenal! It turned out there was a huge audience ready to tune into Tara's show each week, she just needed to reach them. In no time she was getting 1000's of listeners for each episode!

Her Facebook Live video is edited into a YouTube video, therefore providing regular content on her YouTube channel. Bonus! Especially from an SEO perspective.

We create a long-form blog post that can stand alone as a fresh piece of content on Tara's website. The blog post is a multimedia experience, with a written article, video, podcast player and graphics. Perfect for all visitors to the site and it keeps people on the page longer.

We also turn the Facebook Live video into lots of short videos and graphics for Instagram and Facebook. They all get posted out over the course of 3-4 weeks, meaning the social media channels always have great content ready to be published.

So, the moral of this story is one value-packed Facebook Live video can be repurposing into a considerable amount of additional, new content. All you need is a repurposing plan and consistency!

CHAPTER 8

Blogs

Video, podcasts, live-streaming, engaging visual content; all of these different mediums are becoming so popular, does anyone really want to read a blog post anymore? Are blog posts just a thing of the past?!

Of course they're not! Blog posts are still an extremely valuable form of content. People *do* still want to read content online.

Having written content is extremely important for SEO, in other words for being found by the search engines. As such, written content like blog posts are often the way we bring new people into our audience. Even if people later go on to engage with us via our videos and our podcasts, it was the written content that helped us find each other initially.

Creating a video version of your blog can be a great way to communicate your message clearly and concisely.

Imagine taking a 2000-word blog post and stripping it down to a 1-minute video. This forces you to focus on only the most important points of your message. It's a great way to de-fluff it!

When it comes to repurposing blog posts, it's fair to say that they are not the most versatile form of original content for repurposing, not when compared to video, live video, podcast and live events.

However, blog posts do still present many different repurposing opportunities and if you are a regular blogger then you're going to find lots of repurposing ideas in this section. It helps to think of it less as 'content' repurposing and more as 'communicating a message' repurposing. You have communicated your message in one way. Now it's time to communicate it in other ways.

We also must consider the difference between blog *repurposing* and blog *syndication*.

First, what is blog syndication?

Blog syndication is the process of republishing a blog post that you have already published on your website, onto other 3rd party websites. When we write a great blog post we tend to shout about it on social media and maybe send an email to our list but that only gets the content in front of your *existing* audience.

By syndicating it, you put your blog post in front of *new* audiences. You tap into the web traffic of other sites online. When you're just starting out, it's highly likely that those sites will have much more web traffic than your website so this is a huge opportunity!

You *can* republish the exact same article. However, there are benefits to making slight tweaks such that the search engines do not consider it to be duplicate content. There is no penalty for duplicate content despite what many online 'gurus' will tell you (more on this soon ...) but this avoids having the posts (original and syndicated) competing against each other to be found by the search engines.

TOP TIP: Consider changing the title and/or the subtitle of your blog post. Bonus points if you also change the introduction.

Where can you syndicate blog content?

Popular places to republish your blog posts are LinkedIn (as an article) and Medium. You might also consider blogs that specialize in niches that are relevant to you. Many are open to syndicated content in addition to unique guest posts.

For example, anybody with a LinkedIn profile can write an article on LinkedIn. To do so you simply post an article in the same way that you post an update. Note: 'write an article' is the option that you must select. This is not the same as a 'status'.

You can quite literally copy and paste the article that has been published on your own website. You may need to tidy up the formatting a little but, on the whole, it's not the most time-consuming process.

Medium make the process even easier. You don't even need to copy and paste all of your content. Instead, simply provide the URL for your blog post and Medium copies and pastes the content for you.

Very popular sites like Mashable, TechCrunch, Lifehacker, HuffPost and such like will take syndicated content, but you may need more of a profile in order to get accepted onto those sites.

A quick and easy way to find out whether a site accepts syndicated content is to perform a search for the name of the website + "this article originally appeared on". Usually this will help you find out if the site accepts syndicated content.

Will you get punished by Google and the other search engines?

The biggest question I'm asked when talking about content syndication is will you get punished by Google? For a long time, there were a lot of people talking about a 'duplicate content' penalty when this is not true. There is no penalization for duplicate content. However, there are a few things that you can do to syndicate your content in the most effective way:

- **Link back to the original:** Put a link back to the original article somewhere on your republished article - "this post originally appeared on...", or "..was first published on....". When someone searches for the article, if both come up but one links to the other, the original one will likely rank higher.
- **Adapt the article for the audience:** Content works because of the audience and the angle. If you can adapt your original article with a new headline, a different perspective or by adding visuals, you will improve the quality of the piece and increase your chance of gaining authority through outreach.
- **Use canonical links:** This is a tag that Google came up with to address duplicate content online. It tells Google definitively what the original source of the content is. If you are republishing your content from one website to another site that you own, you can place the canonical link on your website quite easily with SEO plugins like Yoast. If you are syndicating an article onto a website that you don't own, you need to ask the publisher to add a canonical link pointing back to your original article.
- **Don't publish everything at the same time:** Publish the article on your website first, give it a few weeks at least for Google and the other search engines to index your article as the original source, *then* start to post the article to other sites.

It's important to note that whilst you will not be penalized by Google if you post the exact same content on multiple platforms, you still want to be wary of overdoing it.

Advantages of blog syndication

The big advantage of blog syndication is more eyes on your

content and more chances of being found by new and different audiences.

But be aware, syndication has no SEO benefit for your website and although it isn't risky, some people would argue that it is lazy! It's a perfectly fine thing to do, with other benefits, but it shouldn't be your *only* blog repurposing strategy.

With blog repurposing versus blog syndication cleared up, let's look at different ways to repurpose your blog posts.

Repurposing a blog post into a video

There are a few different ways that you can repurpose your blog post into video. The option you choose depends, for the most part, simply on whether you want to, and/or feel comfortable, with putting yourself on camera. Let's look at both of these options.

Blog to video, with you on camera

If you're comfortable being on camera then why not take your blog post and use it to form the outline for your video plan and/or script?

You could almost go so far as to read your blog post out on camera. I'm not suggesting that you hold a piece of paper or your tablet in your hand and read the post word for word, that wouldn't be the most engaging video, but you can take the key points from your blog post, turn that into a list of bullet points that you can easily see when on camera, and then video record yourself talking through each of these points.

After all, you wrote the blog post so you should be comfortable enough talking about each point. The list will simply keep you on track and make sure that you don't forget anything!

If you're really fancy, you might have a teleprompter or teleprompter app (the kind of thing that news readers and Presidents use to address the nation!). Using this you can, quite literally, turn your blog post into a script.

Depending on the length of your blog post and where you want to put your video, you may well decide to not just create one video, but many! For example, if it's a short blog post talking about three ways to do something, that may easily be repurposed into a short three-minute video suitable for YouTube.

In addition, consider creating three shorter videos that can be used for Instagram, Facebook and Twitter, one video per point made. Social video generates 1200% more shares than text and images combined. See chapter six on video repurposing for more on this.

Whichever type of video you create, you don't need to invest in expensive video recording equipment. If you have the fancy gear then, by all means use it but most smartphones have pretty decent built in cameras and that's all you'll need. As always, consider the sound quality and consider, at the very least, using headphones with a built-in microphone.

Quite often, it's not the blog post itself that is rewritten into a video script. It's much more common for a blog post to *inspire* a video. You put a lot of time and effort into writing that blog post and during the process you gleaned lots of useful stories and information to share on video so let's take to the camera and talk!

Blog to video, with you *not* on camera

Did you know that you can repurpose your blog posts into a video using online tools/software that mean you don't have to put yourself on camera? This is great for those of us who are a bit camera shy! With the advancement of these tools, you don't even need advanced video editing skills!

There are a few different tools available and the three that I'm most familiar with are Lumen 5, Animoto and Biteable.

What these sites allow you to do is create videos where you pair text, with either images or video footage (from stock libraries or supplied by you), and music (again, provided by you or from their supply). The videos can be animated in fun ways, you select how long each scene is and how it displays. They are generally pretty intuitive.

Lumen 5 in particular is very much designed for blog to video repurposing. All you need to do is provide the URL of your blog post, and through the power of AI and bots it pulls over what it considers to be the most important text and turns it into a video storyboard. You can make any changes that you want to the text until it's just right, and then you select images and/or video to pair up with the text.

It will even bring images over from your blog post if they are in the right dimensions. Plus, you can upload your own images. Or - and I think this is great - it is synced with some of the royalty-free image sites (including my favorite unsplash.com) so you can choose images from those sites without even leaving Lumen 5!

All of the tools/software are free to experiment with but, if you decide you like a particular tool and want to use it regularly, paid plans are generally quite reasonable.

Putting your video into your blog post

Once you have a video version of your blog post, whether it's with you on camera or not, it's a great idea to embed or stream that video into your blog post. Whilst I know that you'll want to share the video in lots of other locations, putting it into your blog post can have many benefits. For example, did you know that blog posts incorporating video attract 3x as many inbound links as blog posts without video? Also, blog posts with a video placed at the top encourage people to stay longer on the page, increasing the dwell time which in turn increases your positive user interaction signals to search engine bots.

Repurposing a blog post into a podcast episode

If you have a podcast then repurposing your blog post into a podcast episode can be a really effective and time efficient thing to do.

For example, for my podcast, The Content 10x Podcast, the majority of my episodes are short solo shows where I share tips advice on specific aspects of content repurposing. They could easily be based on a blog post. Now, whilst we usually repurpose the podcast into a blog post, because that's just the way our content flow/system works, there have been times where we have created a blog post first, then repurposed that into a podcast episode.

I've already discussed using your blog post as a script when I covered repurposing your blog post into a video. All of the points I made there apply here too. So don't read your blog post out word for word or you may run the risk of sounding a bit wooden/it may sound too heavily scripted. Instead, consider listing out the key talking points.

If you decided to create a video based on the blog post then consider extracting the audio from the video and repurposing that into a podcast episode. I cover the whole process of doing this in chapter six on video repurposing.

For any podcaster who also has a blog, I challenge you to look at your blog post archives and future planned posts and evaluate if you have some podcast episodes in there too!

Repurposing a blog post into an infographic

Have you ever created an infographic from your content? Infographics are really popular. Everyone loves infographics, right?! They're visually appealing, highly engaging and they're really good for repurposing certain types of blog posts such as list posts, e.g. 10 Ways To Create Blog Posts.

Infographics are really effective when you're simplifying a complicated concept. Comparisons and explanations work well too. Infographics are not only visually engaging, but they have a tendency if done well to bring topics to life. At a time when scanning is the new reading, infographics enable us to scan and learn. Whilst infographics can be consumed very quickly, you're still able to convey your key message.

Infographics feed our short attention spans!

I consider infographics to be best for your high-end, flagship content. They're probably not something that you're going to create for every blog post but, deployed well, an infographic can convey your message really effectively and enhance your audience's experience.

What do you do with an infographic when you have created one?

Pinterest is an obvious place. When people think infographics, they often think of Pinterest because there are so many infographics on there. That's great if your audience hang out on Pinterest or if you're trying to reach a new-to-you audience there.

One word of caution though, as Pinterest expert Kate Ahl pointed out when she was on my podcast, infographics are good at driving engagement, but they aren't so good at increasing click-through rates. The main reason for this downfall is because infographics tend to reveal too much information, giving a Pinterest user no reason to click because they already know the 'hook'. It's better to provide some information whilst leaving out just enough to encourage them to follow the link to your blog post.

You can also share your infographic on other social media platforms. Facebook and Twitter are the obvious choices but don't forget LinkedIn and SlideShare too. Infographics are popular on social media. They gain three times more likes and shares than *any* other type of content.[12]

Another great place to put your infographic is your own blog post. If you've turned a blog post into an infographic, then displaying the infographic alongside the blog post is often a good idea. It can really bring your post to life.

Another really good strategy is to include the infographic as a download on your website in exchange for an email address,

12 https://www.hubspot.com/marketing-statistics

turning the infographic into a list building tool.

Ultimately there are lots of different places to put your infographic and plenty of people to share it with.

Which blog post should you repurpose into an infographic?

Clearly, it's up to you, there are no set rules, but here are a few pointers:

- You can repurpose your brand new blog post into an infographic, or you can repurpose older posts. Don't forget to look into your archives.
- If you repurpose an older post I recommend using your analytics e.g. Google Analytics, to look at which posts are the most popular.
- If people like a post and the content then it's highly likely they'll love your infographic too. Therefore, consider making the infographic a content upgrade available via email. Or add the infographic into the post itself and share an embed code for people to embed your infographic elsewhere.

The *type* of post needs to be considered too. For example, as mentioned previously, blog posts that provide lists, comparisons and share step-by-step processes work really well.

How to create an infographic from a blog post

Here are the steps that I recommend:

1. Turn your blog post into a storyboard. You need to look at the blog post and decide what you want to include in the infographic. Completely strip your blog post down. Get rid of any words and sentences that aren't needed. Think about what the sections will be and turn long paragraphs and text into bullet points. You want to end up with a clear title, sections, and bullet points within each section, and a call to action at the end. This is your storyboard.

2. Create. There are a couple of options for doing this. One option is the DIY option. You can use tools like Canva. Canva is free, although there is a paid pro version, and it has lots of infographic templates. There are other online infographic-builder options aside from Canva that are free or not too expensive.

3. Caution. It can be quite fiddly and time-consuming to create good looking infographics. If you've got a designer who works in your team then of course this is the perfect job for them. Otherwise, you might consider hiring a freelance designer to do this for you. As well as sharing your storyboard, you'll want to share your logo, brand colors, brand fonts and such like. Find infographics that you think look really good and share those with your designer. Explain that you would like something to be created that looks like that. Or, you could sketch out what you want your infographic to look like. Sketch it out, scan it and email it over to the designer. The more information that you can provide your designer the better.

Always make sure that you focus on quality with your infographic. It needs to look really engaging, really professional and really fun!

Whilst HubSpot has stated that infographics are shared three times more than other forms of content, you need to make people *want* to share it. They're going to want to share it if it provides really good information. If it's really useful, really helpful, people will share it.

Make it easy to share

If you want people to share your infographic then make it easy for them to do so. If you're going to put it on your own website I recommend including some social sharing options e.g. social sharing widgets. You can add the "pin it" button with a Pinterest widget to make it easy for people to share your infographic on Pinterest.

TOP TIP: Track your success. If you put the infographic onto your website it will be loaded there as media and will have its own URL. You can track that URL via your analytics. If you upload and store your infographic elsewhere, like Amazon S3, you should still be able to track it.

On the Content 10x website we have an infographic on how to repurpose a blog post into an infographic - you can download it at www.content10x.com/4. (We repurposed our blog post into the infographic - very meta!)

Repurposing a blog post to a presentation/SlideShare

Have you ever considered creating presentations/a set of slides to communicate with your audience? When I say presentation, you may be thinking that you'd only create one if you were presenting at an event, a seminar, a workshop, etc.

Did you know that creating presentations/slides, like the presentations that you see on SlideShare, can be an effective way of getting your point across and a great starting point for repurposing your blog post?

Firstly, what is SlideShare?

If you're not familiar with SlideShare (and don't worry if you aren't, it's not as well-known as the other platforms I talk about in this book) it's a platform that hosts slide presentations, infographics and other documents.

SlideShare was founded in 2006 and it's grown very quickly. In 2012 it was purchased by LinkedIn, then in 2017 LinkedIn was purchased by Microsoft. This makes SlideShare a Microsoft-owned platform.

Whilst slide presentations are the main content on SlideShare, they are not all boring, stuffy corporate presentations. Many are very fun, creative and engaging. I've seen really good SlideShare presentations that have captured my attention more than many videos on YouTube. In fact, SlideShare is less intimidating than YouTube for those of us who don't want to be on video or who don't have the skills, equipment etc.

It's not SlideShare vs YouTube either, because the presentation that you create for SlideShare can go onto YouTube as well. Record your screen with screencast software and maybe even read out as you go through the slides and then you have a video! Your video need not only be for YouTube either. You can then share it anywhere you like, e.g. your website. See ... lots of repurposing going on here!

And remember, it doesn't have to be a long slide presentation. There are many content repurposing possibilities from a 10 or 15 slide presentation.

Top tips for repurposing a blog post into a presentation and then repurposing the presentation:

- Find an evergreen blog post that addresses and solves a problem that your target market has.
- Shrink it down to an outline. Select the headings and pick out the main points. The main points are anything that without which the post would not make sense. Get rid of anything that is not required.
- Find images to go with each heading and each point. Use royalty-free images from sites like Pexels, Pixabay and Unsplash. Note: See the resource section for links to all these sites and more. Find images that evoke emotion but don't spend too much time on this.
- Create your slides using PowerPoint, Keynote or a site like Canva. 16:9 slides are suitable for YouTube, SlideShare, and most social media platforms. Put words with your images and include text-only slides too.
- Add personality to your presentation. You want people to connect with you.
- For repurposing potential, make each slide represent a

complete thought. I.e. Make sure it can stand alone.

- Save each slide as an image that you can use anywhere. E.g. On your blog post, on social media.
- Always have a call to action. There has to be a goal for every piece of content - it should be to bring people back to your website.
- Save your presentation as a PDF. A PDF is perfect for SlideShare, other document sharing sites like scribd.com, or for providing a PDF download to your audience. Reminder: This is a good thing to do for email list building. Keep reading for more on this.
- In SlideShare, disable the download facility. Instead, include a slide in your presentation offering people the opportunity to download. When they 'click here', redirect people to your website or landing page from where they can add their email address and get the presentation delivered to their inbox. This is great for email list building.
- You can very easily add your SlideShare presentations to your LinkedIn profile since both platforms are linked to each other, and you can easily embed your SlideShare presentation on your website. Put your presentation back into the blog post it was repurposed from.
- As mentioned previously, you could screen record your presentation, with you presenting or even just with music, and then you have a video file that you can upload to YouTube, social media, your website etc. too

Can you think of any blog posts that you have already written that would make a good presentation? Why not give this a go? By uploading your presentation onto SlideShare you have the opportunity to get traffic to your website that you otherwise may not have had.

Creating visual content for social media and your

blog

On social media, images are a must. Can you imagine social media without images?! But the same goes for blog posts too. Imagine clicking on a blog post only to discover that it doesn't have any images. The beauty of repurposing blog posts into images for social media is that you can use those same images in your blog post as well. It's a win-win scenario.

Images that you create for your blog post and/or social media can be key quotes, significant points made, and an image with the title of your blog post. These can double up as your blog featured image and be resized and shared on the social media platforms that you are on. Use Canva or similar sites to create your graphics and visuals.

Note: when you have created your social media images, you will hopefully be able to take well written copy from your blog post and use that (albeit with a little bit of editing) as your caption/copy when posting on social media platforms. This is perfect 'copy repurposing'!

Repurposing a blog post to a PDF

Why would you want to repurpose your blog post into a PDF? Well one reason is that you can use it as a content upgrade. A content upgrade is a type of lead magnet whereby you provide something of value to your audience in exchange for their email address. Turn to chapter 16 to read more about content upgrades.

A content upgrade is directly related to a piece of content and it offers some kind of extra bonus. There are lots of different types of content upgrade. One idea is to offer your blog post as a PDF for download. Why would somebody want a PDF version of your blog post? That's a very valid question but you may be surprised. Many people will find it really useful.

For example, some people may have found your post really interesting and want to print it out, which is a lot easier if they can download a PDF document and print that. They might just like to save PDFs as opposed to bookmark your page. Or, they may want to email it to somebody who they think might find it useful.

A PDF of your blog post is not only useful as a content upgrade, it can also be useful for you to be able to share your post in more ways than one. Not everyone will go to your site and PDF documents can be read by search engines and they rank in search results. What is also great is that your PDF can have clickable links in it, leading back to your website. This is all good news for your SEO. And of course, you can also share your PDF on social media as well.

How do you convert your blog post into a PDF?

It sounds quite time consuming or technical doesn't it? Well it doesn't have to be because there is a brilliant free site/tool called PrintFriendly.com that enables you to convert your blog post into a PDF in just one minute. You simply enter the URL of the blog post that you want to turn into a PDF and it generates a PDF for you. It brings over some formatting, links, and images, but it also gives you the opportunity to make changes too. E.g. There might be some images that you want to remove. It looks nice and isn't anything like a screenshot of your blog post page. For example, the sidebar isn't included. When you are happy you just hit download.

To answer the question then, it's very simple to repurpose your blog post into a PDF. There are some really good reasons why you might consider doing this. Why not give them a go? Offer your PDF as a content upgrade and upload it to a few different places online, including your own website.

Repurpose your blog post into an email

Blog posts and emails have something in common - they are both written content! So, repurposing a blog post into an email doesn't need to be an onerous task at all.

In chapters five and six I talked about repurposing your podcast and video content into an email, and all of what I said there applies here too in terms of the reasons why it is a great idea. It's important to keep in touch with your subscribers and add value to the emails that you send.

You could make subscribers aware that you've just released a new blog post and encourage them to check it out, thus driving traffic to your website. Believe me, they won't all be eagerly checking your site every day for the next new post, no matter how much they may love you, we're all busy and often distracted too.

Or, you could put the whole blog post into the email so they can get the value from it without having to leave their emails. In this case perhaps you have a different call to action than going to the blog post on your site, perhaps you have a product or service that you want them to try out.

The beauty with repurposing a blog post is that you already have written content. It may simply be a case of rewording the blog post to turn it into an email. Whether you send out only the highlights or the whole post, it's up to you.

If you have a neglected email list, but you're regularly publishing great blog posts, fix that disconnect.

Repurposing can turn blog posts into a multimedia experience

One of the benefits of repurposing blog posts is that you often end up creating assets that can be included in your blog post. For example, graphics, videos etc. Most of the content already discussed in this chapter have been mentioned time and time again as examples of repurposed content that can also be put into your blog post.

This is great because, whilst people do still very much want to read blog posts, a text-only blog post has little chance of capturing your audience's attention these days. Why? Because people have short attention spans. Scanning is the new reading. Also, because people crave entertainment. People want a visual experience when they're online.

If they've taken the time to visit your blog, they're usually looking for more than just blocks of text. They might not even realize it, our brains are simply becoming programmed in this way! In fact, blocks of text can be very intimidating and off-putting. Integrating an array of different media into your posts will breathe new life into it.

You can create a multimedia experience by including a variety of content. This includes everything from videos to audio, images to infographics and slide presentations.

If you want to see an example of this, look at almost any blog post on my website www.Content10x.com. We always have a variety of media in our posts: Text, graphics, photos, GIFs, videos, podcast/audio, infographic, embedded slide presentations.

People are far more likely to engage with a blog post that has rich and diverse content. Plus, it does remarkable things for your SEO and helps your site rank higher in search engine results pages (SERPs).

I've already discussed repurposing your blog post into a video and then embedding/streaming the video into your blog post. I've said it before but I'll say it again ... blog posts that incorporate video attract 3x as many inbound links as blog posts without video. Also, blog posts with a video placed at the top encourage people to stay longer on the page, increasing the dwell time which in turn increases the positive user interaction signals to search engine bots.

I've also talked about repurposing your blog post to an infographic or a SlideShare presentation and then embedding them into the blog post. Plus, of course, include any social media graphics that are suitable.

It's important to remember that when a person visits your blog, they're searching for an answer to a question or a solution to a problem but not everyone wants to learn in the same way. We're all wired differently. It's a huge benefit to be able to connect with people in their preferred learning style and you can do this by providing different media within the one blog post, hence a "multimedia experience".

Combining mixed content into one post breaks the article up so it's not just one chunk of text. It feeds the skim readers, as well as those looking for depth and detail. If you're creating the content anyway, for repurposing elsewhere, it's basically a case of recycling your repurposed content!

In conclusion

In chapter seven I declared live video 'the crown with extra sparkle' when it comes to content repurposing. It's so versatile in terms of what you can create and repurpose it into.

Blog posts are actually at the other end of the spectrum when it comes to their versatility - we don't have any content on camera, or any audio, we simply have words. Not so easy to repurpose right?!

Wrong. I hope I've convinced you in this chapter that there are plenty of ways to repurpose a blog post. As well as blog syndication, you can repurpose a post into video content, podcast episodes, an infographic, slides, social media visuals and posts, email...all the while enriching the original blog post by turning it into a multimedia feast!

If blog posts are your core content and you consistently create quality posts then keep it up. Just ensure you repurpose too!

CHAPTER 9

Membership site content

Membership sites are a great way to build a recurring revenue stream into your business. In fact, for really successful membership site owners, their membership site is the main or only revenue generating aspect of their business.

What do I mean by a membership?

There can be many different types of membership sites, as my good friend's Mike Morrison and Callie Willows aka The Membership Guys will attest to. They're the world's number one experts in membership sites. If you want to run a successful membership then check them out!

In general, when I talk about a membership, I'm talking about when people pay a regular recurring fee in order to have access to membership content. This is usually monthly but this can also be for a fixed term and it's common to have the option of annual memberships too.

Memberships are not a fad, or a bubble ready to burst; when ran well and with a solid strategy behind them, they represent a long-term viable business model. As such, more and more memberships are launching.

Memberships can vary considerably in terms of what they offer to their membership but in general, it would be fair to say that they often tend to be content-heavy.

Membership content can sometimes be drip-fed to members on a monthly basis, or alternatively once you become a member you are given access to everything. That content can be an online course, video tutorials, downloads, templates, workbooks, recordings of live events, guides, useful resources and much more. Really, any content that is of value to your audience could be accessible in your paid membership.

Sometimes memberships provide access to resources-only, but often memberships provide live-access to the membership site owners too. For example, I am a member of Chris Ducker's Youpreneur community and every month Chris provides a live Q&A via webinar for his members. Similarly, my good friend Janet Murray has a very successful membership offering called Janet Murray's Love Marketing Membership. She hosts weekly 'office hours' where anyone who joins has live access to Janet and her team plus a monthly masterclass.

Additionally, memberships often offer a community. Whether that's via a forum within the membership site itself, a private Facebook group or something else.

There are many different shapes and sizes for membership sites, but one thing that makes people apprehensive about starting a membership site is the worry about the amount of content that they will need to create. This is where content repurposing can come in useful!

Starting a membership with repurposing in mind

New membership site owners often feel that they need to overcompensate in terms of the content they deliver to paying members. In other words, membership site owners think that their members will expect more than they actually do.

If you're creating a membership site, look at the content you already have and find ways to deliver it in a slightly different format. Remix it. Collate it. Or use your existing content as a jumping off point and create a little bit extra for your members.

Don't underestimate how valuable convenience is.

If you can bundle relevant pieces of content together in one place, e.g. taking ten relevant blog posts and turning them into an eBook for members, the convenience that you have delivered by way of saving time trawling through your blog to find all of those related articles is highly valuable. Saving people time by collating content into the exact way that it should be consumed in order to achieve a desired outcome can often be exactly what memberships are all about.

We live at a time when people place a really high value on anything that saves time. Let's face it, some of the most successful businesses, ones that are relatively new but growing at an extremely rapid pace, all have one thing in common: They offer convenience.

Uber - an example to illustrate the point

If you live in a city you can probably walk out onto the street and flag down a taxi. That's hardly a big inconvenience is it? But who knows how long you'll be out there waiting for one. It might even be raining! Not only that but you have to explain where you want to go and you have to pay the taxi driver with cash (how inconvenient!) or card, and you don't know how much it's going to cost if the taxi is running on a meter.

Alternatively, you can get out your phone and open the Uber app. It already knows where you are so you simply tell it where you want to go, select a driver and a fare. You know exactly where the car is, when it's arrived and payment is taken automatically.

Flagging a taxi down on the street never seemed that much of a time drain or an inconvenience until Uber came along. My point being, people pay for things that make life easier for them. They pay for convenience and they pay for the opportunity to save time.

Offer a little something more

When it comes to repurposing content for a membership, typically you wouldn't just take what has been offered for free and lock it behind a paywall. Instead, use that content as a jumping off point and offer something extra.

For example, bundling all relevant content together (as mentioned already), providing some guidelines or a 'roadmap' to help people consume the content, and perhaps including quizzes, a checklist and some additional worksheets or templates. The 'extras' that you create can form a part of your membership content and people will be willing to pay to access them.

When you publish your free content, reference the extras that members will be given access to as a subtle way to market your membership and entice people to join.

For example, at the end of a video on YouTube, LinkedIn or Facebook (in other words, your free public facing content), you could say "I hope you liked this video and it was super useful. For anyone who is a member of my membership, be sure to watch my bonus video where I provide a step-by-step walk-through of how to do this with a handy checklist to download. If you're not a member then head to ... ". There's something really sweet about this approach because it shows that you are willing and generous with your knowledge to share free content for all to consume, but you also take good care of paying members and give them more.

Let's look at a few different types of content that you can repurpose for use in a membership site and some examples of how:

Creating membership content from your blog post

A blog post could be the inspiration for a live members-only Q&A. You have just published a blog post, it's likely that the topic is fresh in your mind and hot with your audience right now. Do something special for your members and take that blog topic to a members only live Q&A.

A blog post could also be turned into a downloadable checklist or some other form of useful guide that goes into the 'Useful Resources' section of your membership. You could also offer the checklist as a content upgrade to grow your email subscriber list too.

Your blog posts could be collated together into an eBook and again be added to the 'Useful Resources' (or similar!) section of your membership.

Creating membership content from your podcast

If you have a podcast, here are a couple of ideas for using your (free) podcast to create (paid) membership content.

- Video yourself recording your podcast episode. Offer the audio for free as a podcast episode via the usual channels. Make the video recording only available to paid members and perhaps look at how you could add a little bit extra to the video.

- On your podcast, ask guests who you interview to stay on for ten more minutes. Ask them extra questions or do something special with them, just for members. You can let podcast listeners know at the end, "if you want to listen to x, y z, then please sign-up to our membership."
- Similar to the above, create bonus podcast episodes just for members. For example, if your podcast goes live every Wednesday, have another episode that goes live every Friday but that's only available to members. A very popular sport podcast called The Anfield Wrap (about the football team Liverpool F. C. in the UK) based it's membership/subscription model entirely on providing members with access to many more podcast episodes each week, plus the ability to listen to the free podcasts advert-free. It's been wildly successful as a business and picked up many podcasting awards as well!
- You could collate together all of the podcast episodes that have covered a specific topic and create a "highlights of " podcast episode where you take the very best sections from each episode and put them into one super episode, again for members only. A good idea would be to do this in themes. Again, making content easier for people to consume in a way that helps them solve their problems.

Creating membership content from live events

If you are running events, or presenting at an event, whether it's a big conference or a small workshop for an hour or so, consider recording your presentation/talk and putting the recording into your membership area. After all, presenting at events can be time consuming. You take time creating and preparing for your presentation, and you take time out of your day to attend the event. Potentially you have to travel too. Why not get the most value out of your time and benefit your membership too?

For example, when I interviewed Mike Morrison on my podcast, he had recently presented at Youpreneur Summit. All of the video recordings of every speaker are in the private membership area on Chris Ducker's Youpreneur Membership. Chris took the opportunity to repurpose his entire event (in terms of the talks) into his membership. A very smart thing to do and this adds huge value to the membership. In addition, Mike, being the smart cookie that he is, was also able to obtain the recording of his talk at Youpreneur Summit and put that within *his* private membership as well.

TOP TIP: If you are speaking at someone else's event you will need to obtain agreement in advance to have a copy of the recording for your own membership, or whatever you want to use it for. Have this conversation when you are agreeing the terms of your speaking. In fact, there's nothing wrong with making it a condition of your speaking, particularly if you are not getting paid, that you want to be provided with the video of your talk and some photographs too. More on this in chapter 10 on live events.

BONUS TIP: Extract the audio from your live presentation and right there you have a podcast episode! Chris Ducker did this with all his keynote talks and his own talks at Youpreneur Summit. People like Gary Vaynerchuk and Tony Robbins do this too. It works well!

Repurposing your membership content to advertise your membership

So far I've covered how you can repurpose your free content into content for your membership but are there opportunities to repurpose your membership content from behind the pay-wall and into the public domain? There certainly are! If you have courses or long-form content in your membership, it does not diminish the value if you take some of it and release it for free.

Here are some things you can do:

- Take individual stand-alone lessons and put them onto YouTube.
- Take the audio from your membership tutorials and put it out as a podcast episode, as long as the tutorial you re-purpose stands on its own two feet as standalone audio content.
- Take short sections from your videos in your membership, for example member Q&A sessions, and share them on social media. Here you could take video clips of answers to the questions asked and post them onto Instagram (or Facebook, Twitter, LinkedIn...wherever is right for your audience).
- Take images from members-only content and create visual content for social media e.g quote and question graphics.

It's really useful to use membership content for promotion and marketing purposes. Share one piece of the puzzle and provide the call to action to come over to your membership to get more help.

At Content 10x we often help our clients to repurpose their membership content for paid marketing purposes as well, e.g. with Facebook ads. What better way to advertise your membership than to show people a sneak-a-peek of what's included? For example, we created a Facebook video ad from a tutorial within our client's membership site. It converted well because people saw exactly what they would benefit from if they became a member, and video ads tend to perform well on Facebook (if you know what you're doing with the ads platform or if you can hire someone who does!).

It's understandable that you may be wondering if your members will complain that you have given content for free to non-members. When I interviewed Mike Morrison on my podcast I asked him that very same question. He's been in the membership business for a very long time and said that he has never known anyone to complain. Mike's view is that it doesn't diminish the value of the membership and members are usually understanding.

Getting started with a membership site

Don't have a membership site but after hearing that you don't need to create mountains of new content and you can instead repurpose your existing content, you're considering starting one? Here are three tips to help you get started:

1. **Be clear on your role as a problem solver.** It's not about the volume of content, it's about the value and how easily your content solves problems for your members. Zero in on what you need to do to solve your audience's problems.

1. **Decode how your membership will be structured and segmented.** Are you taking your members from step one to an end result? Or, are you creating a competency-based membership and it's more about going from beginner, to intermediate to advanced? Make sure that your content is enough to cover each of those stages as a starting point. E.g. if it's a five stage journey, have content on all five stages as some people will not join at stage one, they will be at stage two, three or four.

1. **Add 10% to your most popular content.** Look at the ten or fifteen most popular and relevant pieces of content that you have produced so far. Find ways to add 10%. For example, create a checklist, create a video, create a guide to print off, bring a guest back for a Q&A. The act of organizing free content in order to take people on a step-by-step journey is also a way of adding value that people will be willing to pay for.

CHAPTER 10

Live events

Live events can be anything from a huge conference attended by 5,000 people to an intimate 15-person seminar. Whether large or small, they can present *so* many content opportunities. In this chapter we'll explore what they are from the perspective of being the event organizer or host, a speaker at someone else's event, and an attendee.

Hosting an event

If you host your own live events, whether it's a 3-day 500+ person conference or a 2-hour 25 person workshop, always try to consider the repurposing opportunities. Putting on an event is a wonderful thing to do - bringing people together, educating, inspiring and it can really position you up there as a leader in your industry or niche.

It's also really hard work and not always super-profitable, on a standalone basis, relative to the level of effort involved! Alongside the many things that you need to do, it usually involves lots of content creation, so constantly assess what content you could make go further.

I'm talking sales pages, promotional material, blog posts, podcast episodes, social media content, video footage, photographs, slides and presentations, live-streaming, handouts and so much more. An event is actually an entire feast of content. The question is, how are you going to repurpose it?

Involve your audience in decision making *before* your event

My good friend Janet Murray is an absolute master when it comes to holding live events and repurposing content. Something that she is really good at is involving her audience in decision making before her events. She will do this for all sorts of different aspects of the event. This creates a buzz and lots of social media engagement, then she repurposes the content for other uses. So it's really a win:win strategy.

There is a famous quote by Benjamin Franklin:

"Tell me and I forget, teach me and I may remember, involve me and I learn."

I think this is relevant here. I'm not quite sure if 'involve me and I'll buy a ticket to your event' has quite the same ring to it but there's something really powerful about involving people.

Some of the things that you can do before the event include:

- Shares design ideas on social media. E.g. share five or six ideas for your event logo and ask for opinions. Share anything to get people talking about the event and pique people's curiosity.
- Share your agenda and ask for feedback, for example, early start and early finish or late start and late finish? One long lunch break or more short breaks through the day?
- Involve your audience in building your sales page. Janet literally got her potential customers to help design the very same sales page they went on to buy from. Isn't that genius?!?

The trick is to share content that will be reused anyway, e.g. a banner, logo, and use that as a tool to get people interested and curious about the event.

If you create content for your event that also generates lots of engagement on social media, that should have a positive impact on ticket sales.

My friend Jess Kupferman, who hosts She Podcasts Live event with Elsie Escobar, involved her audience in selecting the venue. She provided behind the scenes footage via Instagram and Facebook Stories of her tours of the shortlisted venues, and asked her audience their thoughts. What a great way to create content from the event planning process. Imagine if you, as a potential attendee, got so engaged with this social exchange that you wrote a 21-point response on why you favored the Marriott over the Hilton, aren't you going to be a bit more likely to want to go to the event to see for yourself?!

The funny thing is, you might initially involve your audience in the decision-making process without really intending to take their feedback onboard, for example, you know which logo you are going with regardless of what people say, that's entirely your prerogative. But you may find you're pleasantly surprised at what intel you glean from asking others.

Making use of the content created during the event

When your event is underway it's a bit like a content generating machine! Everything is a content opportunity. Plan and take every opportunity to capture what you can from the event, as these are assets you can only harvest in real time.

Photographs and video footage

Firstly, you are likely to be taking lots of photographs. Potentially you've hired a professional photographer. These photographs are going to go on to have so many uses, from your website, to your social media content, to your sales page for your event next year, on your marketing materials. That's why it's really important to put thought into exactly what you want photographed and how. Sit down and run through everything with your photographer and provide clear instructions.

If you don't have a professional photographer, make sure you have a plan in place to get plenty of photographs taken. You can take them yourself but consider that, if you're hosting the event, it's likely you'll be too busy to take photographs. Have a few people on point to take them instead. Remember to give them an idea of what you want photographed. If you don't ask they will never know!

Exactly the same goes for video content too. If you have hired a videographer, work out with them exactly what you want footage of.

For example:

- All of the live talks on stage.
- Testimonials from attendees filmed in different locations at the venue. If it's a big event, could you have a feedback booth even?
- Testimonials from speakers. What was it like to be at and talk at your event?
- Footage of the venue. People turning up, the buzz in the breaks and lunch, the food and drinks served throughout the day. If you are going to edit together a highlights video for your event or a promo video for future events, this kind of footage will be really useful as alternative/supplementary footage.

Be sure to take more 'raw', behind-the-scenes videos too with your phone and to encourage other people to do so too. Videos that will be fun to share on Instagram Stories, for example. Similar to all the photographs, the videos are going to go on to have so many uses. From your website, to your social media content, to your sales page for your event next year, your marketing materials, your membership if you have one.

Your videos can be edited together to create highlight videos, best of videos and promo videos. They can also be broken down into short videos for social media. Take 15 second clips for Instagram Stories, less than 60 second clips for an Instagram post, less than 2 minutes 40 seconds for sharing on Twitter, and so on. Don't worry about these durations at the event, take the footage and do the video editing and snipping later!

Encourage your attendees to take lots of photographs and videos and share them on social media. Have a specific hashtag for your event and make sure everyone is aware of it. Have it written in as many places as possible and tell people. You could even offer a small prize for the most prolific Tweeter, for example! This helps generate interest amongst those that couldn't make your event – also a sense that they may be missing out – planting seeds ahead of your next event.

As well as all the exposure you will get from having lots of content posted on social media about your event, another benefit is that you may be able to repurpose photographs and video content that your attendees took. You could reuse the photograph or video on it's own (after asking permission of the person who took it!) or, take a screenshot of the photo/video with the social media comment, e.g. a screenshot of the Facebook post or Tweet to use in your own content.

I spoke at Podfest event in Orlando, Florida in March 2019 and I've noticed that they got so many photos and videos from the three day event that ever since, that content alone has fueled their social media posts, and they post daily! They post their own photos and videos, and lots of attendee-generated content too!

Even if you hire the best photographer and videographer in the world, you might just be surprised that the best photograph of the entire event was taken by an attendee using their iPhone. You just never know!

Live-streaming video

Figure out whether you want to do anything special when it comes to live-streaming. For example, I've been to a few events recently where there has been a 'live-streaming stage' or particular area at the event where a key-person facilitates various live-streaming activities throughout the event. The idea is that attendees can go and watch the live-streams as they are being recorded, and the audience watching the live-streams have a bit more of an organized and structured experience because it's being planned and managed well at the event. This is as opposed to occasionally jumping into live-stream content in a more haphazard way.

If you do have live content then be sure to save all of the video footage. Some of this could be absolutely priceless when it comes to repurposing.

Audio/podcast content

It's a really good idea to record the audio content from the presentations delivered on stage. If you have recorded the presentations on video anyway then it will be possible to extract the audio from the video. However, it's a really good idea to also record the audio separately.

One way to do this is to purchase a handheld recorder, like a Zoom H1 Handy Recorder, and plug in a lapel mic for you and your speakers to wear. Or, you can use a lapel mic and the audio recording feature on your smartphone.

Your audio files can be turned into podcast episodes. Either the entire talk/event or you could create a 'best of' podcast episode. Even if you don't use the audio for a podcast episode, you could create short audiograms/audio teasers that can be shared on social media (using a tool like wavve.com).

Chris Ducker, my good friend, client and host of the Youpreneur Summit in London, took the audio from his talks and all of his speaker's talks and turned each one into a podcast episode for his very popular podcast, Youpreneur FM. He didn't do this straight after the event though. He waited until tickets were on sale for the next summit and then started to release these podcast episodes.

This is a great idea because not only is it providing you with content for your podcast, but it's also a fantastic form of marketing for your next event. For example, "If you wonder what Youpreneur Summit is like, listen to this week's episode to find out just what the keynotes were like last year".

Incidentally, if you have a podcast, consider inviting your speakers onto your podcast in the run up to the event. For your listeners who are considering buying a ticket, but maybe a little bit on the fence about making their decision, it really helps to get to know who your speakers are and a bit more about them before deciding whether to purchase.

But you're not done yet...when your event is over, the content doesn't stop.

Create content *after* your event to use in the launch of your *next* event.

Here are just some ideas:

- Write a really detailed follow-up blog post about your event. Add photos, videos, banners, artwork.
- Encourage delegates to write blog posts about the event that can later be repurposed for marketing.
- **TOP TIP:** Teach people how to do this, they might not know. Make it super easy for them and give them access to photos and logos, etc.
- If your delegates have podcasts or video shows, encourage them to share their top-takeaways from the event on their show.
- Record a video trailer of your event. Be sure to capture the atmosphere. It's not just about the speakers and presentations. Also film the delegates, the food, the goodie bags and so on. They all play a part in creating the event atmosphere.
- Videos and photographs from the live event can be used

on all social media platforms. Make the most of it all and go for high-engagement with your posts.

- If you have a podcast, record a podcast episode specifically about the event, sharing all of the best bits.

Creating content for membership communities, online courses and virtual tickets

If you have a membership or an online course/s, or you're thinking of starting either, you will have ample opportunity to generate lots of content from your event for both. I also talk more about this in chapter nine.

You may want to structure the event so that each session can become its own mini-lesson and stand alone. If you have hired a videographer then be clear on this in the brief.

You could create a straight digital version of your live event. However, I would highly recommend turning your repurposed content into something different and new. You can, of course, do both for different purposes.

Selling virtual tickets of events is a very popular thing to do right now, which is usually almost exactly a straight digital version of your live event. The good thing about virtual tickets is that they generate an extra stream of revenue for your business for very little additional work.

An option could be to sell virtual tickets to people who are not in your membership, and provide all the content for the virtual ticket inside your membership for free to members. Personally, if I had a membership instead of having a virtual ticket, I would put the content from the event into my membership, and use that as a selling point to get more people into the membership. I'd do this because they may have only joined to access the event content and intended to leave after a month or two, but once they are a member and getting value from the rest of the membership and decide to stay on. It's balancing whether you want a one-time purchase at a higher price (usually) or to take a punt at offering the content at a lower price initially but for the potential long-term customer relationship.

Speaking at an event

Speaking at events can be a great way to reach new audiences, establish your authority, strengthen your personal brand, generate new connections, gain new leads and ultimately grow your business.

Whilst there are many benefits to speaking at events, it generally represents a significant investment of time. Time to research, plan and prepare for you talk, and time to attend the event (which also represents time away from your business and potential loss of earnings, especially if the event is not local).

It's great if you are getting paid to talk, but it's not unusual to either not get paid at all (not even travel expenses), or receive a contribution toward your expenses but no speaker payment. Even when people get paid to speak it's not unusual to accept far less than what they would usually charge e.g. $500 to speak, but you spent 40 hours planning and preparing and it took 3 full days out of your business = $8 per hour.

So, talking at events is often not a key revenue stream for many people/businesses directly (some people do make a living from speaking, that said). But, that's not to say it's a waste of time for all of the reasons I've already mentioned. You do need to ensure you get a positive ROI, but there are multiple ways to do this and measure this.

One thing I know for sure is that you can create lots of content from speaking at events and there are lots and lots of content repurposing opportunities.

Let's look at some...

Repurposing slides and handouts

When you either host an event, or you speak at someone else's event, you're probably going to create slides to present to. Think about how you can go on and repurpose those slides.

This is exactly what I did when I presented at Podcast Movement in Philadelphia in July 2018. Even if I do say so myself, my team and I created the most awesome slides for me to present to! There was no way I was going to miss the opportunity to repurpose them.

The most creative repurposing that we did with the slides was to turn them into a comic book. Yes, you heard right!

The slides were very visually engaging and they told a story about a homebrew beer making podcast and a struggling hobby homebrewer called Barry. Barry didn't listen to podcasts... which was a terrible shame because the homebrew podcast would have solved all of his beer making woes! The slides told the tale of how by repurposing the podcast its message could reach Barry via the content he does consume.

Since at Content 10x our branding has superhero and comic book themes, repurposing our slides into a comic book seemed perfect (and we brought our own superheroes into the story too, of course!).

The beauty of this was that whenever I was able to repurpose the slides again in new talks, I was able to bring the comic book as a handout for attendees of the talk. I've been very proud of our little comic book. It represents a perfect reminder of my talk, something fun to read and refer to, it's educational, and it showcases the talents of my creative agency team.

I have even been able to use the comic book as a giveaway when exhibiting at other events too, handing it to people who have not seen my talk. The comic book stands alone without readers needing to have watched my talk - it's one of those wonderful examples of the repurposed version being bigger and better than the original content on which it was based.

Other ways to repurpose slides:

- Repurpose individual slides that are eye-catching and have a single message into graphics that can be shared on social media.

- Turn your slides into a SlideShare presentation.
- Use your sides to host a webinar. This is great for email list building or you might even consider hosting a paid webinar.
- Record yourself presenting to the slides and create a video that can be shared on your website or YouTube. If you have a membership, share there too. If you were filmed on video delivering your talk, assess the benefit of also recording it separately. It could be more engaging for your audience to watch a focused run through of the presentation, e.g. a tutorial, versus a recording of it being delivered on stage.
- Write a blog post based on the presentation and disperse slides throughout your blog post.
- Go live on Facebook, YouTube or LinkedIn and present to your slides.

With some of the above, you may not want to deliver a repeat of the exact same presentation that you delivered at the event, especially if it's a keynote talk that you deliver at different events (and are paid to do so), but you could take certain slides and sections and give people a teaser of what your full presentation is like.

If there is other content that you created for your talk, for example, handouts for the audience, consider if there are ways to repurpose your handouts. Let's say you provide everyone with a template to fill it. Could that template also be used as a lead magnet on your website or a content upgrade to one or more of your blog posts, videos or podcast episodes?

Repurposing photographs, audio and video content

If you are talking at someone else's event should request beforehand that you'll receive pictures of your talk. If it's been video recorded, be sure to ask for a copy of the video and permission to use it too.

If you have permission to obtain and use the video of your talk you can create lots of short social media videos, for example, less than one-minute videos for Instagram and a ten minute highlights video for LinkedIn and Facebook. The video could be shared in full on your website and YouTube, it could be used to create a speaker reel video, and if you have one, you could put the video inside your membership site. If you provide the whole video of your talk to your members as members-only content, maybe you should only share snippets of the video elsewhere.

Also ask about an audio recording, particularly if you are a podcaster. I mentioned earlier that you can record the audio by plugging a lapel mic into a handheld recorder (like the Zoom H1 Handy Recorder), or even your iPhone. With the audio you have content you can repurpose into a podcast episode (if the organizer is happy for you to do this).

It would be fantastic if you were provided with photographs as well - often they will be of a high quality taken by a professional photographer so it's great to stock up your image archives with some new high-res photographs. The photographs could be used on your website, posted on social media, and used on your website, posted on social media, and used in lots of other online and offline content, e.g. brochures, leaflets.

LIVE EVENT REPURPOSING CASE STUDY

Mark Asquith - Rebel Base Media

TED's strapline is 'ideas worth spreading'. If your TED talk was butter, then repurposing is the knife.

Delivering a TED or TEDx Talk is a highly sought-after accolade for many people. It can have far-reaching positive outcomes.

All TED speakers get a video and photographs of their talk, which can be posted on their website, their YouTube channel etc. For many speakers this is where they stop...which is a huge missed opportunity when viewed from a repurposing perspective. Fortunately, my friend Mark Asquith wasn't about to let than happen!

Mark is the CEO of the podcasting technology company, Rebel Base Media. Over the years, Mark has done a fair amount of speaking at events which has helped him tremendously with growing his personal brand and awareness of Rebel Base Media. When the speaking-bug hit him, something that he added to his bucket list was to deliver a TEDx Talk. So, in 2018 when he was approached to deliver one he jumped at the opportunity.

It can be very time consuming to plan and prepare a TEDx Talk - you have only 18 minutes on-stage to blow people away (no pressure)! You do not get paid to deliver a TEDx Talk. With all of that in mind, Mark was determined to get as many content assets as possible from his TEDx.

He leveraged repurposing to prepare for his talk, and he created lots of new content before, during and after his talk as well.

Mark's talk, titled 'Choose Happiness, Choose Control' was based on talks he had given in the past. He didn't have to start from a blank canvas, he knew the story he wanted to share, he could draw on previous talks (even the slides), he simply needed to reframe the talk to bring a different context for the TEDx stage.

On the day, Mark provided direction to the photographer as to how he wanted his photos to look, to ensure he could reuse them as much as possible.

In addition, Mark took lots of behind the scenes photos and videos, to share with his audience in the moment and afterwards too...for example lots of Instagram Stories, Tweets...etc.

Mark went onto repurpose all of the visual content from the event onto his website and social media. For example, his Facebook page header was a video extract of his TEDx Talk.

But Mark's repurposing journey didn't stop there. Since he typed out his script for his TEDx Talk, he was able to transform the script into a detailed blog post for his website. As a podcaster, he took the audio from his TEDx Talk and published it as a podcast episode. Plus, he created an entire month of podcast episodes (three episodes per week), sharing with his audience how he prepared, designed, executed and followed up on that talk.

With the video footage, we worked with Mark to slice and dice his main video into shorter video clips suitable for each social media platform e.g. for Instagram Stories, Instagram post, Facebook, LinkedIn and Twitter.

It's fair to say that Mark not only delivered a fantastic TEDx Talk on the day, but he knocked it out of the park with his content repurposing thus magnifying the usefulness of his talk many times over.

TOP TIP

If you wank, or indeed *any* talk, and you're provided with a video that you'd like to repurpose, then look no further than our Content TED 10x service. We provide a one-time repurposing package for speakers to ensure your content assets from speaking are maximized to their full potential and reach as many people as possible. Head to **www.Content10x.com/ted10x** to find out more.

Let's look at the content opportunities for an event attendee. If you are a speaker, many of these apply to you too, but to avoid repeating myself please go on and read this section but view everything from attending as a speaker vs a delegate ...

Attendee at an event

From an attendee's perspective, going to events is a fantastic thing to do - it's great for learning and it's great for building relationships. You just cannot beat meeting people face-to-face.

But, they're also often a huge investment - you've investing in yourself which is good, but they can take up a lot of time away from your business and family, and make quite a dent on your bank balance too!

If you're going to be spending anything from a day to a week away from your business (almost all of the key events I go to are in the USA like Social Media Marketing World, Podfest and Podcast Movement take me out for a week), you need to make sure that it's worth it. One way you can do this – well simply create lots of content at live events that engages your audience!

How? Here are eight ideas:

1. Write engaging blog posts

It's a great idea to write a blog post before and after attending an important event. Events are a brilliant opportunity to meet people in your network that you otherwise wouldn't get the chance to see, but if you don't let them know you're going you're missing a vital opportunity to network!

Especially if you're going to a really large event and the likelihood of bumping into people you may know is slim unless you arrange something in advance.

Even if a large majority of your audience aren't attending, it's still very much worthwhile to write about the fact that you are going because it shows that you're investing in yourself and your own personal development.

For your clients you are showing them that you always stay on top of what's going on in your industry. This is bound to impact upon the quality of your service and/or product.

Make sure you write about why you're going, what you hope to get out of it and once you return, write a blog post with the key takeaways from the event. That way, you're adding value for all the people who didn't get the chance to go.

If you're seen as a leader or influencer it's really important for people to see that you invest in your own knowledge and keep up to date on what's happening in your industry.

2. Tweet, Tweet, Tweet - Use Twitter to create content at live events

Twitter is always extremely popular at conferences and events. Attendees will be tweeting non-stop throughout the day, using the event hashtag (be sure to find out what this is...if there is one) and it's important that you join in the conversation and connect with people using Twitter.

You should be sharing your experiences in the run up to the event, during the event and afterwards, too.

Many people add the hashtag to their name on their Twitter profile so that people can find and follow them when they're searching for tweets about the event.

Make sure you take photos of the speakers, share the key takeaways from their talks and don't be shy to do plenty of retweeting. The latter allows you to focus on the talks but still share what's being said with your audience.

Twitter is also a great way to receive feedback on your talk if you're speaking at an event.

3. Make Instagram & Facebook Stories your best friend

People love exploring behind the scenes content and this is one of the reasons why Instagram and Facebook Stories are so popular. Use them to your advantage!

Stories are short, bitesize 15-second videos that force you to be concise (and hopefully engaging). You can have a lot of fun with them - get other people involved, use the geotagging feature and the event hashtags, too.

I am a big fan of Instagram Stories. I post something almost every day, and when I'm at events I always try and ensure I share what's going on.

Consider creating a Highlights folder for the event, so the stories stay on your profile rather than disappear after 24 hours.

4. Have a content plan for all of your social media accounts

This about all of the social media channels that you use. Create a short plan detailing what you're going to be sharing with each network and when in the run-up to, during, and after the event.

You could even consider organizing a meetup at the event using social media. Some events have specific pages on their website to share 'official' meetups (ones that are organized by the event) and 'unofficial' meetups, where attendees organize their own social events and meetups. Get in touch with the organizers to see if they'd be happy to list yours.

5. Let your email subscribers know about the event

Similar to how you should write blog posts to communicate your attendance at an event, don't forget to let your email subscribers know, too!

I always try to ensure that I let my email subscribers know when I'm attending an event and do you know what, there have been many times that because of my email I found out someone on my email list was attending too and we were able to arrange to meet up!

Just a short email detailing which event you're going to, why you're going, what you hope to get out of it and asking if any of your subscribers will be attending is enough. In fact, you can repurpose your pre-event blog post into the email.

Make sure you email your subscribers after the event with all the key takeaways from the event too - you can repurpose your post event blog post for this, too.

6. Use video to your advantage

Events are a brilliant opportunity to develop creative video content that you can use for a variety of different purposes. You could create a vlog, a time-lapse video or even just record some of the speaker's talks (if you are allowed, always check the event rules, especially when it comes to live-streaming).

You could even use the event as a way to get quick, interview style videos with people you wouldn't normally get to spend any face-to-face time with, like the speakers or other attendees.

You don't even need a fancy camera for this. Your phone is usually all you need.

7. Podcast on the go

If you have a podcast like I do, you can easily bring along your recording equipment (if transportable) to record interviews with people whilst you're at events. You can even get quality audio from plugging a mic into your phone and recording from your phone

If you go to podcasting events you will often see a specific recording space set-up entirely for that reason. This is hardly surprising! However, I've been to many other, non-podcast related conferences where organizers are doing the same - Social

Media Marketing World for one.

It can take a bit of courage to approach people, but take the plunge! There's opportunity to get some great audio content from people who you would usually be lucky to even get an email back from because they're so busy. Of course, you can always try to arrange in advance too.

8. Make sure you have a content mindset

Having a content mindset when you're at an event will help you enormously when it comes to repurposing your experience.

There is a content opportunity in almost everything!

Think about all the different types of content you can create based on the conversations you're having with people in your industry and the questions that people are asking.

Make sure you listen and are on high alert - jot down any notes you have throughout the day of what would make amazing content for your audience.

You can get a decent ROI from attending an event from the content alone if you really make the most of all the opportunities.

In conclusion

Whether you are an organizer, speaker or attendee, be sure to look for all the content repurposing opportunities in live events. They are content generating machines. Content repurposing will save you time and help you generate either more revenue from your event, or more ROI from your attendance at the event. Don't let it be an afterthought though. You can't turn back time after the event, it's frustrating to think about all of those great pieces content you could have created but didn't. Have a plan and execute!

CHAPTER 11

Webinars

Webinars present numerous repurposing opportunities. You can repurpose content to create a webinar, and you can repurpose webinar content for other uses as well.

A webinar is like a virtual classroom. It's a class or seminar that's delivered online. They are often live, but you can also record them for use at a later date. We've probably all been invited to a webinar at some point.

Many people hold webinars as a means to connect with their existing audience and to reach new audiences. They provide their time and share (hopefully!) valuable information in exchange for the contact details of attendees for following-up. Webinars can be great for audience building but they are also a marketing tool and very good for email list building.

If people attend your webinar and stay for the duration, it's fair to say that they are quite a warm lead. They clearly like what you have to say and are engaged.

But remember: webinars are not just a marketing tool to reach new audiences. Many people hold webinars for their existing audiences too. For example, membership site owners hold webinars for their members.

How to deliver a webinar

You don't need the latest tech or any fancy equipment to start your webinar journey. However, if you want to take webinars seriously you may want to consider upgrading your equipment to offer high-quality results. The two main pieces of equipment you'll need is a camera (or a webcam) and a microphone.

Thanks to the software available online specifically for running webinars, delivering a webinar does not need to be too complicated. There are plenty of webinar software options to choose from. For example, the video communications software Zoom makes it easy to run webinars. There's also EverWebinar, GoToWebinar and WebinarJam. If you're not ready to invest in software then you can use YouTube Live or Facebook Live to host your webinar. However, the issue with doing a webinar with Facebook Live for example is that it makes obtaining emails a lot more difficult. Typically webinars are not totally public facing and will be accessible once you have provided your email address.

If you do your research and offer educational presentations on topics that your audience care about, people will attend. Be sure to stay close to your audience, find out what they want to learn about, and strike while the iron is hot!

TOP TIP: You can find out what people want to learn by engaging with your audience on social media. For example, spark discussions in Facebook groups. You could also survey your email subscribers.

You may be able to promote your webinar in other people's Facebook groups but be sure to check that the owner of the Facebook group is okay with you doing this.

Your webinar structure

If you are delivering webinars to launch a new product, training course or program, or to entice people to join your membership it's of course important to include a pitch in your webinar. But don't make it all about the pitch. You need to add value first and foremost.

When people attend a free webinar they understand that at some point there is going to be a pitch, there is going to be a next step. If someone is giving up their time and valuable content for free then there's always a catch, right?! We generally accept this if the content is good.

A good webinar format is:

- Introduce yourself and the topic of your webinar.
- Deliver valuable training for around 30 minutes.
- Answer questions from the audience. This is what many people love about live webinars!
- Deliver your pitch. What do you want people to do next? How?

Once you've created a webinar, it's time to think about how you're going to get your viewers to take the next step or obtain your viewer's email addresses, if that is your goal (if you didn't obtain them to begin with). The main way you can do this is to point them in the direction of your landing page. Make sure that the look, feel and copy on your landing page aligns with your webinar and any ads that you use. If there is a stark misalignment, people will click off the page because it isn't what they expected to see or what they were promised.

As with any presentation, whether it's an in-person seminar, or an online webinar, if it's going to be of value to your audience then you're going to put time and effort into creating and delivering it. What next? That's where repurposing comes in.

Ideas for repurposing webinars

There are a number of ways you can repurpose webinars to help grow your business:

- If you have a podcast, extract the audio from the webinar and create a podcast episode.
- Use a snippet of the webinar to create a short teaser video and share it with your followers. Consider using this snippet to advertise future webinars. Video ads work well on social media, especially Facebook.
- Create standalone visuals for social media platforms using a key quote from your webinar paired with an eye-catching image. Consider a still image from the webinar itself.
- Transform your webinar into an impressive slideshow for SlideShare or other similar document sharing sites. See the section on chapter six about SlideShare.
- Create a downloadable PDF of your slides. Offer this as a content upgrade on your website.
- Write an engaging blog post or create a fun infographic based on the ideas you explored in your webinar.
- Host a live workshop using the slides you used for your webinar.
- If you have a membership site, repurpose your webinar into your membership as member-only content.

Webinar replays

Have you ever been invited to a 'live' webinar only to find that the webinar is not live at all. I have, and I have to say I find it really annoying! Especially when it's glaringly obvious that the webinar is a recording, but you are still being spun the line that it's live.

Nonetheless, this is one way that people repurpose webinars. They essentially record it once as live and then they continue to put out recordings of the webinar whilst advertising to attendees that it's live. People sign-up to attend the webinar at a set time, click a link, usually wait in a waiting room for a little while, then get plunged into the 'not really live at all' webinar!

The webinar recording software is simply configured to play a recording at a set time to everyone who signs-up and has the link. You can probably tell from my tone, I am not a big fan of doing this. I have no problem whatsoever with showing people a recorded webinar. I just object to pretending it's live when it's not!

I don't appreciate the whole song and dance of running the webinar on a set date and time, scarcity marketing and so on, for a recording that you could just provide people access to at any time in exchange for their email address. You still get the email opt-in and they get honesty.

In summary, replays are good way to maximize take-up of your webinar, but be sure your audience knows what they are getting before they join!

In conclusion

If you want to launch a successful webinar you need to find out what your audience wants from you and then create a webinar that delivers it. Survey your existing audience and then choose a topic that gives them real value.

When you have done this you will not only have a webinar that delivers value, but you'll have lots of repurposed content to create from your webinar. This will go onto add even more value. Your repurposed webinar content will enable you to reach people who didn't attend your webinar and put you even more front of mind for those who did.

CHAPTER 12

Emails

This section looks at email from two angles. It's about the content you can repurpose to use in the emails you send to your email list, as well as how you might repurpose original email content into other formats. Having an email list is essential for any business.

It therefore felt important to include this section on emails, outlining how you can leverage other content for email marketing. It's so important to have a way of keeping in touch regularly with people who have expressed an interest in your business and people who have bought from you in the past. That's where this section can help.

When I first started out in the world of online business and digital marketing, growing your email list was everything. A phrase I recall was 'the money is in the list' and that's as good advice today as it was then.

Social media is all well and good but an email list is something that you own. If you get booted off a social media platform for whatever reason or social media platforms just change how they do things, you lose those connections. Email lists are more solid because the list is yours. Also, very importantly, email lists are important because people are more likely to make buying decisions in their email inbox versus on social media, where there are many other distractions.

Email lists are crucially important but there are two important factors:

1. How aligned is your list with your business and what you're selling?

It's all well and good having a list of 20,000 people but if 15,000 of those people have been on your list for a long time and potentially came onto your list via a lead magnet or offer that isn't closely aligned with what you sell today, then it's likely the majority of people on your list are never going to buy from you. That's why it's always important to review your email list and clean it up once in a while.

In Europe, the introduction of GDPR in 2018 forced us to clean up our email lists. Many people complained but, aside from the administrative burden of it all (at the time it was rather annoying and time consuming!) I think the end result is actually a good thing. We have better quality email lists as a result.

When I refer to cleaning up your list, I mean removing people who do not open your emails. The people who never open your emails need to be removed. For the people who hardly ever open them, send an email asking if they still want to receive your emails, kind of like a 'one last chance' email, then remove them.

It's hard building an email list, and it can be costly too, but if those people on your list shouldn't be there, you have to let them go.

2. How regularly do you email your list? What are your open rates?

Your open rates should improve if you follow some of the steps I mention above and work towards having a list of email subscribers that want to receive your emails, removing those who don't. But it also comes down to how regularly you email your list.

You must send emails that your subscribers want to open and get value from opening. If you mostly send emails that are valuable and helpful, then when you send emails that are selling something, your subscribers will be in the habit of opening and reading your emails and are more likely to take note of what you have to offer.

What should you send to your email subscribers?

I often find it interesting when I speak to new clients and potential new clients, and the conversations often goes something like this:

Me: Do you have an email list?

Them: Yes, I've got 15,000 subscribers.

Me: Excellent! How often do you email them?

Them: It's terrible really, I hardly ever email them. I know that's bad but I don't really have a process for emailing them and I often don't really know what to say.

This same person is publishing a great podcast episode once per week, or blog post, or a regular vlog, or is going live on Facebook weekly.

They have email subscribers but they are not letting them know about their content. You cannot assume that, just because someone is on your email list, that they are avidly consuming your content. You can't assume that email subscribers are also podcast subscribers and listen to your episodes each week. You can't assume that they are following your content at all. Some will be. Many won't. Because the fact is, people can be really busy and have many things competing for their attention all day long.

My recommendation is to stay in touch with your email subscribers by letting them know about your content. Get into a regular rhythm of doing this. Turn it into a repeatable process. I'm not suggesting that you email them too often, or that you email them every time you publish a blog post, a Facebook post or a video.

Instead, why not consider a weekly round-up? You could send a weekly email letting your subscribers know about all the content that you have published that week. This could include content on your own platforms, e.g. blog posts, podcast episodes and videos, but don't forget to let people know if you have been featured elsewhere too.

For example, I regularly contribute guest articles to sites like Chris Ducker's Youpreneur.com and to The Podcast Business Journal. I also regularly appear as a guest on other people's podcasts and video shows and I run masterclasses and training inside of other peoples' memberships. All of this is great content and it's well worth letting your subscribers know about it.

I also make sure that in my weekly emails I let subscribers know when I'm going to be talking at events. It's great to let your subscribers know beforehand in case they are going to the event too - ask them to let you know. After the event you can let people know how it went.

I have a client who repurposes her blog posts into an email in its entirety. She doesn't send a summary or 'round-up' of the content. Instead, she sends the full blog post out as an email every week. At first, I questioned this, I wondered if it was a good idea to provide the whole blog post in an email when, ideally, it would be good to provide a teaser and then entice people over to her website for the full blog post. But in actual fact, it worked well for her niche.

Her audience are extremely busy medical professionals, and given the blog posts are full of valuable content, it's best to provide this to email subscribers within the email, making it nice and simple for them to consume. The subscribers will be thankful for the information. This put my client front of mind for her audience regularly and there were plenty of calls to action at the end of the email and hyperlinks within the email that still benefited her business and generated website traffic.

Repurposing your content into an email list building challenge

Have you heard of online challenges that people use as a lead magnet or email list building activity?

For example, the folks at Simple Green Smoothies ran a really successful challenge. When you landed on their website, the first action that they asked you to take was to join their 'FREE 7-Day Green Smoothie Challenge'. This smoothie challenge comprises smoothie recipes, shopping lists and tips. It has enabled them to grow their community, their email list, and ultimately grow their business to become hugely successful.

Challenges are so good because they are designed to get people to take action. If people do what they are being challenged to do, it's likely they will see results. This makes it a win for the participant and for the person running the challenge.

As the person running the challenge, you get to help people and get their email address, helping you to grow your all-important email list.

Unlike other kinds of lead magnet, like a PDF checklist for example, challenges can often spark a lot of discussion on social media plus create a great sense of community. Sounds good, but aren't they really time consuming to manage? They don't need to be. The beauty lies in automation and, you guessed it, repurposing!

Challenges usually consist of a series of steps or actions guided by pre-written content and delivered to people via email. Each challenge has a specific end result. For example, to double your followers on Facebook, lose five pounds in weight, or try a different smoothie recipe every day. The end result must add value to your audience.

You don't need to manually send emails every day to the participants of your challenge. Automate the delivery of emails by using an email auto-responder like Active Campaign or ConvertKit.

You can create your email list building challenge by repurposing your existing content.

Here's an example of how you can run an email list building challenge:

Step one: Decide on the end goal of your challenge

The first step is to think about what people are going to achieve at the end of the challenge.

TOP TIP: The more specific the end goal, the more likely it is that people will sign-up!

Participants join your challenge because they want the result that you promised them. Consider what your ideal customer wants and then deliver it to them. You can find out what your target consumers want by carrying out a survey on social media. A simple Facebook, Twitter or Instagram poll will work fine. Or, you could send an email to your subscribers.

The goal is to find out what your ideal clients need help with, something that is more of a quick-fix versus a major intervention, so that you can create design a challenge that delivers a the solution to their problem within a short time frame.

I suggest you ask your current followers and subscribers one fairly broad question. Something like, "What's the biggest challenge you face when <insert something relevant to you/ your business>?"

Once you've got enough feedback, you can analyze your survey results, spot a problem that you know you have already created content on (because remember we are repurposing here) and there you have it, you have come up with your challenge idea.

Step two: Map out the journey with your existing content

Once you've come up with the end goal for your challenge, start mapping out the journey that people will take to achieve the end result.

You know that you have already created content that can be used so review that and make a list of all of the content that you know will provide people with the most value. This may be varied content from blog posts, podcast episodes and videos.

You need to map out the journey people could take if you were to guide them through your content to complete the challenge and achieve the desired end result. Remember, the challenge will be delivered via email and each email will request the participant to complete a daily task.

- Maybe they'll watch a video and follow the advice from it on the first day of the challenge.
- On the second day, they could read a blog post and follow the steps suggested.
- On the third day they are asked to listen to a podcast episode ...

Don't be afraid to play around with the framework of the roadmap until you're happy with it. Think about what actions you want participants to take each day and remember to make each step of the challenge solution orientated.

The good news is that you don't have to spend hours creating new content for the challenge because you already have the content. You'll simply have to come up with the daily action related to the content in your email.

Step three: Deliver the challenge via email

Now that you have all of your content mapped out with the end goal in sight, it's time to think about how you're going to bring it all together and deliver it to your subscribers via email.

Construct a series of daily emails that will take people through the challenge. Each email takes them a step further towards achieving the end result.

Perhaps within the email itself you add a little more oomph to the call to action, but you don't need to create oodles of new content. Hooray!

If you want to, you could create a series of pre-recorded instructional videos and send those out with your emails to add a little more personality into the mix. New subscribers would get to know you better - always a big bonus.

Set up your email challenge using an email service provider. You *could* send out the emails manually but why do that when you can let an email service provider to do all the work for you? You have to pay for the service but at prices as low as $10-$15 per month, and the time saving associated with it, it's worth the investment. Think how much you value even one hour of your own time. Email service providers save you hours and hours!

Having an automated email service in place ensures that you can use the same email list building challenge again and again, without doing extra work each time.

Step four: Market your email list building challenge

Online challenges can work wonders for growing your email list but how can you spread the word about your challenge to attract more participants?

Create a buzz surrounding your challenge on all of your social media channels. Encourage your followers to sign-up and mention it in any Facebook groups you're in (if they allow it. Check first with the group moderators!).

It's worth taking the time to get in touch with your current email list to let them know about the launch of your challenge. They might be interested in joining the challenge and, if not, you can ask them to pass the information if they know someone else who would be.

If you have time before the challenge, find some podcasts that you could be a guest on and ask the host if it's okay to mention your challenge on the podcast.

Paid advertising on social media is one of the fastest ways to grow your email list and invite more people to take part in your challenge. Run paid ads across your social channels and make sure you emphasize that all-important end goal to capture people's attention and make them want to sign-up.

When you have run the challenge once or twice and you have people who successfully completed it, get testimonials from them. Nothing beats social proof on social media! Run paid ads to your testimonials. Ensure your testimonials are on your challenge sign-up/landing page.

In conclusion

Don't neglect your email subscribers. Keep in touch with them regularly, and don't assume that they are aware of all of the awesome content that you are publishing. Instead of spending hours and hours every week on your email content, repurpose the content you already create into an email for subscribers.

Look at ways that you can use email as a tool to grow your list via an email challenge. It does not need to mean creating lots of new content because you can repurpose your existing content into your email list building challenge. It's all about repurposing and automation. Remember: curating your existing content then guiding people through it toward a specific goal or outcome saves them time and can add enormous value.

CHAPTER 13

Transcripts & repurposing

Transcriptions might not seem like the most exciting form of content, but they represent huge repurposing potential if you use them correctly and that's why I decided to give them their own chapter in this book!

A transcript is simply the spoken word, your podcast and video content for example, turned into the written word. However, it's not always necessarily word-for-word. There are different ways to transcribe your content, but good transcribers and transcription services don't include "ums" or "ahs" for example, and they'll edit lightly to prioritize comprehension over literal accuracy.

Why should you create and use transcriptions?

There are a number of reasons for creating and using transcripts for your podcasts or videos. You make your content more accessible, it's good for SEO, it makes your content easier to refer back to, and (here's the biggie) it makes it significantly easier to repurpose your content into other written forms.

Let's look at all of these in more detail:

1. Make your content more accessible

Having a transcript available creates a better user experience for a potentially large portion of your audience.

Transcripts make your content much more appealing to:

- Those who are hard of hearing.
- People who speak other languages than yours as their first language.
- Those who don't like listening to podcasts or watching videos or, for whatever reason, prefer to read.
- Scanners or busy people who might scroll through your transcript while listening to you, to find a place they want to skip to.
- Employees or commuters who don't have their headphones plugged in and aren't in an environment where they can blast out the sound.

2. Improve Your SEO

The web is constantly crawled by bots that read and catalogue content so that it can show relevant content to searchers. While they're getting better at cataloguing the spoken word, it's still far easier for these algorithms to read and index the written word, than the spoken. They can't scan audio or video very well, even now.

On your website, if you have a transcript below your podcast or video, perhaps under your show notes, it allows Google and other search engines to know everything you were talking about during the episode and helps them to index you properly for future search engine results.

Interestingly, Google are introducing a way to transcribe podcasts in the Google Podcasts app using AI (in the back end, not for the public to see) so that they can return more podcast content in search results and help more podcasts get discovered. Apple are doing the same on their podcast app too.

Whilst transcripts are great, well written show notes and blog posts are generally better for SEO than transcripts, because the search engine bots find transcripts on their own confusing. Transcripts are a written version of exactly what was said, and we don't all talk in the structured, coherent way that we would write. SEO these days is all about finding quality, well written content, which is why transcripts can be a little confusing to crawl for the bots.

3. Make it easier to refer back to your content

Listeners don't always have the time to listen to a whole podcast episode when they come across it. With transcripts, it becomes much easier for listeners to come back and find the content they want or to skip to the point in the episode that they care about the most.

4. Fast & easy repurposing

Just as video is the richest content format in terms of repurposing potential, transcripts are a fantastic basis for any written repurposing. They make it easier to create articles and social media content.

How to create transcripts

You have three options for creating transcripts:

1. Type them out yourself (or delegate to a member of your team).

2. Use an online transcription service.

3. Hire your own transcriptionist.

1. Creating your own transcriptions (with a little help from AI!)

It is unlikely that your time would be best spent typing your own transcriptions straight from the audio since transcription services are quite cheap and, unless you are a blisteringly fast typist, it will be quite time-consuming. However, A.I. software dramatically cuts the time it takes to create transcriptions, especially if your audio is clear and well-enunciated.

One well-known A.I. transcription app is Trint and it's reasonably priced. You can also use otter.ai for free. You'll need to edit the text after the software has done its best to transcribe it, but the time it takes to correct these errors will likely be far less than if you were to do it from scratch.

2. Use an online transcription service

There are transcription services available where real humans rather than AI are writing your transcripts. At Content 10x, we've used Rev.com to create our caption files and transcripts from day one. Because humans create the transcriptions, the accuracy is considerably better than that of A.I. software. The cost is very reasonable and the turnaround time can be as short as a few hours. You'll still need to make a few adjustments here and there. The accuracy is not 100%.

3. Hire your own transcriptionist

If you have a bit more of a budget to devote to transcriptions and you don't want to have to spend any time correcting errors, get a professional on your side. Search for transcriptionists on freelance platforms such as Upwork, Fiverr, and PeoplePerHour.

How to get maximum value out of your transcripts

Six ways you can repurpose your transcripts:

1. Offer Your transcript as a download

Some content creators offer their transcripts as downloadable PDFs to offer convenience for their listeners and to give them a way to save the episode on their computer without having to download the audio file. Others offer their transcripts in exchange for an email address as a "content upgrade" list-builder.

2. Include your transcript as searchable text on your website

You get significantly more SEO value from hosting the text in HTML format on a page on your site, making anything you said searchable by Google or Bing (or whatever search engine used). Therefore, rather than place your transcript as a PDF on your site, consider adding it in the main body of text.

You can still offer your transcripts as downloads even if you've posted them on your site. Some people prefer to save the content they like on their computer and will appreciate the PDF option.

3. Repurpose your transcript into a blog post

Instead of simply posting a transcript as-is, you can use it as the basis for a blog post. In this case, you're using your transcription service to get you halfway to a blog post and to save you a lot of time. From the transcript, you would edit out anything unnecessary, tighten up the language, add formatting, headings, and structure to either expand on the points you raised or make them easier to read.

By turning your transcript into a high-quality article you can then post it on LinkedIn, Medium, or on someone else's site as a guest post. You could also send the blog post to your email list. Publishing high quality articles is really going to help you with SEO.

4. Use your transcript as a resource for social media content

It's much easier to find Tweetable quotes from a podcast episode if you have a transcript. You could tweet out quotes as they are or create visual graphics to make them more eye-catching and better able to promote your content. If you create longer-form posts on social media, a transcript is extremely useful. You could take one transcript and wordsmith chunks of it into five or ten (or more) social media posts for all the platforms.

5. Repurpose parts of your transcripts into a book or eBook

If you're planning on writing a book or ebook, having transcripts of all your podcasts and videos might take you halfway to writing it. With transcripts, you don't even need to write it yourself to have it sound like your voice. You could take your transcripts, choose a working title and basic overview, and hand that over to a ghostwriter to turn into a well-written book that reads as though you wrote the whole thing yourself.

6. Use your transcripts to help you create a course

Course creation feels like a daunting task. Writer's block can show up in a big way when you're creating content that you'll put behind a pay wall. With all your podcast or vlog episodes in hand as transcripts, along with the data on which ones were most popular with your audience, you can create valuable lessons and workshops faster and more confidently.

Also, however you're creating your course, it's generally expected these days that online lessons are available as downloads in both audio and written form so your students can take your course content on the go.

In conclusion

When you want to repurpose your audio or video content, a great starting point is to generate transcripts. Having converted your audio and video into a first iteration of written content, you can have fun multiplying the value you get from your transcripts in many of the ways that I've talked about in this chapter. Also, see chapter eight on blog repurposing.

CHAPTER 14

Social media

There are so many ways that social media can, and should, be incorporated into your content marketing and content repurposing endeavors. I could write an entire book on social media and content repurposing alone. The next one perhaps?!

So many social media platforms. So many uses for social media to grow your audience and business. So many ways to incorporate your existing content into your social media strategy.

The world of social media is forever changing too. In fact, during the time it takes to write this section of the book, Instagram will have probably deployed a new update ... oh, they just did! Nonetheless, I'm going to share with you my ideas for repurposing content for the main social media platforms. Just bear in mind changes will take place, as they always do.

- Instagram
- Facebook
- Twitter
- LinkedIn
- Pinterest

Instagram

I love Instagram. I would say it's my favorite social media platform. It's my favorite because it takes me away from the noise of Facebook and the chirping chatter on Twitter, to a more fun, and generally positive place. Although, maybe that's because of the people, businesses and brands that I have chosen to follow. I'm pretty ruthless with who I follow. If someone puts out regular content on Instagram that is not to my liking in any way I don't hesitate to unfollow them in order to keep it a platform that I enjoy.

More so than any of the other social media platforms, it's all about the visuals. I'm a very visual person. After all, a picture speaks a thousand words, right?! Plus, I have a pretty short attention span when on social media, and so I like scrolling through Instagram, taking in short bite-sized nuggets of content, whether that's in the main feed or in Stories.

That's enough about me. The question is, how do you use Instagram to maximize the promotional value of your business? More importantly, how do you repurpose your content on Instagram to make it go further?

You can think of Instagram as having five main elements that you need to master to maximize its promotional potential for you:

- Posts
- Hashtags
- Stories
- Live video
- IGTV

I'm going to take you through each one, to give you a basic understanding, then I'll provide a practical example of repurposing a blog post on Instagram. As you read on, remember, it's not about large follower counts or likes. It's all about the right followers *for you*, engagement and conversions.

The basics of promoting your content on Instagram

First thing's first. How do you send people back to your website from Instagram? Historically, Instagram have not made this easy. Unlike Facebook, Twitter and LinkedIn, Instagram post captions and comments don't support hyperlinks. You are only allowed one link in your bio, although there are some notable exceptions in the other elements which I'll come onto soon. This is less than ideal.

You could consider using Linktree which enables you to generate one single link that, when clicked on, takes people to a list of other links to your content. For example, my Link Tree link offers links to my blog, my podcast, and my services at Content 10x. In my Instagram bio I can ask people to find out more about me by clicking the link and, for any post that I create where I reference a podcast episode or blog post, I can say 'click the link in my bio' and at least it will take people to my blog or podcast page. I know some people are far more specific with this and they regularly update their Link Tree links with direct URLs to their most recent content.

Another option to consider with the link in your bio is to create a trackable link using Bitly.com. This will allow you to see exactly how much traffic you're getting from Instagram.

Posts and caption guidelines

When I refer to an Instagram post I mean a post that appears in your main feed and in your grid, as opposed to in your 'Stories' feed. You can post images and videos of up to 60 seconds as a post.

When I interviewed Instagram expert, Jenn Herman, on my podcast, she recommended that you should post about every blog, podcast or video of yours at least once. You can quote a favorite line or take an image from the article, a snippet of audio from the podcast, a video clip, or even a photo of your desk space with the article on the screen.

It's great to have a process in place for how you repurpose your content onto Instagram, and follow that process regularly. For example, if you are repurposing your YouTube weekly video, turn the video into three 60 second video clips that you can share on Instagram.

Or, if you have a weekly blog, turn that into a quote image plus one video where you go onto camera and talk about your blog post to let people know more and why they should care.

When you create a post on Instagram you also need a caption, the text that accompanies your post.

The general structure of a caption promoting content is:

- New post, podcast, video is live. Brief intro to the topic. Humor is a plus and emojis a bonus!
- A teaser, such as a tip or two from the post. Why should they care? What will they get from it?
- CTA. "Click the link in my bio". Whether this is to your main blog page where all your content is or a link generated from Linktree or similar.

Or, you can flip the first two so that you start with your teaser to draw people in and get them interested, then you mention your new content, then the CTA.

Some people change their bio link every time they upload a new article so it takes people straight to the article. The downside is it can cause confusion for future readers. If you have 200 posts that all say 'click the link in my bio' and only one post takes you to the right place, and 199 posts take you to the wrong place, that's far from ideal. That's why, as mentioned previously, using either a tool like Link Tree or having a link to your blog page versus individual blog posts in your bio, is preferable.

You can put the URL of your content onto the image or video as well. I won't be clickable but at least people can see it. In this case, make sure you use a nice, easy to read and memorable, hyperlink. At Content10x we use the Pretty Link WordPress plugin to generate 'pretty links'.

The hashtag formula

Using hashtags is a great way to get noticed on Instagram. In fact, if you have a really small following then hashtags really will be the main way that you will get found by others. It's not quite so simple as #just #putting #a #hashtag #on #any #word (which I see people do all the time).

Did you know...

- You can use up to 30 hashtags in one post
- More is better. Instagram "culture" is perfectly happy for us to use plenty of hashtags
- You can either incorporate them into your captions, put them out of the way at the bottom of your caption, or add in the first comment. They work the same either way.

A good hashtag strategy mixes broad vs narrow and popular vs niche hashtags.

For broad vs narrow, imagine you're a chef in San Diego. A highly broad hashtag would be #food. That won't help you much. But the narrower option, #sandiegorestaurant ... now we're cooking! You could also tap 'Add Location' to drop a location tag on your post. Geotags also help you get found on Instagram, particularly useful for location-based businesses.

Popular vs niche is all about the numbers. How many posts use a particular hashtag? Open Instagram right now and search a relevant keyword for you. Tap the 'Tags' tab. You'll see a whole list of similar tags, each one displaying how many times it's been used. We'll use these numbers to divide our hashtags into groups.

The hashtag formula we use at Content 10x is generally:

- 3-5 very popular hashtags - 500k to 1m

- 3-5 moderately popular - 100k to 500k
- 3-5 targeted niche tags - less than 100k (as low as 2k or even 1k)

If you follow this formula, this is what will happen: The popular tags give you a quick burst of exposure that dies down in minutes. Then your moderate tags kick in and give you exposure lasting for hours or days. After that, your small, targeted tags continue to provide a trickle of exposure for weeks.

This perks up Instagram's algorithm. Instagram sees your initial burst followed by long-term attention and assumes you're a bit of a rock star!

Get this right and you'll probably outperform the other posts in the narrow, niche hashtag categories, which will put your post in the short running for being made a Top Post. As a Top Post, you'll be seen first by everyone searching those hashtags.

TOP TIP: Don't include hashtags with over one million uses. It's not worth it. You'll probably only get a handful of real human eyeballs. The rest will be automated bots swarming your comment section leaving things like, "Great post!" and "Awesome photo" and "I love your page, check mine out too". If you use hashtags with over, say five million, you'll see *so* much spam coming your way, you'll need a shower afterwards!

Using Stories to promote and repurpose your content

Stories took Instagram by storm. If you're not familiar with Instagram Stories, they are photos and videos that you can post and they vanish after 24 hours. They don't appear in your main Instagram grid, instead they appear in the Stories section at the top of the page.

Videos shared in Stories are vertical and up to 15 seconds long, keeping the content crisp and snappy. You can upload videos that are longer than 15 seconds but they will automatically get chopped into 15 second segments when published in Stories.

Or, you can upload still images to Instagram Stories and they display for about six seconds.

I use and consume content within Instagram Stories a lot. Stories is all about sharing micro moments and I think that's what makes it so interesting. There are lots of fun features to help you engage with your audience too. From polls, to a sliding scale voting feature, to 'ask me anything'.

If you have created content you want to use Stories to get more eyes on there are a number of options:

- If you create video content, you can repurpose snippets into 15 seconds clips for Stories. Of course you can also repurpose your video content into less than 60 second video posts in your main grid too.
- If you your content is not video, then there's nothing stopping you from jumping on Stories and recording a video to let your audience know all about your content. I do this every time I release a podcast episode. I enjoy telling my Instagram following that a new podcast is live and what it's all about. I often get good feedback.
- If you have a podcast, take snippets of audio and create 15 second audiograms for Stories. I talk more about audiograms in chapter five. Remember to choose snippets that are really interesting to get people to want more!

If you have over 10,000 followers and have a business profile (based on current criteria and I expect this to change), any Story you post can have a "swipe-up" feature to send people straight to your content. If you're not there yet, write "link in the bio" on top of the video, or write out the URL.

Whilst Story posts only last for 24 hours, you can keep them alive in Highlights. Highlights are those bubbles that show up on your profile above your photos. Highlights stay in place as long as you like on your main Instagram profile page. You can create themed highlights folders then add whatever Stories content you want to them. You can immediately add Story content to a Highlights folder, or you can resurrect expired Stories by fishing them out of the 'archive folder' and turning them into a "highlight". I have a Highlight folder of podcast clips, but I also have an "About Me" folder and "Client Testimonials" too.

Other engaging fun that you can have in Stories includes polling your audience by adding the YES/NO button or the 'emoji slider'- or any of the other engagement options that exist. They add to this all the time.

If you have just recorded a podcast episode, video, or any other form of content, and you asked certain questions in your content, maybe even sparked a debate, why not take it to an Instagram Poll?

You can also use Stories to ask for feedback on content, or poll your audience on article ideas. It's perfect for those times when you think, "How many times can I write about this one topic??" Then you poll your audience and people say "more please!".

Live video

Another option is live video - as you'll have read, I'm a massive fan of live video content if used well.

Here's how you can incorporate live video into your content repurposing strategy:

- Go live at the same time every week to discuss your most recently published content. By doing this you provide regular access to you and doing so at the same time every week aspect really helps your audience to know what to expect and when. Let's face it, we're all creatures of habit. This kind of behavior makes it easier for you to become someone else's favorite.
- Use Instagram Live to build trust. Live video's biggest benefit over the other types of content is its ability to

build significant trust and likability in a single session. When someone asks you something and you provide a great answer off the top of your head, you've just proven genuine expertise. Make sure that you provide the opportunity to ask questions versus just broadcasting.

- Show transparency. When you publish content, let's say a new blog post, if you then turn up live to talk about it in more detail, you're able to show that there is depth behind the words and that you're the real deal! But equally, when you're asked a question that you don't know the answer to right away, and you're totally transparent about that, it builds even more trust. In this era of fake news accusations and 'insta-famous influencers' you can't lose so long as you stay transparent and honest. Live video helps you do this.
- Enhance your likability. You can do this via all forms of content and not just live video, but there is something about live video that allows people to get to know your personality on a more intimate level. They hear your off-the-cuff tone and the passion in your voice, e.g. when you go off on a rant perhaps! People even like to see you stumbling over your words, not to point and laugh, but to see that you're human, just like them.

IGTV

When IGTV, Instagram's foray into long-form video, first came out, it rode on a wave of hype and excitement for a month or so before experiencing a bit of a dip. Time to bail? Not quite. The exact same thing happened to Stories in 2016. Then people kept using it after the novelty wore off and it's been growing steadily in popularity ever since.

IGTV can be accessed within the usual Instagram app or you can download a separate IGTV app. Videos must be between 15 seconds and 10 minutes and, at the time of writing, you can't record IGTV live or record video in the platform itself. Instead, you need to upload a video.

Instagram have been working on making IGTV more a part of the overall Instagram experience to get more people interested in it. For example, they have enabled users to post a video to IGTV and select to share the first minute as a post in the main feed. They've also made it very easy to share IGTV videos directly to Stories.

In terms of content repurposing opportunities and IGTV, it is possible to repurpose your videos that are used elsewhere onto the IGTV platform, if you think this would work for your audience. There is the slight challenge in that most videos that we create are not in portrait form, but please read the section in chapter six where I explain how you can overcome this. Plus, in June 2019 IGTV started to accept horizontal videos, so you can now repurpose your YouTube videos onto IGTV.

A good feature of IGTV is that you can put any link you want in the description and it's clickable, regardless of your follower count. This is a great benefit and is very different to main Instagram posts where there are no clickable links.

A simple way to get started on Instagram by repurposing your blog posts

Having gone through the various features of Instagram, let's consider a super simple way to repurpose blog content onto the platform. This is particularly useful if you're just getting started.

1. Pull quotes from your blog post

Think about grabbing your audience's attention with impactful imagery. Don't worry, you don't have to be a professional photographer or graphic designer. You just need to know a few of the basics of image editing such as overlaying text and using templates. If you have The Content 10x Toolkit then take a look at the super useful guides on how to do this.

Go through your latest blog post and pick out a few key points. Try to find a quote that's interesting and sure to grab people's attention. Pick an image that will go well with your chosen quote or the title of your blog post. You can use a picture you've taken yourself (which I highly recommend, people love the personal connection). Or, use a stock image from a royalty-free website such as Unsplash, Pexels or Pixabay.

Instagram images are square, 1080px by 1080px. I recommend going over to Canva and resizing/editing your image there. You can add the quote to the image itself or keep it simple and communicate your message in the Instagram caption.

2. Create an Instagram Story (or several!)

Jump onto Instagram Stories and talk about your most recent post: what it's about and why people should care. Don't want to go on camera? Create an image to use for Instagram Stories. You need to create a rectangular dimension of 1080px by 1920px with an aspect ratio of 9:16.

Make the most of Instagram Stories animations and special effects too plus engagement features like polls.

When you tell people that your blog post is live don't forget to provide the URL in the image, or tell them in the video, so they know where they need to go to read your blog post.

3. Create a video 'trailer'

You don't need to spend a fortune on a fancy camera or high-tech equipment to make an excellent video on Instagram, your smartphone is more than good enough!

Get your phone out, film a one minute or less video, and tell people why they should check out your post. What will they get out of it, what's 'the hook'? How will your post add value to your audience's life?

These are three simple things you can do every time you publish a blog post to get in front of your audience on Instagram.

Instagram conclusion

Instagram is a high engagement platform. You don't need to struggle with wondering what to post on Instagram. If you are already creating content then start by simply repurposing it. Create quote images, record short videos, go-live to talk about your topic, jump into Stories. There's so much you can do to get your content on Instagram. As with all content strategies, it's about testing. Find out what works with your audience and try to be consistent.

Facebook

There's no doubt that Facebook is an extremely powerful social media platform, and it's going nowhere. There are still over two billion active users on Facebook each month.[13]

If you know how to use the platform correctly, if you can create engaging content that people enjoy, then you have the potential to reach millions of people. But more importantly, you have the potential to reach your ideal audience. This doesn't need to be millions of people, it just needs to be the *right* people.

The question is, as a content creator, what are the best ways to repurpose your content onto Facebook to get in front of your ideal audience on the platform? Or, if you're already creating lots of content on Facebook, how can you repurpose it?

Elsewhere in this book I've covered how you can repurpose podcasts, videos, live videos, and blog posts. Within those sections I've discussed repurposing onto social media. In this section dedicated to Facebook, I'm going to focus on five Facebook-specific features and how you can leverage repurposing to make the most of them:

- Facebook algorithm and engagement

---

13 https://zephoria.com/top-15-valuable-facebook-statistics/

- Facebook advertising
- Video content on Facebook
- Facebook Pages and Groups
- Facebook Messenger bots

Facebook algorithm and engagement

What Facebook wants to see, more than anything, is engagement. Facebook is simply looking for quality content that engages people and is frequent in its production.

But please note: when I say "frequent", I don't necessarily mean putting out multiple posts a day on your main page. It can be tempting to think: 'I haven't seen much meaningful engagement on my page recently, so I'll just up my post frequency through the roof'.

Stop right there! Facebook wants excellent content, but it's about being regular and consistent in your approach rather than blasting posts multiple times per day.

It's about having a content schedule.

How much exactly? Posting three times a week is a good number to work with, but if you have high-quality content ready for every single day of the week, and can commit to posting it, that's even better. Remember though, it has to be quality content.

When I interviewed Facebooks ads expert, Liz Melville, on my podcast she shared a great tip: "Post quality content once a day, for thirty days, and you should see the algorithm kick in and your content reach more people."

It's about focusing on great quality content first and foremost and then asking yourself what more you can do to widen your reach. Once you've settled into a good content rhythm, that's when you should consider boosting/advertising your

Facebook posts. More on this in the next section. Boosting posts selectively on Facebook can double down on your success, but be careful not to overuse it.

When it comes to repurposing content onto Facebook, there's a lot that you can do. Video in particular is really good for repurposing. I'll come onto that shortly.

You can create and share images and graphics related to your video, podcast or blog post. However, beware of overloading your quote-based images with too much text. In fact, if you've got more than 20% text on your image, it will almost certainly harm your reach.

In short, when it comes to pleasing the Facebook algorithm and thus extending your reach, images are great. Videos are even better!

Facebook advertising

Organic reach on Facebook (i.e. getting found without paying for it) is without question a challenge. It has diminished considerably in the past few years for business pages in particular, damn that pesky algorithm, but it's fair to say that few platforms can rival its advertising and marketing potential. The Facebook ads platform is without question the most powerful advertising platform in the world of social media. The audience targeting features are incredible.

But there's a problem.

The Facebook advertising platform isn't intuitive so content creators aren't getting the most out of it. The advertising platform is powerful, with custom audiences, lookalike audiences and retargeting. In fact, I'm sure we've all experienced looking at a website, thinking about buying something, and the very next time we go onto Facebook we see an ad for the exact item we were just considering purchasing. This is no coincidence!

If you are not careful, a lot of money can be wasted on Facebook ads. You need to know the best ways to reduce the cost of your ads. I interviewed Facebook ads expert, Julia Bramble, on my podcast.

Here are her tips:

- Make your ad a video. This will cost you less.
- Target a proven audience and use retargeting.
- Build gradual trust with a sequence of ads.
- Use a chatty tone of voice like you're talking to a friend over coffee.

Repurpose your videos for ads

Just because your video is being used as an ad does not mean it has to be highly produced. The video can be as ghetto as any others you create! This is where repurposing comes in handy. You don't have to create brand new videos just for Facebook ads. Instead, repurpose the videos that you've already created and use them for ads.

Although it is an ad, as in you are spending money to get it in front of a target audience, it's important that it feel 'native' and natural on people's Facebook feeds. They do not want to see ads when they are on social media so it should not appear like one.

Find the best audience for your ads through trial and error with small tests. You can dip your toe into Facebook ads with a budget of just a few dollars a day.

When choosing your audience, filter people who have "liked" pages devoted to books or tools (e.g. software) that indicate they might be interested in what you offer. For example, if you offer a course on increasing personal productivity, you might want people who have liked 'Getting Things Done' or 'Todoist'.

Facebook will ask you what your objective is for the campaign and then help you to optimize your post for what you want. I recommend choosing "Engagement" for your first ad. The idea is to get a feel for how the system works. The engagement goal will get you more responses and therefore more data and Facebook won't "mark you down" for not making a sale or conversion.

You can use Facebook ads to attract more people to your upcoming Facebook Live session. You could just pull out your phone and record a one-minute video explaining what you'll be talking about and why people should attend. Include a few useful tips in the video itself.

This kind of video is short, sweet, and endears you as a "real person", since you're not trying to be flashy. It provides some value in the ad itself, and the rest is a very soft sell. Because you are advertising something that's (a) free and (b) still on the Facebook platform, this maximizes the chances of getting a positive reaction from people.

Anyone who watches it can be caught in your web, aka your Facebook retargeting audience! You can send additional content to viewers who watched 20 seconds, and different content to those who watched 45 seconds. This is when the Facebook advertising platform comes into its own.

More repurposing...

After your live session has been published you can repurpose it into a few different new ads in no time and continue to draw more traffic in. Engagement will build up through comments and likes, and eventually the Facebook algorithm should kick in and start bringing organic traffic.

This is just one example. You don't need to start with a Facebook Live event. The point here is to not send people away from Facebook the very first time they interact with you or your brand. That can come later. Right now you're gaining trust.

TOP TIP: If you're starting with a $100 ad budget and you want to be sure most of it goes to the right people, devote the first $30 of it to running a little test. Define three audiences using the tips below, run each one for a few days with a $10 cap. Then, simply see which one performed the best and put the remaining $70 behind that one. None of this needs to be guesswork.

Getting your audience right for your ads

Before you dive into the Facebook Ads Manager, research is required. For the people you want to reach, what interests do they have that would separate them from the rest of the rabble on Facebook!? Are there particular books that they would have read or organizations they would belong to that would suggest they are actively doing something to address the problem that you can help them with?

Consider:

- Books, authors, or specific online influencers.
- Organizations and networks.
- Tools or equipment they might use like email marketing software, membership software, invoicing software, etc.

Too many newbie online advertisers use Facebook's "interests" fields but they rarely tell you where someone's head is really at. For example, someone might have clicked that they're interested in entrepreneurship because they watched The Apprentice or Shark Tank once on TV!

In addition to their interests, brainstorm and research your audience's behaviors and demographics. What age range are they in? Do they have kids? Are they married? Do all this research and brainstorming on paper *before* you go into the Ads Manager, or you're likely to feel a little overwhelmed by all the choice in there. Know what you're looking for *before* you dive in.

If you are a local business, define your audience only by location and perhaps one or two other broad attributes such as age or marital status. For example, if you're a wedding photographer, you could target people within 100 miles of your home who are engaged. You can even target friends of an engaged couple.

With a local business, don't drill down too much or you'll wind up with such a small audience that Facebook probably won't run your ads or will run them very slowly.

By contrast, if you're not constrained geographically, you'll benefit from drilling down much more. Be sure to do your research and test.

Video content repurposing on Facebook

Facebook is heavily focused on compelling video content that engages people. Video content is the top priority within their algorithm - just knowing this fact can allow you to get ahead of the game.

What sort of video content should you post on Facebook?

You can of course create native video content on the platform but when it comes to repurposing, if you are already creating video content elsewhere, e.g. for YouTube, your website, your membership community, you can repurpose them into shorter videos that make a point, engage and connect with your audience. This is covered in more detail in chapter six: video repurposing.

As I mentioned in the section on Instagram, I recommend recording short 'trailers' for your content that are less than one minute. Tell your audience about your most recent blog post, podcast episode or video; state why they should care and what's in it for them.

Facebook Live, in particular, offers many ways to repurpose your content. In fact, at Content 10x, almost half of our clients have a Facebook Live repurposing service, where we take their video every week and repurpose it into lots and lots of new content.

A good duration for a Facebook Live is 15 minutes, but really that does depend on your audience and your niche. You need to allow time for people to turn up. You also don't want it to go on so long you start to take up too much of other people's time!

It's important to get people engaged in real-time on the platform. However, frequently you may see fewer people than expected turn up to your ive session but they watch the replay. Don't worry - it's quite common for more people to watch the replay than join you live.

How do you repurpose your Facebook Live video?

You can cut up your Facebook Live video, turning it into multiple short videos, each with a specific point in mind, to generate an emotional reaction from your audience. Attention spans these days are short and are shortening, so you need to think really carefully about what your audience wants to consume. These smaller videos are a perfect way to test out what formats work, what lengths work, and what people do and don't respond to.

You can also turn your Facebook Live video into a written article, into a podcast episode, into graphics, into a YouTube video, and so much more. It's all about having a repurposing mindset and all of this is covered in chapter seven: Live video.

Facebook groups, pages & profiles

Facebook groups are another part of the platform that people devote their time to. Whilst anybody can like and follow your page, a Facebook group is something that you 'belong' to. They can be secret, private or public. You usually have to submit a request to be a member of a group. Group owners and admins control who is or is not in the group.

Groups are great for discussions and for building a community.

If you have a page and a group, while it's great to repurpose content across Facebook, ideally you shouldn't be posting the same content to your Facebook group as you do your Facebook page or personal profile. It's good to really think about the purpose of each and keep them separate in terms of the content that you serve up. What does the group want to see? What do people on my primary page want to look at?

Facebook groups are successful when it comes to building a community of people, so you need to keep that in mind. Your Facebook page, however, is more about raising the initial awareness of your business.

When you repurpose content from your blog, video or podcast onto Facebook, have a strategy for the kind of content you want to put on your page to raise awareness and, if you have one, in your group, to build community - or whatever your reason is for having a group.

The key point here is just because you have different places to post content on Facebook doesn't mean you should post the exact same content everywhere. Be strategic. You can repurpose but do so with intention and make appropriate changes here and there.

Facebook Messenger bots

Chatbots are a rising force in digital content marketing and Facebook Messenger bots in particular are becoming more and more popular. Chatbots and content repurposing can be used together to maximize engagement on Facebook. What's more, chatbots can really boost your ability to get your content in front of your audience.

In short, a chatbot consists of a flow of "decision logic", something you've undoubtedly come across before. Think back to a time you found yourself trapped in an automated phone conversation where you have to press buttons when prompted. Or, even worse, voice recognition - where your voice just isn't being recognized! That sort of technology used to be relatively expensive and complicated to set up. Now, with the advent of chatbots, automated decision logic tools are available to all of us.

If you're wondering what you can do with chatbots, the possibilities are endless, and they go really well with content repurposing. Uses range from simple menus that direct people to FAQs or somewhere else on your website to complex sales funnels that integrate with Facebook Messenger. What makes it so exciting is more and more people are using the Messenger platform and preferring it to things like phone or email. As of April 2019, 1.3 billion people use the Facebook Messenger app every month.[14]

It's growing so fast! Michael Stelzner, CEO of Social Media Examiner, talked about Facebook Messenger and messenger bots in his keynote speech at Social Media Marketing World in 2019. His view was that Facebook Messenger is a really powerful marketing tool and chatbots are not to be underestimated.

How do you make Facebook Messenger chatbots if you're not a coder?

You used to have to write code to build chatbots. You can still build them from scratch using Facebook's app developer platform if you want to create amazing bots with unique features. For most of us, however, 3rd party tools like Manychat and Chatfuel are more than enough to create what we need.

I interviewed Facebook Messenger bot expert, Kelly Noble Mirabella, on my podcast and she shared that ManyChat is her favorite, mostly because it has an easy visual builder to create your automation flows, similar to InfusionSoft. Either way, both have free trials so you can figure out for yourself which works best for you. There are other options out there as well as ManyChat and Chatfuel.

Whichever tool you use, first and foremost, you'll need a business page to have a chatbot on Facebook. People need to engage with you through a trigger you previously set up, and only then will they get added to a chatbot list.

Note: It's not enough for someone to simply 'like' your page.

14 https://www.socialmediatoday.com/news/facebook-messenger-by-the-numbers-2019-infographic/553809/

You can set up your bot so that a person is added to a chatbot list if they send you a message. Or, you can encourage visitors to engage with something, e.g. "[Comment below/Message us] to let us know what you want to see from us next, and we'll send you a message right back."

It all starts with setting up the trigger and to do this you need to create what Facebook calls a growth tool. In the back end of your chatbot software, you'll see the option to create a bunch of growth tools. For example, you can create a Facebook post that triggers a chatbot when someone leaves a comment.

Kelly Noble Mirabella explained that a great growth tool is a URL/link that you can generate that when clicked, it will take people straight to your Facebook Page Messenger, this is referred to as a "Ref URL". You do can do loads of things with these, such as adding them to buttons on your website or putting them into emails. Plus, you can easily track who comes through which URL, which is really important for audience segmentation. Once someone triggers a growth tool, your chatbot will send them a message. Use this first message to confirm what they're subscribing to.

Common chatbot mistakes

I'll be honest, I was skeptical about chatbots at first. My first exposure to them was people using chatbots to trick others into getting on their list. Like any brand new tool, short-term marketers quickly swooped in and did their best to ruin the party!

Don't make these mistakes:

Mistake one: Not being clear about people being signed up to your chatbot

The "black hat" chatbot marketers made this mistake (a deliberate omission) right from the beginning. They would publish a post encouraging people to "leave a comment below." What they neglected to mention, however, was that leaving a comment would sign you up to a chatbot!

It is against the Facebook terms of service not to tell people that they'll be subscribed to a chatbot.

You don't need to use the word "chatbot", however. You just need to say that they'll be hearing from you via Messenger. e.g. "Comment below and we'll send you a message to say hi."

Mistake two: Making it hard to unsubscribe

Include an unsubscribe button in every chatbot message. Why would you want anyone there who doesn't want to be? If you make it hard or confusing to unsubscribe, you're only going to create a bunch of frustrated people who don't even want to hear from you. Very bad for your brand!

Besides, under GDPR regulation, you need an unsubscribe button in every single message sent to anyone in Europe. The unsubscribe button is not a built-in feature, so make sure you find it and switch it on right away.

Mistake three: Being tempted by big numbers

You'll see big numbers from gaming the system, but don't be tempted. Building things correctly will yield better results and keep your brand safe. As with email subscribers, it's better to have 100 engaged subscribers who are really happy to be there than 10,000 random people who don't care one way or the other about your content.

Your mother might have told you to "treat others the way you want to be treated" and in marketing I say "market to others the way you want to be marketed to".

Aside from the mistakes and, quite frankly, unsavory things that some people do with messenger bots, there are also some pretty awesome benefits from using them if used correctly.

Let's take a further look ...

Audience segmentation

Chatbots are amazing for audience segmentation. You can

track what people click on and, over time, you can serve people more of what they love and less of what they ignore. This drives click-through rates (and audience happiness!) through the roof.

For example, let's say that every week you create a video, a podcast episode, and a blog post on a particular topic. You send a message in Messenger, telling your subscribers that you have new content on a particular topic. You say 'select below whether you want to watch the video, listen to the podcast or read the post'.

Over time you'll see that some people only ever want to watch video so you can segment them as people who prefer video. And the same for the other options. This in turn allows you to start serving up more of the content that they like, and less of the content they don't like.

Lead magnets

You can deliver lead magnets using chatbots. It works in a similar way as an email list lead magnet except, instead of emails, you're sending them instant messages.

Have people engage with the bot before giving them the lead magnet, e.g. by replying with "yes". Doing so gives you extra privileges when it comes to broadcasting promotional content to them.

Retargeting with online ads

If you use Facebook ads, chatbots are your best friend for building custom audiences. When you export your chatbot data into the Facebook ads manager, you'll see close to 100% import rate. Importing data from an email list is closer to 50% because people sometimes use different email addresses for different things so you may not have the email address they use on Facebook. Furthermore, as hard as it may be to believe, not everyone on your email list is on Facebook too! Chatbots, however, save people's Facebook user ID. The only way you won't get a match is if someone has left Facebook.

How to use chatbots to support & promote your repurposed content

So chatbots can be great for building a new audience, segmenting your audience, delivering lead magnets and building custom audiences in the Facebook Ad Manager, but how can they help you with content repurposing?

When you're multiplying your content by repurposing it, you can use audience segmentation to send each audience member exactly what they want to see. If everyone gets to consume your content in the way that they find most comfortable you'll see your listenership, open rates and click-through rates all increase. This is similar to the example I provided previously on segmenting people who like video, podcast and blog posts.

Create a "choose-your-own-adventure" sequence. If they click on all the videos, you can tag them as such and then, when you come up with a bonus video, you might not send it to everyone, but you *would* send it to people who have shown reliable interest in that type of content.

Using chatbots with repurposed Facebook Live sessions

We have a lot of clients who use Facebook Live as the core of their content repurposing strategy. Say you have a weekly live show, which you then turn into a highlights video, a podcast episode, and a blog post. You can use your bot to reach out to your audience and say something like:

"If you missed the Live Session (or it's just not your thing), you can catch the highlights video, download the podcast, or dive into the blog post guide."

Your message would end with buttons to each of those destinations. You're serving people a content buffet and they can choose exactly what they want to 'eat'. They get to choose the medium they prefer, and the more you know about their preferences, the more you can serve them the content they will engage with.

TOP TIP: You can also use bots to encourage more people to attend your Facebook Live. Let's say you have a segmented audience of people who like your Facebook Live videos. You can send out a message before, during and after a live video. The first lets them know, in advance, when your next live video will be. The second reminds them that you're going live right now. The third, after your live video,, serves them your list of repurposed options, e.g. check out the blog, podcast or short video summary based on the live video.

The simplest way to get started with messenger bots is to set up a welcome message with a menu attached to it:

"Thanks for getting in touch. Here are some places you can go:

[Latest blog]

[Learn about us]

[Work with me]"

Once you have that basic setup in place, you can start dabbling with the next level. Make sure that everyone who comes through that entry point is tagged as such so you can send them specific broadcasts.

Finally, once you've repurposed your content into text, audio, and video, notify everyone with a broadcast that gives them the three options of how to consume your content.

Track who chooses which option and put them in different segments so you can send more video options to the video-lovers and so on. You'll soon have built the most highly engaged audience you've ever seen, all by combining chatbots and content repurposing into your strategy. Sounds good, right?!

Facebook conclusion

There's lots that you can do to repurpose your content onto Facebook, particularly your video content. Whether you like the platform or not, there is no denying that a) a lot of people use Facebook everyday including, most likely, people you want to reach, and b) the Facebook ads platform is by far the most powerful advertising platform in existence right now. Are you making the most of this?

Going live on Facebook is a great thing to do and you can really grow your audience and build a community by regularly going live, but don't let your live video content go to waste. Look to repurpose each video into shorter videos, written content, visual content and so much more.

If you have the appetite for it, explore what Facebook Messenger bots can do for you and your business. Being able to dish up content to your audience in the format that they like the most is a real win!

Twitter

When it comes to Twitter and how you can repurpose content, there's lots that has been covered elsewhere in this book that can be applied to Twitter. For example, repurposing long form video content into bite-sized videos, repurposing podcast episodes into audiograms, and creating visually engaging content. Similar to the Instagram and Facebook sections therefore, I'm going to focus on platform specific features.

Something that is very specific to Twitter is the short lifespan of a tweet. Tweets are reported to have a lifespan of around 18 minutes. What does this mean? If your followers haven't seen your tweet 18 minutes after tweeting it, they probably won't. It'll be lost in history.

Twitter is about concise communication. Tweets can't be longer than 280 characters, videos can't be longer than 2 minutes 20 seconds. It's fast paced, concise and, as such, there's a lot of 'chatter'.

Reposting evergreen content on Twitter

When I first got started on Twitter, and I was late to the game, Twitter was a place where content marketers would tweet the same content again, and again, and again.

People would use social media scheduling tools like Meet Edgar and SmarterQueue, where it's possible to set-up a re-posting schedule for your content. You'd load content into categories and then set-up a publishing schedule for when those categories post content. The content recycles through the queue and keeps getting tweeted until you remove it.

There was nothing wrong with doing this given the lifespan of a tweet and if the content was relevant to your audience. It might not be the most imaginative approach but there was nothing 'wrong' with it per se. However, Twitter made changes to its platform back in early 2018 to improve the quality of content on the platform and to crackdown on spam and bots.

Twitter, along with other social media platforms, had been (and still is) under a lot of pressure to try and reduce the amount of spam and fake news spreading and manipulating their networks. Problems associated with multiple fake accounts attempting to amplify or inflate specific tweets and hashtags artificially came under the spotlight worldwide following the last U.S presidential election and the vast growth of fake social accounts and fake news. Twitter decided to make significant changes to help reduce automation on their platform to crack down on spam and bots. Here's what changed:

1. You can no longer post identical content across multiple Twitter accounts

If you have a number of Twitter accounts and you would usually post the same tweet simultaneously to save yourself time via tools such as Buffer, Smarter Queue or MeetEager, you can't do that anymore

There is an easy way around this problem - retweets! You can post content to your main Twitter account and then retweet the same post from your other Twitter account, within reason. Don't enlist thousands of helpers to retweet your post or you risk getting Twitter's attention for all the wrong reasons!

2. You can't post duplicate content on your account

When you create a fantastic piece of content, it's understandable that you want to shout about it again and again. On Twitter you may want to tweet about it again and again. Because the lifespan of a tweet is so short it became common practice to post the same tweet many times using social media scheduling tools but this is no longer permitted on Twitter.

Recycling your tweets is not as straightforward as it used to be. You can't just copy and paste your content and tweet it again in the way you once could. You have to really think about your tweets so you don't post identical content and break Twitter's new automation rules.

An alternative option is to create five to ten re-written versions of the original post. If you are repurposing a blog post, podcast or video into tweets to help promote your content, take key points from the original piece of content and repurpose it into many engaging tweets.

Taking time to review your content and harvesting a few key points or a quote from a guest, for example, allows you to come up with a variety of reworded content for your tweets. Now you've got a selection of great tweets that won't be classed as duplicate but that still effectively promote your original piece of content.

3. You can't cross-post content from other social accounts to multiple Twitter accounts

Another addition to the automation rules is the fact that you can't cross-post content from other social networks to multiple Twitter accounts. Don't worry, you can still cross-post if you want to, but you can only do it for *one* of your Twitter accounts. You should also keep in mind that you can't simultaneously perform actions such as liking, retweeting and following from multiple accounts.

Creating impactful content on Twitter

Overall, the crackdown on posting identical content, cross-posting and automation is a good thing. When you think about it, with the presence of spam and bots dramatically decreased there are more opportunities for your content to reach people and get noticed.

Here are some tips on what to focus on with Twitter:

- **Focus on delivering valuable and high-quality content**

You only have 280 characters per tweet, so make them count. Focus on creating and publishing high-quality content that gives the reader value. Think about each tweet and come up with good quality content for each one. When you focus on quality, the platform will reward you for it!

- **Include graphics to make your tweet stand out**

A tweet with an image, video, animation or GIF is more likely to be retweeted. What's more, if you post a short video clip such as a teaser of your latest podcast or YouTube video, it's six times more likely to be retweeted than tweets without one.

You might not even need to create images and artwork specifically for your tweets. For example, if you're tweeting about a recent blog post, do you have images that you included in the blog post itself that you can share? If you're tweeting about a recent podcast episode and you interviewed a guest, perhaps you have a headshot of the guest that you could share.

- **Ask for retweets and you'll get retweets**

Did you ever hear the saying, "ask, and you shall receive"? Well in Twitter's case this is very true! Asking for a retweet improves your chances of actually getting your tweet retweeted, so don't be shy!

- **Ask questions to engage with your audience**

Get a conversation going and increase engagement on Twitter by asking your audience questions. It doesn't have to be a question of epic proportions. Even a simple question will be enough to encourage someone to respond with a comment.

While some may say it was great to be able to save time and recycle tweets, these Twitter changes are for the best. You can expect higher quality content, more active users and increased engagement. Thanks to the changes, we now have a better platform with fewer bots, less spam, and less fake news!

Repurposing Twitter chats

When it comes to repurposing content, we spend a lot of time thinking about what we can post to Twitter rather than repurposing content that's already there. I ask you to consider Twitter chats.

I had a wonderful guest on my podcast, Madalyn Sklar, and she blew me away with her approach to her weekly Twitter chats and how she makes the content go so much further than simply the chat itself.

A Twitter chat is a way to have a conversation on Twitter by using a specific hashtag, e.g. #content10x. They usually happen at a set time each week and the host of the chat will ask questions in their tweets, labelling them 1, 2, 3, and so on. Participants can then reply to those tweets using the hashtag to join in the conversation. It's a great way to make friends and share knowledge with people around the globe.

Would you believe that the #TwitterSmarter chat, hosted by Madalyn Sklar, has amassed over six billion impressions in its 6+ years of being held? Let that sink in for a moment .... Six billion impressions.

What can you do to repurpose a Twitter chat? Here are just a few suggestions:

- **Facebook Live:** After you have completed your Twitter chat, invite your guest onto a livestream and take the conversation to video. Madalyn does this with her Twitter Smarter chats and she finds it works brilliantly because people are able to ask questions in real-time *and* they allow Madalyn and her guest to really dig deep into the subject, beyond just 280 characters. They also appeal to a whole host of people who prefer content in video format than social media posts - one of the main reasons we love content repurposing! The people who turn up to the livestream might not even be on Twitter. That is okay.

- **Create additional video content:** After you have recorded your Facebook Live following the Twitter Chat, edit your video into short teasers for sharing on social media. You could also edit (if necessary) for YouTube or IGTV, and put the video on your website. If you put your video onto YouTube, create a specific playlist just for post-Twitter chat video Q&As.

- **Audio:** There may be potential to repurpose your Facebook Live video, or edited video, into an audio file which you could use as a podcast episode if you want to. In chapter seven, live video, I share all you need to know about video repurposing

- **Twitter moments:** Tweets seem so fleeting, there one minute, gone the next. But did you know that there is a way you can eternalize your best tweets on Twitter? You can do this by creating a Twitter Moment. That's exactly what Madalyn does for each of her Twitter chats. Twitter Moments provide an engaging way to curate a group of tweets. Twitter chats can be very fast paced and it's hard for people involved to see every tweet and every great takeaway. Twitter Moments provide a way to curate a group of tweets into something that lasts permanently on your profile. Just like Instagram highlights but for Twitter! You can create a Moment from your own tweets, about an event, or testimonials that other people have given you. By using Twitter Moments, people who missed the chat *or* people who want a summary of the event can click on the Twitter Moment and see a round-up of what's been discussed.

- **Blog post roundups:** You can create a blog post about the Twitter chat. This is such a great idea because you share all of the value from the Twitter chat in one place. You could share the questions asked and the main comments from participants. You can do this by embedding the tweets into your blog post. Each tweet has an "Embed Tweet" option in the dropdown menu and you just copy and paste this onto your website.

You could even consider writing a stand-alone blog post, with no embedded Tweets at all, simply an article about the Twitter chat topic. This is another brilliant way to give Twitter chats more longevity and repurposes them into a format that can be seen again and again. By writing a blog post you will improve your SEO as well. Do some keyword research and try to make your blog post keyword focused.

- **Other social media platforms:** If you have an audience on other social media platforms, such as Facebook and Instagram, then it's a good idea to create content about the Twitter chat on those platforms. Shoot short videos before the Twitter chat letting people know about it and explaining how to join.

But the reality is there will be a lot of people who would never join a Twitter chat and might not be on Twitter at all. A good idea therefore would be to film short videos after the Twitter chat where you share with your audience on other platforms the questions asked and the key takeaways.

You don't have to film videos, that's my suggestion simply because video performs so well on social media platforms. On Facebook you could simply write posts about the Twitter chat. On Instagram you could share screenshots of the Tweets. Lots of people like to do that.

- **Livestream on Twitter:** Twitter have released

live-streaming on the platform. This feature works on the mobile app. Once you open the app it will show you who, out of the people you follow, is live-streaming. After you have completed your fun and engaging Twitter chat, much like hosting a Facebook Live after-party, you could host a Twitter Live after party instead!

The good thing about doing this is your audience who took part in the Twitter chat are obviously already on Twitter, so you know they are there and possibly ready to engage. I guess the downside is simply that you are not then putting yourself in front of a new audience and entering into new discussions on a different platform.

If you have the time and resources, why not do both? That would be my advice. There's so much to be gained from Twitter chats and so much repurposing that can be done from them. They are without question something a little bit different and unique to the platform, which is why I've enjoyed taking you through what a Twitter chat is and the repurposing potential.

LinkedIn

LinkedIn has had a big resurgence of late. In fact, at the start of 2019 Gary Vaynerchuck declared 2019 to be the year of LinkedIn.

LinkedIn is a professional networking platform. It used to be a place for employers to post jobs, for job seekers to post CVs, and not much else. It's where we went to update our career history when we were in the market for a job. And if we were recruiting, it's where we'd go to not only advertise a position, but also find out more about a candidate.

Year ago, I remember only really logging onto LinkedIn once in a blue moon and it was usually when I'd met someone and was keen to find out more about what they did for a living or their career history. Today it has evolved into something much more than that. It is a thriving social media and content platform, but retains its unique professional, business and employment focus.

On LinkedIn you create a profile and then form 'connections' with people to build your LinkedIn network. You can send anyone a connection request, it's up to them to decide whether to accept it or not.

People use LinkedIn to post status updates, post content (including visuals, videos and articles) and there's lots of interaction and engagement taking place. It's still very much a professional/business platform, but it's not boring or stuffy like it once was.

Other social media platforms, like Facebook, are making it hard for businesses to gain any traction without spending a lot of money on ads. By contrast, LinkedIn still has decent organic reach (for now!) and that's one of the things that people love about it.

Essentially, things that used to work years ago on Facebook, that fall flat on their face today, work on LinkedIn. Hence the resurge in interest and usage of LinkedIn. Also, since 2003 when it launched, LinkedIn has gone through lots of changes. LinkedIn was acquired by Microsoft in 2016 and that brought about many changes, for example, with the addition of video content and now *live* video.

Social selling is critical on LinkedIn

LinkedIn is the place to focus on social selling, which is the art of selling without selling! When I interviewed LinkedIn expert, Sam Rathling, she emphasized just how important this is. There are a lot of people who approach LinkedIn in the wrong way whereby they focus on advertising and pushy sales techniques. This is simply not going to work. Instead, the focus should be on attracting the right clients to you by creating high value content.

If you connect with people and then immediately start trying to sell to them in their inbox you're doing it wrong. If your posts are all salesy, you're doing it wrong. You can get leads and business on LinkedIn, but in a non-salesy, less overt way.

Repurposing content on LinkedIn

If you are already creating long-form content elsewhere, for example, videos, a podcast, a blog, livestreams, and are now deciding what you should post on LinkedIn, the good news is you will be able to repurpose your content in many ways.

Firstly, get your profile set-up correctly.

Before creating and repurposing content on LinkedIn, let's get the basics right with your profile.

A few tips:

- Pay attention to your headline and have a decent (appropriate/on-brand) photograph of yourself.
- On your LinkedIn profile description, make sure that you mention that you have a podcast, blog, video show, etc. and add a call to action for people to check it out with guidance on how. Don't assume they will know.
- In your profile you can add links to your contact information so it's a good idea to add a link to where people can go to consume your content, e.g. if you have a podcast, add a link to the main location that you'd like people to go to listen to it
- You can add media files to your profile as well. For example, you can add images and videos to your profile. This is an opportunity to add images related to your content. If you have a podcast you could add your podcast artwork, quotes from your show, reviews from your subscribers, audiograms (snippets of audio from your show paired with an image) or video clips.

Posting status updates

LinkedIn (like other social media platforms) makes its money by keeping people *on* the platform, so you fall out of favor if you do things that take people off the platform. When you post an update, don't post links to your website or YouTube or any external site in the post itself. Instead, post the link in the first comment. If you post links to external sites in the main body of your post you will get hardly any views on that post.

If you are posting a video, then upload the video directly LinkedIn. If you put a link to YouTube you will reach hardly anyone. Videos must be native to LinkedIn.

You get up to 1300 characters for your update so you can create a pretty lengthy post. LinkedIn likes this. They like posts that are like mini blog posts. Even if you are posting a video or a graphic, if you accompany it with a long post, you will get more reach for your post. It comes back to keeping people on the platform.

In fact this is where blog repurposing could work well. Why not repurpose your short blog posts as LinkedIn updates? Put the whole post in the update or cut it down. Link to the full blog post in the first comment.

TOP TIP: The first three lines of text are always shown in the feed followed by 'see more', so a good way to get people to click on 'see more' is to consider the first three lines as a teaser for the post. Don't give away the answer or your point straight away. The more people click on 'see more', the more popular your post will appear to the algorithm, and the more people will see your post. Again, similar to Facebook, it's all a popularity contest!

Video is king

The best form of content to post on LinkedIn is video. Your video should be uploaded to the platform, with captions/subtitles on the video for those who don't have their sound on when watching, and it should be accompanied with a long text post that has no external links This would be the optimal post on LinkedIn.

Videos on LinkedIn can be up to 10 minutes long, but according to LinkedIn expert, Sam Rathling, the optimal duration is actually as short at 10-60 seconds. If the video is educational and high value then 60 seconds could be too short so it's fine to go over that, but aim to stay below five minutes. People are busy and they don't really go to LinkedIn for long-form content, so you need to grab attention - and keep it. Whist attention spans are longer on LinkedIn than say, Twitter, they still aren't really that long.

When it comes to repurposing content on LinkedIn, if you are repurposing video content then a great idea is to cut down longer videos into shorter 'teaser' videos. Find a clip from your video that can stand-alone and will grab attention, share it on LinkedIn and provide the link to the full video in the comments. Some people may never watch your longer video, but will get value from your shorter clip.

Or, film a completely separate short video, letting people know about your longer form video. Be sure to explain why anyone would want to watch it and what value they will get out of it. For example, explain the problem and the solution that you're offering in the video. This separate short video notifying people of your content can be created for all kinds of content. A new blog post or a new podcast episode could all be supported by you taking to camera and filming a less than one-minute video letting people know all about it. This is what I mean when I refer to a content video trailer.

Visual content on LinkedIn

LinkedIn is not really a visual platform. Interestingly, unlike Facebook and Twitter, plain text posts do really well on LinkedIn. They have even been known to do better than posts with images. People are more prepared to digest information on LinkedIn. That said, adding visuals that grab attention can be impactful, but only for certain posts.

If you are going to post images, social media manager Cathy Wassell shared a top tip to not post five images! Post less or more than five, because if you post more than five you will get the 'see more' button. If people click it, that's engagement and it sends out an 'I'm popular' message to the algorithms. It's all about testing what works for you and, most importantly, what works for your audience.

LinkedIn articles

Articles are great for building your credibility. However, they don't get a lot of readership. LinkedIn used to send a notification when you publish a new article but they don't anymore because so many articles are published every day. So, creating articles is a good idea but don't go "all in" on articles.

A great thing about creating articles for LinkedIn is that they don't need to be written from scratch, just for LinkedIn. Repurposing comes in handy once again!

You can repurpose your blog posts into LinkedIn articles but you need to allow a few weeks or longer between posting on your site and posting on LinkedIn. In fact, Sam Rathling suggested as long as three months. This is so that the original article on your website gets ranked as 'the original' by the search engines. At the end of your article it's useful to include a note, 'This article originally appeared at <link>'. Tweaking your article, changing the headline and the introduction, all helps too.

A great thing about articles is that when you publish an article it will appear on your LinkedIn profile. It always shows the most recent article that you published. New people landing on your profile will see this which is great for your credibility. Articles also help with your Social Selling Index, which is a score that LinkedIn gives you out of 100. It helps to establish your brand on the platform and your status.

Another great thing about articles is that you can send people to other locations in an article - it's okay to use links. For example, you can write an article all about a podcast episode and direct people to listen to it. Remember, in status updates we stay clear of external links, leaving them in the first comment only.

TOP TIP: Write your bio at the bottom of your article with information about where the reader can find you and links to things like lead magnets.

Engagement is critical

With LinkedIn, as with most social media platforms, it's less about the type of content you post and more about the engagement your content gets. LinkedIn loves comments!

A great way to get engagement is to ask a question. Invite people to comment and then engage with them when they comment. Ask questions back as well. E.g. 'thanks for your comments, what did you learn the most from ...' or 'thanks for your comments, is this something that you do too...' and so on. Get a conversation going in the comments.

When you post content, the first hour after posting your content is critical. If positive vibes get sent to the algorithm in that first hour, you'll reap the benefits for days or weeks. A happy algorithm means more reach. Therefore, don't post content when you are not going to be free to respond to comments.

Tagging people

Many people tag others in their posts as a way to drive more engagement and comments. Only tag people if it's relevant to them. Ask permission first if you don't know them so well or if it is clearly just appropriate to ask e.g. an attendee of your course or a client. For example, let's say it's someone you recently met at an event and you want to tag them in a post about a conversation you had, or get their thoughts on something, whatever it may be, if in doubt just ask them if it's okay.

Don't tag people in the hope that if you tag someone with a large following or influence it'll help your post. Unsolicited tagging is annoying and should be avoided. If this happens to you then you can un-tag yourself from a post. In the top right-hand corner of the post you can choose to un-mention yourself.

Frequency

How frequently you post depends on how much you want to dominate the platform. If you want to dominate then post on LinkedIn every day, or more. But as with all platforms, it's more about quality than quantity.

Unlike other social media platforms, posts have a longer lifespan on LinkedIn. They can last for a few weeks as long as people are still engaging with them. It's not unusual for a post that someone posted three weeks ago to pop into your feed. That's why quality is important.

Business pages versus personal profile

Unless you are a big brand, like Amazon or Apple, you do not need to use a business page on LinkedIn. You're far better focusing on your personal profile. This is especially true if you focus on personal branding and clients are buying into *you* as the business owner or head of the business. It's hard to get traction and followers on a business page and people buy from people, so there is little to gain from a business page and a lot to gain from posting great content consistently from your personal profile.

How to grow an audience and following on LinkedIn

There are two main ways to grow your following on LinkedIn. The first is an inbound approach, i.e. people finding you. They will find you when you have the appropriate keywords on your profile. You'll also get found by sharing great content consistently.

The other way to grow your following is to proactively build your network of people in your target market. Search and find people, whether in your local area, by their job role, or profession. Figure out your target market, they will be on LinkedIn regardless of whether you are B2B or B2C. Whatever you do, most people you want to connect with will be on LinkedIn!

LinkedIn conclusion

There is huge potential on LinkedIn to make connections and grow your audience. You need to create a strong profile. In particular, pay attention to your headline, have a decent headshot, and link to your best content, e.g., your podcast, your video channel, your blog. Add media files to you profile, e.g., videos, testimonials, photographs.

Build your connections and send personal messages when asking to connect with people. Think strategically about who you want to connect with, then look at who does business with them, and so on.

When you post content it's all about quality. Quality over quantity. Plus, it's about being sociable and creating posts for engagement. You can repurpose your content, for example, your blog posts, YouTube videos, etc., but make sure you respect each platform and adapt the way the content is presented so it's platform-specific. Only by testing will you work out what works best for you and your audience. Find what works and stick to it. Also, remember that you do not want to post links that will take people off LinkedIn. This will be harmful to your audience reach.

Pinterest

Pinterest is included in this section on social media but it's important that we're all on the same page: Pinterest is a search engine and *not* a social media platform.

If that statement surprises you, I understand. People regularly talk about Pinterest as a social media platform. In fact, even at big events like Social Media Marketing World, held annually in San Deigo, talks about Pinterest are included and here I am, including a chapter on Pinterest in the section about social media. It seems I'm just as bad! It deserves a mention somewhere in this book though, because it has great repurposing potential, and here is as good a place as any.

When Pinterest first launched back in 2010 it was tempting

to brush it off and continue concentrating our content marketing efforts on the 'big players'. However, Pinterest proved itself to be a worthy competitor for our attention and has over 250 million users per month[15] with half of them likely to complete a purchase after seeing a promotional pin that caught their eye.

When I spoke to Pinterest expert, Kate Ahl, owner of Simple Pin Media, an agency that helps content creators and small businesses grow their business using Pinterest, she revealed that a change in Facebook's algorithm in 2013 acted as the perfect launch pad for Pinterest's rising success. The Facebook algorithm changes meant that businesses struggled to receive the amount of free organic traffic they had once enjoyed on Facebook. They went on a quest for an alternative platform and many of them found Pinterest the perfect platform to replace the organic traffic that they lost. In fact, it was Kate's keen eye for recognizing this movement that led her to start managing Pinterest pages for bloggers. She later launched Simple Pin Media and it's been hugely successful.

Here are some of the key things to consider when it comes to Pinterest:

Pinterest is an online scrapbook

Unlike other social media platforms that are like online parties (Facebook, Instagram) or networking events (LinkedIn), Pinterest is a unique digital space. It shares some of the traits of a social media platform butmuch more with those of a search engine, as I've already mentioned. It's social in the sense that, unlike a search engine like Google, you can gain followers, re-pins and generate monthly engagement, but search is its key function.

Pinterest is like a scrapbook because users can save ideas, images and articles and categorize them into different boards. Users collect and preserve ideas with the intention of taking action at a later date. So, whether you want to plan a wedding,

15 https://marketingland.com/pinterest-says-it-has-250-million-active-monthly-users-247779

discover new recipes or decide on the destination of your next road trip, there's a board for that!

Driving organic traffic

If your primary goal is to use Pinterest to drive traffic to your website, ask yourself this:

What type of person are you trying to attract?

In other words, who is your ideal customer and are they even on Pinterest?

TOP TIP: Type this link into your search bar: pinterest.uk/source/"your-domain-name.com" Enter your own domain name where is says "your-domain-name.com. For example, I would enter pinterest.uk/source/content10x.com

The source page displays what is pinned on Pinterest from your website. You can see what type of content people are sharing. This gives you a more precise depiction of which pieces of content are valuable and preferred by your followers on Pinterest. It's genius!

So, what do you do if you discover that your content is attracting a Pinterest audience? It's simple: You get active on Pinterest! How can you do so when you already create content? And are there repurposing opportunities?

Repurposing blog content for Pinterest

When you create a blog post image, be sure to also create a vertical image that can be used on Pinterest. Pinterest has a vertical image ratio of 600x 900px so try to avoid posting square pictures. Stick to a vertical format. Add text to your images: the title of your blog post, statement that encourages someone to click on the image, or a question that your post provides the answer to. The aim here is to get someone to click the image and read the blog post. You want them on your website.

You can, and should, create multiple images for one blog post, all with a slightly different image and different words used. Whilst on the subject of blog posts, if you post your podcast or video content to your website, follow this same process for them too.

Create a variety of boards

Images are pinned to boards so you want to create lots of different boards for your own Pinterest account. It might sound excessive but it would be great if you could create 15 or even 20 boards. Think of this like breaking your content down into categories and each category is a board.

When you have created your boards, remember the 80/20 rule. Aim for 80% of content on your boards to be your own, and 20% to be content created by other people. Pinterest do not want you to only think of yourself, they want you to be interested in others too!

Consistency is key. Pinning every day is a good strategy.

If you create a weekly blog, podcast episode or video and you are able to create seven vertical images for each piece of content, each image with different words on, then you are building up a great set of pinnable images to help you pin daily.

Pinning to other boards

Engaging with your followers and other Pinterest users is a great way to drive traffic to your profile and your company website. You can pin your content to your own board but you can also pin it multiple times on different boards. If you see that one particular pin gets a lot of attention from Pinterest users, it's worth re-pinning it to various boards over the course of a few weeks or months.

Keyword optimization

There's no keyword search tool on Pinterest. However, that doesn't mean you should toss everything you know about SEO out the window. Instead, you should take inspiration for keywords from the Pinterest search bar and the Google search bar too. When you type a search term into the search bar, Pinterest will give you keyword predictions and recommendations of keywords that people are already searching. Those are the main keywords that you should target because they are popular and more likely to generate traffic to your profile.

You can also use the guided search boxes along the top of your screen to find out how Pinterest categorizes keywords on the platform.

Once you've defined your keywords, you should use them in the following areas:

- Pin description
- Board names
- Board description

Promoted pins

You can pay to get your pins in front of your target audience by promoting a pin. A promoted pin on Pinterest is evergreen. The shelf life is anywhere from six months to a year, giving you an extended period to advertise your brand to your target audience. Pinterest doesn't have as many ad restrictions as other social platforms such as Facebook. However, you want to avoid adding prices to your pins or anything to do with alcohol because pins like that get flagged and rejected. The critical thing to remember when creating a promotion pin is to make sure it's clear and easy to understand.

Repurposing blogs, video and podcasts by creating infographics

Sometimes you may cover a topic on your blog, your podcast or in a video you create and you're thinking that you could also create an infographic. Maybe you have talked through a step-by-step process, or you have compared two different options, and you can visualize how well the concept would look if explained via an infographic.

Infographics looks great! Pinterest is full of wonderful, visually engaging infographics.

Infographics are good at driving engagement but they aren't so good at increasing click-through rates because infographics tend to reveal too much information. They leave a Pinterest user with no reason to click through to your website because they already know the 'hook'. It's better therefore to provide some information, whilst leaving out just enough to encourage them to follow the link to your video or podcast.

Kate Ahl provided me with this tip and I found it really useful. It's very appealing to provide all of the information on your infographic but she is exactly right: by doing so you're keeping the user on Pinterest

You could always create two versions of your infographic. The slimmed down version with a 'hook' to your website for Pinterest, and the full version that goes onto your website that visitors can download if they provide their email address.

Best performing content

What kind of content performs well on Pinterest? High-performing pins have a number of key traits.

They:

- Give solid tips and tools to their audience.
- Answer your audience's big, burning questions.
- Share content that helps your audience solve their problems.

If your content focuses on these three things, you'll soon be the king or queen of Pinterest!

Pinterest conclusion

Pinterest has a lot of potential and most consumers using the platform are active users that either want to shop, create or research. If you're new to Pinterest, it may seem a little daunting or confusing at first, but it doesn't have to be.

If you are getting started, keep it simple and create ten boards about the top ten things that you talk about. The next step is to start sharing your content on your Pinterest boards, and other people's content too, and be consistent.

When you create content for your website, for example, new blog posts and podcast episodes, create pins for your content and pin them to the most appropriate boards. Create more than one pin per post and ensure you share with a keyword rich description.

Social media conclusion

As I mentioned in my introduction to this chapter, there are so many ways that social media can, and should, be incorporated into your content marketing and content repurposing endeavors.

I've shared some of the ways that you can make the most of your content on Instagram, Facebook, Twitter, LinkedIn and Pinterest (focusing on unique features of those platforms).

If you consistently create content, you have no reason to feel you have little to post about on social media - you do, it's all in your existing content!

You need to focus on the platforms that your audience hang out on, rather than focusing on all platforms. Make sure you create content that is platform-specific and your audience will engage with. Engagement is key.

Try and keep up with what's working and not working on social media. The world of social media is forever changing!

CHAPTER 15

Book & eBook

"I love your content, have you ever thought about writing a book?" How many times have you heard that? Or maybe you've even said to yourself, "maybe one day" or "I'd love to, if only I had the time".

Writing a book is certainly not an easy task. It's not just the writing, it's the planning, editing, designing, publishing, and promoting. A book is quite an undertaking with many different components. But if you are a prolific content creator then the reality is that you are probably sitting on a potential book just waiting to be written.

You have already communicated the thoughts and ideas that might go into a book in a number of different forms. Perhaps in blog posts, podcast episodes, videos, or something else, and now it's simply a case of repurposing that content into a book. Sounds easy, right?!

You are reading an extample of book repurposing

This book, yes the book that you are reading right now, is an example of repurposing. The content of this book is based on over a year's worth of blog posts and podcast episodes that I created for Content 10x. I'd been thinking about writing a book for a while and I knew that if I kept creating content on a consistent basis, there would come a point where I had enough to form the basis of a book. When I knew that a book was in sight, this even helped me plan out my content creation.

Let me share with you the method I used:

- I created a plan for my book, what I wanted it to include at a high level, then the main sections and the chapters within each.
- I went through all of my content and worked out where I had blog posts and podcast episodes that could be used in the different chapters. I think it's important that I followed the first step before doing this. I wanted to make sure the content of the book wasn't dictated by repurposing existing content, rather it was developed based on what would make a great book and, in my opinion, simply what *had* to be in the book.
- I identified the gaps, i.e. the chapters in the book on topics that I didn't already have any content on.
- I updated my content plan to create new, fresh blog and podcast content to fill in the gaps, meaning that not only would my new content be relevant and useful for my audience, but it would also be utilized for my book.

There aren't any instances where blog posts were literally just lifted and put into the book, a fair amount of editing was required, but using blog posts and podcast episodes as the starting point meant a lot of the 'heavy lifting' was already done.

As you create you content to fill in the gaps, it's important to be mindful of really sticking to your plan. When you are continuing to record new podcast episodes every week, you have to be pretty ruthless at drawing a line under what *will* make the cut and what will have to just wait until the *next* book. However tempting it might be to keep on creating more and more content, if you're not mindful of your book outline, content creation for the book will be never-ending!

This approach goes to show just how valuable it can be to repurpose podcast episodes into blog posts. Almost every blog post I have ever written is based on a podcast episode. Therefore, this book is really an example of podcast, to blog, to book repurposing.

Similarly, if you create video content, it's a good idea to turn your video content into blog posts because when you have written content, that opens up a whole new world of repurposing.

Being able to plan and write my chapters based on blog content as opposed to starting with a blank canvas made the whole process easier.

Repurposing a podcast into a book

Repurposing a podcast into a book is a novel ideal, and it's something that I've seen done well quite a few times and I love the concept.

Tim Ferris used his podcast as the entire source for his book Tools of Titans. The best quotes, tips, and concepts from hundreds of episodes of Tim interviewing really interesting people were curated into a bestselling book. Avid podcast fans will grab a copy of the book, as will people who do not listen to the podcast. If non-listeners love the book, perhaps they'll go and subscribe to the podcast too.

Similarly Gary Vaynerchuk published a book called #AskGaryVee which is based entirely on the questions asked on his popular podcast show with the same name, where listeners put forward questions to Gary. In the book, some answers are expanded upon and some are his answers verbatim from the podcast.

Emily Prokop is a podcast producer and podcaster, and when I heard that she had repurposed her podcast into a book, I invited her onto my podcast to share more about her process.

Emily shared a really interesting story. Her podcast, *The Story Behind*, closely examines everyday objects, from their ancient beginnings through to the present, within 5-10 minutes.

When I spoke to Emily she explained that from even as young as seventh grade, she knew she wanted to write a book. However, it was 20 years later when her opportunity finally arrived and it was all due to her having a podcast (a podcast that was leveraged through the power of repurposing).

After her podcast had been out for around a year, a publisher, having listened to her podcast, approached her and said that her episodes were short enough to be tuned into chapters in a book. They wanted her to put a story together about 50 different items. Emily never thought about turning her podcast ideas into a book and was stunned by the offer. After all, who'd have thought that putting yourself out there as a podcaster could see you being offered a book deal?!

Emily had only seven months to write the book. There were certain things that Emily did that made the process more straightforward than it otherwise could have been, in particular her shows were scripted. Meaning, Emily already had the written content for each show in the form of a script. This was a great starting point. Even with edits to complete, this was minor compared with starting a book from scratch. I was in a similar position to Emily with my blog posts. They formed a great starting point for my book.

Similar to me, Emily planned out what to include in her book, assessed the content she already had, and worked out what fresh new content she'd need to create to 'fill in the gaps'.

Before the book was even finished, the publisher sent her ideas for the cover and the book was published just 10 months after the publisher first got in touch with her. Of course, when it comes to writing and publishing a book, the writing is often seen as the 'easy' part. Okay, I know it's not easy and never will be, but honestly? That's the least of your problems.

The real challenge comes in finding people to purchase and read your book. Marketing. Nobody knows your book is a masterpiece if they don't even know it exists! Luckily for Emily, her podcast and its existing audience meant she had an audience of potential book readers ready and waiting. That's not to mention that her audience were genuinely excited for her and prepared to support her efforts all the way.

How did she get them excited? Emily took her audience on the journey with her. They helped her select the content for the book and what the book cover should look like. They knew what she was doing every step of the way. This is a great tip to pass onto anyone with an audience when you embark on a project like writing a book. Always take your audience with you on the journey. The journey is important and just the kind of content that people love! If you are not convinced, check out Social Media Examiner's YouTube show, *The Journey*. It follows their journey to host Social Media Marketing World.

Upon the successful publication of her book, Emily found an even bigger audience for her podcast, once again as a result of the book. In a nutshell: people found the book and then they listened to the podcast. It converted them over. So when you think about it: her new book drove people to the podcast, and the podcast's content fueled the book. It doesn't get much more satisfying than that, does it?

Once the book was published, Emily received feedback from her audience and in fact, they helped market the book for her. The key was having that audience already in place. It was a blessing that made everything smoother.

Other book repurposing opportunities

When my good friend and mentor, Chris Ducker, published his book *Rise of the Youpreneur* in 2018, I expected the book to be a result of a lot of content repurposing. After all, Chris had been creating lots of content for 5+ years and he's a very savvy person who wouldn't miss repurposing opportunities. However, whilst Chris did repurpose content for *Rise of the Youpreneur*, he didn't do it in the way you might expect.

I invited Chris onto my podcast to dig into how he leveraged his content for the book. Chris is the founder of Youpreneur.com, the entrepreneurial mastermind community that helps experts become the go-to leader in their industry. As a prolific content creator, I anticipated that Chris would talk about the many aspects of his book that were based on his blog posts, videos and podcast episodes. Interestingly, Chris explained that just *one* blog post was directly lifted and put into the book. Everything else in the book is fresh content.

However, the *entire* book is basically a repurpose of content within his Youpreneur mastermind community. I found this fascinating! Chris explained that when he and his team launched the Youpreneur community, they listened a lot to what the community were talking about and studied what people were asking for help with.

Where there were gaps, they filled them. They then started to siphon content off into three distinct sections: building, marketing and monetizing. This ultimately became the *Youpreneur Roadmap*, which is ongoing and evolving all the time. The roadmap was a huge success because people were better able to see where they were in their own journey. They could jump straight to the right point for getting the support they needed for that stage of their journey.

Since the roadmap was incredibly successful and helped so many people, Chris essentially took the entire roadmap content and put it into a book. This included content created by Chris and his team, and user-generated content too.

This is an example of repurposing at its best. Thinking outside of the box. Making the most of the hard work and effort already put into creating something, in order to create something else that adds considerable value in a different format.

Repurposing content from your book

It's not all about repurposing content to create a book. The flip side is that you can use a book to create more content. One way that you can do this is to create promotional content in order to help you market and sell your book.

For example:

- If you have a podcast, you could read the introduction of your book, or another part of your book, as a podcast episode.
- Create articles and guest posts from sections of your book to publish on different websites around the time that the book launches. If you are allowed to, make sure you mention your book and provide a link to the sales page or somewhere they can go to find out more and purchase.
- Can you repurpose content from your book for your website? Excerpts of interesting copy, images and diagrams could all go onto your website
- Pull the best quotes from your book and create quote images that can be shared on all the social media platforms. Have your quote images created and ready to share for your book launch and beyond.
- Create a social media campaign with user-generated content. For example, authors often encourage readers to share photos of themselves on social media with the book.
- When you get reviews and testimonials for your book, be sure to share them in lots of different places. Don't just leave them sitting on Amazon. For example, share on your website and your social media accounts.

There's so much great content in your book, it's possible to scatter parts of your book in many strategic places prior to the launch but it doesn't have to end there. For as long as you have the book and the content is relevant to your audience, there will be lots and lots of content within the book that you can repurpose.

For example, if you're a podcaster and you're struggling to come up with your next podcast episode topic and outline, review your book and see if there's anything within it that you could use as the basis for your episode. Is there a related topic you could cover, for example?

Similarly, if you're a video content creator and you're struggling to come up with your next video topic and outline, review your book and see if there's anything within it that you could use as the basis for your video. Is there a topic you could explore in more depth or maybe has evolved since the book was published?

The same goes for bloggers. Can you take parts of your book and turn them into blog posts?

The same goes for membership site owners too. Maybe a whole section of your book could be repurposed into membership content?

The potential content repurposing opportunities from a book are endless!

Creating an audio book

After you've published a book, consider going one step further and publish an audiobook as well. Audio books are so popular thanks to sites like Audible making it so easy to buy and consume audio books.

If you create an audiobook, you can repurpose it into lots of audio content. For example, use parts of your audio book as podcast episodes.

In conclusion

You never know who is listening to your podcast, reading your blog or watching your video. It took just one person who loved Emily Prokop's podcast, who just so happened to be a publisher, and the rest is history. She published a book!

Is there a future book waiting to happen for you?

If there is and you have the appetite to embark on a book project, ask yourself:

- *Who* are you writing it for?
- What is the *big problem* that you're solving for them?
- What is the *end result* for them, after having read your book?

Once you are clear on these points you can start delving into your content. Find relevant pieces, categorize and start to structure and plan how you could use your content to create your book. If you have a lot of useful content then the power of repurposing could put you on the road to publishing a book.

The truth is: anyone can repurpose their content into a successful book, as long as their content is of a high quality. It's about having the right approach, the right tools and keeping that excitement alive and real. It's hard work, yes, but the best things in life are, right?!

Likewise, if you have a book, you are sitting on mountains of content. Make the most of it in the most creative ways possible.

CHAPTER 16

Other content repurposing opportunities

There are so many ways that you can repurpose your content. Whilst I have talked in detail about video, podcasts, livestreams, live events, blogging, membership sites and the rest, in this section I want to briefly shine a light on a number of different and interesting ways that you can repurpose content.

We'll look at:

- Smart speaker flash briefings
- Press releases
- Content upgrades
- FAQs

Smart speaker flash briefings

Smart speakers, such as Amazon Alexa and Google Home, are electronic 'gadgets' that seem to have gone from "relatively new" to "fairly common place" in many households at an alarmingly fast rate. In fact, Edison Research in 2019 found that 34% of the adult population in the US own a smart speaker. Say whaaaaat?!

Their research also found that the longer people have owned a smart speaker, the more they listen to it (meaning that their usage doesn't "fizzle out", unlike many gadgets) and they confidently predict that smart speakers are likely to become the dominant audio player in people's homes. Smart speaker media consumption is resulting in the diminishing use of other media, e.g. radio, TV and even reading magazines and newspapers. Fascinating.

People use smart speakers to listen to music, make calls, get traffic and weather updates, listen to podcasts, order food and groceries, control household devices, and so much more.

Did you know that listeners can subscribe to a flash briefing?

Flash briefings are short, informative pieces of pre-recorded audio up to 10 minutes long. They are like a podcast or radio show, but you subscribe to the briefings you want to listen to.

Now here's the interesting part: Did you know that you can create your own flash briefing 'skill' to supply short bursts of content to your audience via their Alexa-enabled device? Plus, if you have a podcast then you're already halfway there because you can potentially repurpose your podcast into a flash briefing.

Repurposing content into an Alexa flash briefing is not as difficult as it may sound and can be incredibly powerful. For many people, flash briefings are an integral part of their daily routine and if they aren't now, the stats show that they very likely will be at some point. If you can inject a snippet of your content into their routine in the form of a flash briefing, it gives you the opportunity to connect with your audience in a new, more personal way.

To create an Alexa flash briefing is all you need is:

- **A (free) Amazon developer account**. In your Amazon developer account go to Alexa, choose 'Create a

Skill' and follow the guidelines.

- **An RSS feed via your podcast host**. Not all podcast hosts support Amazon Alexa so you will need to check. E.g. Libsyn support this. Some hosts are specifically for Alexa, e.g. Sound Up Now.
- **Optional: An Alexa device**, to test how well your flash briefing works!

As with most things, you don't have to do it all yourself. There are plenty of people who offer services whereby they will set up your flash briefing for you. The important thing to remember when creating a flash briefing for Alexa is that each episode has an expiration date. It's valid for one day only. You've also got to keep it short because you have up to a maximum of ten minutes. This is true at the time of writing. As this is a growing medium I'm sure things are going to change quite fast.

You need to decide the frequency e.g. daily, multiple times a day, a few times a week, weekly. You'll need a small square icon for your briefing and have your description ready. The good news is that you don't always have to start from scratch. If you have a podcast you can consider taking sections from your podcast episode and transform it into a flash briefing for Alexa.

On my podcast, I spoke to Sigrun who has embraced flash briefings as part of her repurposing strategy. Sigrun is a mastermind business coach, lifestyle entrepreneur, business strategist and international speaker.

Signrun told me she has repurposed her podcast content into a flash briefing. She tries to keep her flash briefings under 90 seconds long. She doesn't take the audio and turn that into a flash briefing. Instead, she uses the transcripts from her podcast episodes, and she repurposes those original episode transcripts into short 60 or 90-second scripts for her briefings.

If you don't have a podcast there are still repurposing opportunities. For example, do you have blog posts you could use as the basis for your flash briefings? Old or new, as long as they are still relevant, they can still be used. Similarly, video content could be used as the inspiration for flash briefings. You could take videos, transcribe them, and use them to create flash briefing scripts, or maybe even take the audio from the video directly and use that.

After you've taken the time to create flash briefings that you know your audience will love, you'll need to think about how you can get your audience to add you to their daily briefings. If they don't know what daily briefings are then you'll have to educate them on that as well. Sigrun told me that she emailed her entire list to let them know about her new venture into Alexa flash briefings. She even gave them a list of instructions explaining what flash briefings are and how to add hers to their daily rundown. Don't assume people will know how to do this. Make it easy for them.

Press releases

Have you ever considered creating press releases in order to get your content in front of your desired audience in the newspaper, on the radio and on TV? Perhaps you're wondering why you'd want to do this? Why bother with press releases in the digital age when we can reach so many people via social media and other means? However, getting attention in the press and knowing how to create a press release can be really useful for you and your business.

Despite the emergence of social media, press releases still remain a popular method of providing news and promoting brand awareness. What's more, perhaps you can repurpose existing content into a press release so it doesn't take too much time and effort, yet reaps many rewards.

One hundred years ago, press releases were the only media available to reach large audiences via newspapers so creating written press releases formed an important part of a business's content marketing strategy. They ensured your content and message were shared and seen. I'm quite sure they wouldn't have called it a 'content marketing strategy' back then, during the times of horse-and-cart, but I'm also sure Henry Ford *was* creating press releases for his Model T Ford.

However, fast forward to today and, as you would expect, press releases have been reinvented. They're no longer blocks of text. They need to be interactive and visual if they are going to grab the attention of a journalist.

The impact of technology has meant content can be presented in a multimedia format. We've seen radio, TV, video, and now the internet, all come into our lives. These varied media channels all present great opportunities for businesses to get content in front of their audiences. Every time new media channels become mainstream, press releases evolve too.

In fact, in the early days of the internet, text became the dominant media again, because download speeds were too slow for our computers to handle video or even graphics. Today of course, the online landscape is very visual and video-heavy. Press releases have evolved in this way too. They're no longer just about getting an article in a printed newspaper. They are about getting your content in front of large audiences via mainstream media, and in various media formats.

Press releases enable you to tell your story in a different way than you would on social media or in a blog post. It's a 'news' story and this can be presented from a different angle. Therefore, if you want to create press releases, you may want to look at content that you have already created and repurpose it into a newsworthy story for the press.

If you get featured in large publications, on the TV, and radio, you can add this to your website 'As featured in', which helps you establish more credibility. People still care about these things!

On the Content 10x podcast I spoke to Sally Falkow, an accredited PR practitioner with the Public Relations Society of America who has been working in PR for many years and has been a pioneer in the change to Digital PR. On her blog, **ProactiveReport.com**, she writes about the impact of technology on the media, PR, and marketing.

Sally made the great point that newsrooms are not what they used to be. Newspapers and TV stations have been massively impacted by the internet. There are fewer journalists and reporters than there used to be. Those left still need to find lots of content to report on so we find there are newsrooms with less people having to create *more* content. They are interested in press release content if it tells the story that people want to hear. Therefore, if you have an interesting topic for a press release it's not sufficient to simply alert journalists to a story for them to investigate further. They simply don't have time. Instead, you need to bring the *entire* story to the journalist, including visual content. *Then* they will be interested.

Tips for repurposing content into a press release

Look at the content you already have. What content can be repurposed into a news story? What are your most interesting stories? Look with a critical eye. What is interesting and new? Do you have important statistics, unique services or products? It must be a story and it must be newsworthy.

Avoid boring facts and think about what a reader would like to find out or enjoy learning.

As well as answering the classic questions included in all press releases the world over - who, what, when, where and how - it is a good idea to include links to provide more information or content to download. Make it interactive with links to your social media accounts too. If you have research that you have put into a white paper, that will be very easy to format into a press release.

Now is the time to show off your visual content. Think infographics, images and video links that help tell your story. Your visual content must be relevant. You may be able to repurpose images that you have created already for your website and social media.

Think about what media you want to feature in. Wall Street Journal? Your local newspaper? A TV show? Find journalists that cover news where you want to be featured. Build good relationships with those journalists via social media channels such as LinkedIn or Twitter. Connect with them, engage with them, and send press releases to them directly to increase your chances of being noticed. Building relationships and working with journalists directly is a great approach

TOP TIP: Don't clog a journalist's inbox with huge attachments. Instead, put the whole press release on your own website (not a public URL), send them an email with the highlights and then add 'Read the full release here' and give them the link to your site.

On Twitter there are hashtags you can follow to look for journalists writing specific stories. In the UK #journorequest is a popular hashtag.

Content produced for a press release can easily be repurposed in a variety of ways. If you have created a press release, here are some content repurposing opportunities to get the most out of your time and effort:

- **Visual content:** If you created visual content for your press release, use it on social media, your blog and, if you shared statistics, create an infographic.
- **Blog posts:** Create a post on your own site or guest post on other sites. Most press releases are not long so consider extending the story for other written content.
- **Video:** Create a video about your press release. This could be for YouTube, Facebook, or your website. You could even go live on Facebook, LinkedIn, YouTube or Instagram to share your press release with your audience in an interactive way.
- **Audio:** If you create audio content, why not cover the content of your press release in a podcast episode?

In conclusion

Press releases can form an important part of any content marketing strategy. Getting your stories into mainstream media can be an effective way to increase awareness and get your content in front of large audiences.

When looking to utilize content you have already created for a press release, it is important to always look for a story that people will want to read. What information will attract them? What is newsworthy? Don't tell the story *you* want to tell. Tell the story *people* want to hear.

Always provide visual content to increase the appeal of your press release and the likelihood of the content being used and shared. Your visual content can be repurposed for your website and social media.

Content upgrades

You can repurpose your content into content upgrades. A content upgrade is usually some form of lead magnet. A lead magnet, sometimes referred to as an 'ethical bribe', is something of value that you offer to your audience in exchange for their email address. So basically, it's something that helps us to build our email lists.

You might have a number of different lead magnets on different parts of your website. For example, on your homepage, your about page or your blog sidebar.

A content upgrade is a form of lead magnet but it's very specific to a piece of content. It's an extra bonus related to that content, kind of like saying, "hey, if you liked this then guess what? There's more!".

Content upgrades are brilliant because if people are already interested in your content then they're likely to want your free upgrade.

It may be that you have another lead magnet that you offer on your website but, for whatever reason, a website visitor simply doesn't resonate with it. They don't perceive it to add much value to them so you lose them as a lead. By contrast, it's easy for them to see a lot of value in your content upgrade, especially if they already loved your video, podcast episode or blog post, and they want more.

Amy Porterfield, an online marketer, offers content upgrades a lot, after almost every post. Pat Flynn from *Smart Passive Income* also offers content upgrades with a lot of his content too. These guys have huge followings and know what they're doing so I'd say content upgrades must work!

If you're thinking of creating a content upgrade, I recommend it meets with the following 3 criteria:

1. Easily consumable: Content upgrades need to be high value but not necessarily high volume. It does not need to be a 50-page ebook when it can be a one-page checklist or cheat sheet.

People are more interested in having quick and easy ways to solve their problems rather than long and convoluted ways to solve their problems. This is hardly surprising!

2. Address a problem: Don't just address *any* issue, address a really *specific* problem. The more specific the problem, the higher the perceived value because people know exactly what you are going to help them with and they probably have a good idea of what it would mean to them if that problem was solved.

3. Actionable If your content upgrade is focussed on getting people to take action and in taking that action they see a result, then that's a huge win-win situation.

You might not be able to hit all three criteria every time, but it's something to aim for.

TOP TIP: Ensure everything is aligned with your product

or service. For example, if you help people who are currently at A and want to get to the end destination of C, then design your content upgrade to take them from A to B. Then, when they are ready to move onwards to C and are looking for someone to help them, they are likely to go to the person who got them to B rather than a complete stranger. You are already on the journey with them because you helped create real action and results for free.

Examples of content upgrades

Here are some examples of content upgrades created by repurposing existing content:

- **Checklists:** Who doesn't love a checklist? Maybe you have recorded a long podcast episode or video, with lots of tips or maybe some step-by-step guidance? Why not turn that into a simple checklist that your audience will love?
- **PDF version of your blog post:** You may be surprised how many people would be interested in having your blog post in PDF form. Something so simple can be useful.
- **Transcript:** If you record podcast episodes or videos then you could offer a transcript that you'll email to them. If someone loved your episode and they want to refer back to it, a transcript would be really useful. I recommend using Rev.com for transcription services
- **A list of tools & resources:** If you have provided examples of tools and resources in your content, why not create a PDF that simply lists them out with some details about each one?
- **Quick guide:** If your content provides instruction or step-by-step guidance, why not slim it down into a simple and easily consumable quick guide? This would add value to the original content

- **Bonus video or audio:** Film a video or record an audio file where you talk about a topic in more detail. In the original piece of content, make the offer to learn more. "If you want to learn more about this I've filmed a short video/recorded an extra bonus podcast episode where I talk about it in more detail." They provide their email address and you send the link to access the bonus content.

- **Bonus interview:** If you have interviewed a guest for your podcast or video, record an additional, separate interview with them. This could be anything from a quick-fire round, to answering a really specific question. You can say to your audience that they can get hold of the bonus interview if they provide their email address. It's a good idea to stick to the criteria above and offer an interview that helps solve a specific problem.

- **Infographic:** Create an engaging infographic. Visuals can really bring topics to life. You could display the infographic on your website and let people know that they can have a copy of it if they give you their email address.

- **Templates:** For example, email templates, blog templates, plan templates. Something that people can use really easily and will save them time

- **Swipe file:** For example, if you are an internet marketer, perhaps it would be to provide 50 of your best Facebook ad templates. The idea is people 'swipe' your content and tailor it for themselves.

- **A challenge or free course:** This can be automated but still highly effective. An example is emailing your list every day for a week as part of a one-week challenge. Every day your email has guidance and instruction. Sometimes people just like to be reminded and told what to do.

Content upgrades are all about enticing your audience with something of value that they will want, related to your piece of content. They can be really effective for email list building plus really effective in growing a highly engaged audience who view you as someone that really goes the extra mile to add value.

You have already created the content, your upgrade doesn't need to be created totally from scratch, because you can repurpose.

FAQs

If you're anything like me you probably get asked a lot of questions. Don't get me wrong, I don't mind answering people's questions and providing thoughtful and considered answers but sometimes it can feel as though you're stuck in a continuous loop, answering the same questions time and time again. The good news is it doesn't have to be this way! Instead of repeating yourself each time, why not repurpose your questions and answers into valuable, evergreen content?

There are so many ways you can convert your questions and answers into creative, original and impactful content. Here are six ideas for what you can do with your questions and answers:

1. Create a spreadsheet

I recommend keeping spreadsheet listing all of the common questions you get asked, along with the answers you provided for each one. You can use something like Google Sheets for this, which is perfect if you want to share the spreadsheet with other people.

You can also categorize your questions and answers into specific topics or subjects to make the organizing and finding process easier. Once you have all of your questions and answers in one place, you'll have a repository of discussion points you can convert into different forms of content.

2. Write a blog post

A blog post is a great way to generate engagement with your audience and build credibility within your industry. After all, the primary purpose of a blog post is to provide the reader with a solution. Whether you use your blog to establish yourself as an expert in your field, promote your product or service or express your thoughts and opinions to like-minded people, a blog post has the power to make a real impact.

Refer to your spreadsheet of questions and answers and find one for which you provided a great solution. Take this topic and create an original blog post by elaborating on both the question and the answer. Writing a valuable blog post that answers the questions your audience want to know the answer to is a great way to give them what they need.

3. Write a social media post

If you don't have a lot of time to repurpose your questions and answers into a long-form blog post, why not create a simple social media post instead?

If somebody has asked you a particular question, there's a good chance other people will also want to know the answer. Once you've chosen your question and answer, you can publish a post on whichever social media channel you think is the most appropriate.

Facebook is a great platform for answering people's questions because your post can reach a wide audience and you also have the opportunity to interact with your readers via the comment section. Try posting with links to your website, and without. You'll likely find your longer form posts, without links, achieve a greater reach because Facebook want to keep people on Facebook!

If you want to give a short and snappy answer, a quick tweet will do the job. If you prefer the visual aspect of Instagram, post a relevant image that will grab people's attention and include the answer to the question in the description.

4. Video record your answer

A video is one of the most popular and influential forms of content. According to Forbes, video claims more than 80% of web traffic - and that's increasing!

If you're having a hard time thinking about what type of video content you can create, take a closer look at your spreadsheet of questions and answers. You have an entire pool of potential ideas at your fingertips. Create a simple Q&A video to get started or focus your attention on one specific topic. All you have to do is find the best question and answer that you think will make an excellent, short and value-packed video and then post it to YouTube, the social media platforms and/or your website.

Are you on Instagram Stories? Posting short Q&A videos to Instagram Stories would be a great place to start with your video content.

5. Create website content

Now that you have a list of your most frequently asked questions and your well-crafted answers, you have everything you need to form an informative FAQ section for your website. An FAQ page saves you and your audience time because all of the answers are in one place. It also gives you the opportunity to improve SEO, build trust with your target audience and establish yourself as a leader in your industry.

If you notice that some of the questions and answers are quite important or relevant to your business, you may need to consider incorporating them into the main copy of your website. Perhaps you could expand your product and/or services page to provide potential customers with the answers they need upfront. This also helps to increase the chance that visitors to your website will take whatever the next step is that you want them to take on your site.

6. Email the answers

Many people have an email list but they never use it. The most common reason for this neglect is because they don't know what to include in their email. However, if you keep getting the same questions day in, day out there's a chance that there are a lot of people on your email subscriber list that also want to know the answers to those questions. Why not start to send emails/newsletters to your subscribers that are helpful in answering frequently asked questions that come your way?

In conclusion

There are lots and lots of different ways that you can repurpose your content. In this section I provided a fairly brief overview of repurposing with smart speaker flash briefings, press releases, content upgrades and your FAQs.

I think perhaps one of the most important points to make here is to ensure that you develop a repurposing mindset. Don't let repurposing be an afterthought. Instead, let repurposing be something high on your radar so that you can make the most of all of your content.

Similarly, when viewing new content opportunities, be sure to weigh up the potential to repurpose content before dismissing it as too much additional work. That may not be the case when your repurposing mindset is fully engaged!

PART 3

Approach & Strategy

CHAPTER 17

Mistakes to avoid

Welcome to Part Three and congratulations on making it this far! In Part One I shared with you what content repurposing is, plus lots of reasons why you should be repurposing your content. There are so many be benefits to you as a content creator and so many business benefits. I hope I've inspired you to give content repurposing a try!

Having done so, in Part Two I shared lots and lots of different ways that you can repurpose content. We looked at all sorts of different content formats and many different strategies for expanding your reach and your ability to connect with as much of your target audience as possible, in ways that suit their preferred learning style.

So far so good, right?

Repurposing content is, without question, a great thing to do but, like anything in life, there are good ways to do it, and not so good ways. I'm about to share with you some of the biggest mistakes I regularly see people make when they're repurposing content.

Do not 'post and forget' on social media

Imagine the scenario: You've been invited to a party and you respond, "hell yeah! see you there!" But then you get invited to another party at the exact same time. What are the odds? You hardly ever go to parties and now two come along at once! You can't be in two places at the same time can you? That would be madness!

Or, maybe you can. If you had the option to send a large, life-sized cardboard cut-out of yourself to the party that you're not going to, would you? Or, would you send a mannequin dressed up like you?

People might comment on how it was nice to see you there (if they were totally unobservant and didn't notice that you were a cardboard cut-out!) but they'd say that you were pretty antisocial. You didn't really speak to anyone. In fact, you didn't talk at all. Even when people asked you questions you remained silent. Quite frankly, you were pretty darn rude!

This sounds absolutely ridiculous doesn't it? But I see people do this too often when they repurpose their content on social media.

You cannot ignore the *social* in social media!

Don't post your content onto social media platforms where you have no intention of showing up to engage with people. Either you, or at the very least a member of your team, should follow that content and monitor responses and interactions.

For example, let's say you decide to repurpose your blog post into a series of tweets. You use a scheduling tool like Buffer, SmarterQueue or Hootsuite to schedule all of your tweets. No more action required from you. You don't actually use Twitter yourself, you can't remember the last time you ever logged in. You have no idea if people are following you, or commenting, liking or retweeting any of your tweets. You have a presence on Twitter but you do not interact with anyone. Result: the people you are working hard to attract will be turned off if they can see you ignore social engagement.

Social media is about socializing, being social. Think of it like turning up to a social event. We could call Facebook the party, LinkedIn the networking event and Instagram an art gallery (a sociable art gallery!). One important reason why you should be present and engage with people is because you wouldn't turn up to in-person social events and not interact with anyone, so don't do it online. The added bonus is that you'll start to build relationships.

But, there is another really important reason why you should engage with people on social media: Bots are watching!

Let me explain...

Jumping back to my party analogy, let's say that you put the cardboard cut-out of yourself in the kitchen. All the cool kids hang out in the kitchen at parties. I like to because it puts me closest to the food and drink! People come over and talk to you (cardboard cut-out you) and of course you're not engaging, you're actually being very rude and ignoring people, because you're not really there. You're just a cardboard cut-out!

Somebody is (Big Brother style) monitoring the party and wants to make sure that only the most popular and interesting people are in the kitchen. You're being very rude and ignoring people. Big Brother notices that "most popular and interesting" is *not* you and they move you out of the kitchen. In fact, you've been so disinterested in people, they put you in the cupboard under the stairs. Even if you try to speak now, not many people will hear you. Sounds outrageous, doesn't it?

But guess what? Something similar to this takes place on social media thanks to the algorithm. An algorithm is a process or a set of rules to follow. In social media, it's basically a program that sets out the rules of how it treats content and how users are treated. Bots observe behavior and implement the algorithm (they're the party police, if you like!).

Social media algorithms look at certain factors when deciding what to do with your post. For example, how many people to put it in front of (your reach). If they see that you are not engaging with others and that others are not engaging with you, that you basically don't appear to be particularly interesting or popular, they will stop prioritizing your content. They won't put you in front of as many people. You're heading to the virtual cupboard under the stairs! No-one wants that, but it's the price of being boring, antisocial, or both.

What should you do instead?

When you repurpose your content you take the ideas and concepts from one piece of content and share them in different ways with a new audience. This is a great thing to do. Just make sure that you are there to have conversations with people. Make sure that you respond to comments and engage with people. In fact, better still, make engagement a priority. Ask questions and invoke discussions.

You will build relationships, build trust with people, show your human side, and you'll send positive messages to the social media robots! And guess what else? You'll probably have fun too!

For the purposes of this conversation, I've focussed on social media but the same goes for any platform you send content to where others have a chance to comment and interact. For example, YouTube, Medium, SlideShare. It's not about spending all of your time monitoring interactions, you need to be sensible, time is precious, but don't embark on a one hundred per cent 'set and forget' strategy.

Respect the platform

Content repurposing is about taking content and sharing it in new and different ways. It's about changing the format of the content and it's about changing the location, i.e. where you post it. Respect plays a huge role in this. Specifically, I mean respecting the platform that you put your content onto and the audience associated with that platform.

I often get asked, “Can I repurpose this piece of content exactly as it is from one place to another?” My answer? It always depends on the content and the context.

For example, you have an article on your website and you want to repurpose it onto LinkedIn, without making many changes. If it’s the right content and context for the LinkedIn audience that may be perfectly fine, e.g. does it have a professional tone, is it ‘work’ or career related, etc? Would you put that same article on your Facebook page? Probably not because people are on Facebook for different reasons.

Another example, you’ve filmed a hilarious short video of yourself falling over and you share it on Snapchat. You decide to share the exact same video on Instagram Stories. Go for it! Facebook Stories? If you think your audience there would like the video and it’s what they have come to expect from you in terms of the type of content you share, no problem. LinkedIn? I’d hazard a guess that you’re not going to share that same video on the more professional platform.

When it comes to sharing content, what is appropriate really does depend on the platform and the audience. You need to respect *why* people are on the platform. What do they want to see? What do they expect to see? What will they respond to?

This comes back to my point regarding algorithms. By respecting the platform and the audience, people will engage with you. This signals to the algorithm that you’re “popular and interesting” and they’ll put your content in front of more people. Get it wrong by posting content out of context and you’re going to struggle to get engagement.

People love authenticity online. But what people also love, probably to a greater extent, is consistency. You need to get your content strategy lined up in such a way that whatever the platform is, your audience on that platform come to expect and benefit from a certain level of consistency.

Let’s look at some of the major social media platforms and explore generally what people expect to see when they are on them.

I'm a wine lover (I almost said connoisseur but that's taking it way too far. Let's just say, I like wine!) By way of illustration, imagine I want to share my wine drinking experiences on the social platforms. Let's explore what that might look like:

Facebook: "I like wine with my friends!"

Facebook is like a party or social gathering. I might share that I'm drinking wine with my friends and I could post a few photos or videos, maybe get a few 'likes' on my posts and comments from friends and family.

Facebook is all about being sociable (mostly!). It's about bringing people together and sharing thoughts, ideas and experiences. This kind of post would be perfectly normal on Facebook, it would fit naturally into people's News Feeds as they scroll through, and it would be exactly what they might like, comment or share.

Facebook Live: "I'm drinking wine, right now. Join me!"

Facebook Live is about the real time experience. It's about the here and now and it's about sharing experiences with people far and wide via the wonder of the internet and live streaming.

In this instance, I could share my experiences of tasting different wines. I could ask people to join me in a virtual tasting and we could talk to each other about the wines. This would be an amazing thing to do if you had an online wine store or you were a wine producer.

For the purposes of content marketing, if you're going to 'go live', be sure to make the most of the live aspect. Interact and engage with people watching and make it a fun and shared experience. Build your community. If you don't acknowledge your viewers and you 'go live' but for all intents and purposes you treat the video like a pre-recorded video (without live viewers), then why go live? You might as well do a pre-recorded video.

I use Facebook Live as an example, but this conversation includes Instagram, LinkedIn and YouTube live streaming, as well as other options.

Twitter: "I am drinking a bottle of #amarone tonight, anyone doing the same?"

When I think of Twitter, my main thoughts are concise communication and conversation. Twitter is fast moving. It's a real-time information platform. You can find out the latest opinions, news and stories on Twitter, often before it reaches the mainstream media. You can find and reach people with hashtags, plus jump onto trending hashtags to grow the discussion and potentially grow your audience.

Twitter is great for local businesses. For example, maybe I want to find out whether a local wine shop has a certain wine in stock. If they are active on Twitter we could converse.

In fact, it's funny how Twitter has become so many things really. It's certainly a place where people go to have conversations. It's also become a key customer service and customer communication channel for many businesses.

In my example of sharing my recent wine experience, I could have conversations with other people on Twitter who like drinking wine too. I could talk to people I know, my friends, family and followers, and I could talk to people I don't know but whom I find, or they find me, through hashtags or other people retweeting my posts.

Also, I could converse with the wine shop/supplier whom I purchased the bottle from, or even the wine producer, whether it's a small rustic back-of-beyond vineyard in Italy or a wine merchant in the UK. The great thing about Twitter is you can reach all sorts of people, from all over the world, and have a conversation.

Instagram: "Here's a photo of my bottle of wine tonight!"

Instagram is a visual platform and generally we share content that is aesthetically appealing to our audience. Here I might share a photo of my bottle or glass of wine. I'd try for some nice lighting, make use of the Instagram filters, and make it look as pleasant as possible. In order to get found on Instagram you can make use of hashtags and geotags, both of which will help you to reach new people. For example, I could tag my location and could research hashtags related to the wine that I'm drinking.

Your Instagram content doesn't always need to be staged or fancy. You certainly don't need to invest in expensive camera equipment, the camera on your phone is going to be just fine. It is a visual platform though. Always bear that in mind.

You can share video content and images. Your videos are *less* about the visual appeal. That said, be sure to select a nice thumbnail to show in your Instagram grid from the video itself. If you don't, Instagram will take the halfway still shot from the video, which you can almost always guarantee will be when you're pulling the worst face!

Instagram or Facebook Stories: "Here I am buying wine. Can you help me choose what to buy? Now I'm drinking the wine. Oops I fell over, too much wine. Now I have a hangover!"

Instagram and Facebook Stories are casual and fun. It's in the name, but it is about our 'stories'. It's about sharing micro-moments and the 'behind the scenes' content.

With my wine example, I'd take images and videos during the day then share them all together as a story. I would even consider getting people involved by doing a poll. "What wine shall I drink tonight: French or Italian?". Or I could make it less about me and more about my audience by asking, "What is your favorite wine: French or Italian?".

Take people on a journey to find out a bit more about you. With Instagram, Stories don't have to be as visually engaging as Instagram posts because they are a subtly different kind of format, the context is not the same and stories disappear after 24 hours. Think of them more as raw, vlog-style content.

With Stories you can have a mix of video and images and you can have fun with features like GIFs, polls, countdown times, music, rating sliders, questions, filters and emojis.

YouTube: "Tune into my YouTube show where I interview a wine producer every week. Remember to subscribe!"

YouTube is a place to be entertained, educated and inspired. People go to YouTube for many different reasons. It's important to remember that YouTube is a search engine. It's *not* social media. Unlike social media, you don't know much about the person finding your content but, with a search engine like YouTube you know exactly what that person wants and what they're thinking.

The person who finds your wine video on YouTube was almost certainly looking for wine related content.

In this example, there's so much I can do with my wine content on YouTube. I could vlog about my wine drinking exploits, I could even have a wine tasting show. In fact, that's how Gary Vaynerchuk got started online with his YouTube channel, Wine Library TV.

LinkedIn: "I am a fully qualified wine drinker"

Whilst LinkedIn is a more 'professional' social media and content platform, with a focus on career, business and job opportunities, that doesn't necessarily mean it's dull and boring.

I might share my wine qualifications, if I have any. For example, *The Wine & Spirit Education Trust* (WSET) is the largest global provider of wine, spirits and sake qualifications and if I happened to have a WSET qualification then LinkedIn would be the place to let people know.

Realistically though, unless I work in the wine industry that's probably not that interesting to any of my connections on LinkedIn. A sommelier sharing WSET qualifications is extremely useful on LinkedIn, a recreational wine drinker like myself sharing wine qualifications is about as useful as sharing what colored belt I am in karate or what my handicap is in golf!

That said, there is nothing wrong with using LinkedIn to share social aspects of your life as well as work and business. You might not use it socially to the same extent as Facebook and Instagram, but you can still share a photo of your bottle of wine and let people know that you're letting your hair down at the end of a long week! It really depends on whether you think that would be appropriate for you and your brand.

My point here is that LinkedIn is not so stuffy that you can't share fun and sociable posts, but the focus does tend to err on the professional side to it, more so than any other platform.

This is exactly the kind of topic that would get people engaging on LinkedIn though: "Is it okay to share updates on socializing and drinking wine on your LinkedIn profile?". People would have a great time responding to that. Engagement is the name of the game with LinkedIn, just like it is with all the platforms. Anything that sparks something of an intellectual or controversial debate always seems to get people responding!

Pinterest: "Take a look at my 'Wine & Cheese Pairing' Infographic"

Pinterest is all about the visuals, and it's about providing tons of visual inspiration and ideas. If I were posting about wine on Pinterest, I'd like to think I could create a really visually engaging infographic. Or, I'd create a Pinterest board (like a scrapbook) full of images and ideas about, for example, pairing wine and cheese (mmmm, sounds like my kind of Pinterest board!).

I'd be sure to make content that led back to my website

though because Pinterest is a search engine. We want to get found on Pinterest and bring people over to our own website.

In conclusion

We must always engage with people on social media. Simply having a presence but not engaging with anyone will do you more harm than good.

Also, we must speak the language of the platform.

We must understand and respect why people are on social media and other online platforms and take into account what they expect to see.

Effective content repurposing is not copying and pasting content from one place to another because what works in one place is not necessarily going to work somewhere else.

Maybe all that is needed is a little change here or there to make your content in-line with what people on a new and different platform expect. You may not have to spend a lot of time making adjustments for platforms, you simply need to be mindful and put some thought into it.

Platforms are different. Respect why people are there and show your respect by adjusting your content for every platform.

CHAPTER 18

DIY approaches to repurposing

In this book I have shared lots of different ways that you can repurpose almost every type of content imaginable. But, you have a lot of other things to do in your business alongside creating and repurposing content, so you need to work out how you're going to do the work and, very importantly, who is going to do the work.

What you can achieve with content repurposing does depend to a large extent on the time and resources you have at your disposal.

Let's first start by looking at content repurposing when are you going it alone, when you don't have a person or team of people to help you.

The DIY approach

Creating content and then repurposing it can be time consuming. Obviously it depends on how much content you have and how much repurposing you do but, nonetheless, it all takes time.

In fact, when I talk to people about content repurposing, especially when I'm interviewed on other people's podcasts, I get very enthusiastic about all of the different ways you can repurpose content. And the person I'm talking to gets excited too, and then immediately stressed in equal measure. "It's exciting to do all of this but when will I get the time?!".

Content repurposing sounds so good that people often feel they must immediately do everything they can to repurpose all of their content. Realistically that's just not possible. It's often not even possible when you have a team like I do (and I have a team of content repurposing experts covering every skill-set needed. I have the dream team for this work and yet *still* we can't do everything!), so it's certainly not possible when you are doing it all on your own.

There are lots of reasons why you might be doing the work on your own but it usually comes down to budget. When we're starting out there isn't necessarily a budget to get help with producing and repurposing our content so we roll our sleeves up and we learn how to do it ourselves.

Regardless of whether you have the budget to hire help with your content or not, it's often a good idea to first learn how to do the work yourself so that you are better able to guide and manage the people who you will later hire to help you.

Getting started tips

If you don't have the budget to hire help, I'm going to assume that you also have limited time too. After all, you may be doing this work yourself but you also have a business to run. Creating content is really important but it needs to fit in around other priorities. Here are my step-by-step tips for getting started, bearing that in mind:

Step one: Decide on your primary content method

First, decide what the primary content is that you want to

focus on, whether that is a podcast, video, live-streaming or blogging. Decide what your core content will be. This is what you'll repurpose.

It's really important to hone in on *one* content medium instead of trying to do everything. Don't be creating videos, vlogs, podcasts, *and* Facebook lives. It bears repeating: You're far better focusing on *one* core content medium.

Choose something that you enjoy and choose something that you know your audience consumes. For example, if you enjoy recording Facebook Lives but your audience don't tend to turn up to Facebook Lives, that's a bad choice. On the other hand, if your audience love Facebook Lives and would turn up, but you hate recording them and can't stand the thought of the next time you need to go live, then that is not the core channel for you. Find something you enjoy creating *and* your audience enjoy consuming.

This is your long form content. This is the content that you're going to put time and effort into planning and producing on a consistent, regular basis and this is what you're going to repurpose. Decide what this is and stick to it.

Step two: Get consistent!

Consistency is key. Commit to creating your primary content. Draw up a schedule and plan in advance.

When it comes to creating content, if you can create your content in batches this will prove to be a big time-saver. Putting aside one day per month to record four or five videos, podcasts or write blog posts can be immensely satisfying and hugely productive.

When it comes to publishing the content, commit to a regular schedule that your audience will get used to.

As vlogger, author and content marketing coach Amy Landino said on the stage at Youpreneur Summit in London, 2017, you should "become somebody's favorite". She likened being consistent and always turning up with watching our favorite TV shows. Believe me when I tell you I know exactly what night Game of Thrones was on and I would not miss it!

That's probably not the best example since these days shows like Game of Thrones are only on TV for short periods of time and half of the time we can binge watch them, as they're available on-demand but the example still stands for weekly TV dramas and soap operas.

This is also true for my favorite podcasts. I know exactly what day of the week certain podcasts release new episodes and I look forward to it.

Your production and release schedule should suit you and what you know you can stick to. For example daily, weekly, bi-weekly. Whatever you deem realistic.

Do not embark on anything more than weekly unless you can truly commit to it because creating content is hard. Don't make it any harder on yourself by over-committing to how much you'll create. Remember, quality over quantity. Better a twice monthly absolutely amazing episode than a daily podcast that is mediocre!

Step three: Create processes/standard operating procedures

There will be processes that you follow in order to create and publish your content. As you become more consistent, those processes will become self-evident.

For example, if you have a podcast, the process probably includes planning your episode, recording, editing, writing show notes, creating artwork, uploading to your podcast host, and so on.

If you have The Content 10x Toolkit you'll see within it we provide example processes/templates to use.

Think about what your processes are. Standardize them and document them.

If it's only you doing the work then documenting your process may seem a bit over the top, but at the very least having a checklist can be a good idea. Documenting your processes will come in really handy if there comes a point where you hire help.

Step four: Add one new step to your process, a content repurposing step!

As I've mentioned already, you don't want to try and do everything at once. Quite simply, you don't have the time and you most likely don't have the skillset either. We can't all do everything and nor should we want to!

Take your content repurposing one step at a time. That's why I recommend just adding one extra step to your existing processes when you repurpose your content.

For example, if you have a podcast you could create two audiograms per week/per episode and share them on social media. See chapter five on repurposing podcasts.

Or, if you have a weekly Facebook Live, download the video every week, do some editing of your video and put it onto YouTube and your website.

There are lots of things you can do to squeeze more value from the content that you have already created and for ideas and advice, all you need to do is read Part Two of this book!

TOP TIP: Consider the way that you are connecting with your audience via your primary content, e.g. verbal, social, visual, etc. then explore the different ways that you can connect with your audience through factoring in the different learning styles.

For example, a podcast is great for the aural learners but with your extra repurposing step, what kind of learners do you want to reach out and connect with in addition to the aural learners? Perhaps a blog post to connect with solitary learners? See the section on learning styles in chapter three for more on this.

Step five: Get consistent with your new step before adding the next!

Once you have added *one* new repurposing step to your regular processes it comes back to step two again: Get consistent!

Continue with your content creation process and new repurposing process until it's baked in. This may mean following this method for a couple of months or even longer. Get to the point where your content repurposing step isn't a 'new' step at the end of the old process, it's actually just a part of the process.

Then, consider adding your next content repurposing step. Assess how much time you have, stay within your skill-set or look to develop/hire new skills, in order to implement your next step.

Go back to Step four and repeat!

In conclusion

Take one step at a time. When you are taking a DIY approach you must not try to do everything at once. Don't get frustrated if you aren't making the most of every possible content repurposing opportunity. It's far better to acknowledge your time and resource limitations and get consistent with what you are comfortable with.

Too many times I see people get so excited about all the content repurposing opportunities, and they try to do too much. They do a lot of repurposing for about a month before it becomes too much and they stop *everything* and go back to square one.

It's better to be consistent with a smaller number of content outputs than inconsistent with a lot.

CHAPTER 19

Small budget & hiring help

In chapter 18 I shared tips and advice for content repurposing if you are doing the work on your own. It's time to look at the options available to you if you have a small budget to invest and decide to get help.

What should you get help with?

If you have decided that you'd like to invest in getting some help with your content repurposing efforts then firstly you need to decide what you want help with. It's really important to consider your skills and where your time is best spent.

What can you do and what can't you do? And remember just because you *can* do something doesn't mean that you *should* be doing it.

There are tasks where someone else is far more suitable to complete the work than you. Quite often this is the more procedural tasks, freeing you up to do other things like sales, liaising with clients and working on higher level strategic tasks.

Then, very importantly, think about what you *like* to do and what you *hate* to do.

You might like to do something and have the skills to do it, but it's not the best use of your time. Or, perhaps you'll find you have the skills to do certain tasks and it seems like you're the appropriate person to do it, but you hate the work!

It comes down to acknowledging what you *can* do versus what you *should* do. Keep your focus on what you should do.

Consider time versus money

When weighing up what you should or should not be doing, remember this: your time has a monetary value associated with it. It sounds so cliche, but time is money. Every hour that you spend doing one thing, you could be doing something else instead.

Because there is a value attached to your own time it's useful to put a price tag on an hour of your time. Then, when working out what to outsource always ask yourself, should I be doing this task or is there someone else with the skills who could do this at a lower cost to the business?

If the answer is yes, then that's almost certainly something to consider getting help with.

The person you hire may not be as skillful as you but if they have the skills to do the job to the required standard, that is usually good enough. Guess what? They might actually be *more* skillful than you and do a better job!

As business owners, it's common to suffer from 'superhero syndrome' where we think that we're the only person who can do everything well, but the reality is, we're not! Plus, there is more than one way to do something, so sometimes you just need to let go for the greater good.

Hiring for the task

Whilst it's important to make sure that you don't suffer from 'superhero syndrome' yourself, it's also really important to bear in mind that other 'superheroes' don't really exist either. What I mean is that you're not likely to be able to hire one person who is a 'superhero' and can do everything.

If you bring an employee, VA or freelancer on to support you, they are unlikely to be able to do video production and editing, audio editing, designing and creating graphics, writing content, planning content *and* publishing content. It's unrealistic to expect to find one person who can do everything. Instead, hire for the specific skill-set and task.

If you are just getting started and haven't hired in your business before then you are probably considering the pros and cons of hiring a VA, a freelancer or a part time member of staff.

There will be a number of considerations related to this decision. You need to be clear on whether you see the position as long term or short term. What kind of flexibility are you looking for versus stability?

Hiring a freelancer

Hiring a freelancer to provide you with some support when you're just dipping your toes into having a team is a great, flexible thing to do. This is exactly what I did when I was getting started and realized that I needed to hire in some help.

If you decide that you want to hire a freelancer, here are a few of the places that I have sourced freelancers from in the past:

- **Fiverr** A marketplace for digital skills. All jobs are no longer US $5 but they were at first and that's how it got the name! Prices vary more now depending on the job. Always look at ratings and feedback of the freelancers
- **Upwork and People Per Hour** Post a particular job and freelancers go ahead and apply. You can set all sorts of filters on applicants. E.g. location, skills, feedback ratings, experience level on the site. You can also invite specific people to apply for the job. If you have worked

with someone in the past you can continue working with them without posting new jobs all the time

There are plenty of other sites too, including far more niche sites for niche skills and you may find the right person on LinkedIn too.

TOP TIP: Always be clear on the job that you want someone to complete. State the outputs you are looking for and standards you expect. Spell out the deadlines, rate of pay and the skills required. The clearer you are, the better for everyone.

Of course you don't always have to look online. Another option is to hire someone locally, for example look into local freelance job boards and agencies.

Working with freelancers offers a really flexible work arrangement. It's a much quicker process to find and recruit a freelancer to complete a job for you than it is to hire an employee into your business. Plus, it's a lot smoother to let a freelancer go than it is to let an employee go!

You can hire people for single, one-off jobs or you can find freelancers who are willing to commit to regular work. For example, a certain number of hours every week. Be aware of local labor/employment laws if go down this route though in case your work arrangement is deemed similar to an employer-employee relationship, in which case you can get into trouble in some countries.

The main benefits of hiring freelancers are flexibility, freedom, access to expert skills and a global talent pool.

Downsides of hiring freelancers are similar to the benefits but they work against you! The flexibility and freedom works both ways and this can mean that you need to ensure that you don't become dependent on a freelancer because they are not committed to you. If you want that level of dependence and commitment then it's time to discuss employment with them.

Otherwise, a freelancer can stop working for you at any

time, including right when you have that huge client deadline coming up! From past experience, it's not unheard of for a freelancer to just disappear and there is little that you can do if this happens. It works both ways in that of course you can discontinue working with your freelancer too so the vulnerability is on both sides. It's the price of freedom that comes with a freelance relationship.

You also may not be a priority for your freelancer. They are likely to be working for other clients as well as you, especially if you're not providing them with the full-time amount of hours/ income that they're after.

When a freelancers leaves, either by agreement or unexpected, you have to find a replacement and this can be a time consuming process. During the time that you're sourcing a replacement, you may also have to pick up the tasks that they were managing, meaning your own time can become consumed with tasks you wouldn't normally be doing. The work you should be doing can suffer as a result.

Another downside is that when you work with freelancers it's difficult to build a strong team spirit. When there is no long-term commitment it's probably unrealistic to instill your core values when they have no real skin in the game.

Hiring a Virtual Assistant (VA)

Similar to a freelancer, you can hire a VA to work for you from pretty much anywhere in the world. The whole 'virtual' aspect of hiring a VA means that there is total geographic independence.

You can hire someone either onshore (in your country or even in your town) or offshore. For example, there are a lot of VAs who work from the Philippines supporting small businesses and entrepreneurs in the USA, UK, Canada and Australia. Whilst the Philippines is a popular place to hire offshore VAs (English literacy levels are very high in the Philippines), you can find people offering VA services from almost anywhere in the world.

The usual arrangement is that the VA is not an employee. Instead, they are a service provider. You don't provide office space to them because they work from their preferred location instead. Again, this is very similar to a freelancer so you could argue what's the difference between a VA and a freelancer?

Generally (not always) VA arrangements are entered into with a longer term lens. VA positions often look similar to a job that you would give an employee: regular, repeatable tasks. Usually you draw up a service agreement with your VA which states the service that they will provide to you and the finer details regarding hours, availability, notice of termination etc.

You can find VAs on websites that you would also go to for freelancers like Upwork.com and Peopleperhour.com. There is a website called Outsourcely.com that distinguishes itself more on helping people establish longer-term virtual work arrangements. In the Philippines there is a website called **OnlineJobs.ph** that helps you find VAs in the Philippines only. If you are looking to hire an onshore VA then you may be able to advertise on your local/national job boards.

LinkedIn can often be a good source for finding suitable candidates for onshore and offshore VAs too.

Be prepared to train your VA and have the time commitment to review their work and support them. I highly recommend bringing your VA on for a two-week trial initially to see if they are the right fit. In fact, during the recruiting/interview process I recommend asking them to do some tests/trial pieces of work to test their abilities. You can offer this as paid or unpaid. I usually offer a paid trial.

Don't be backward about asking for and following up on references too. This is something that I always tend to do, and whilst it's wonderful when a referee comes back saying how great somebody is, it's also eye-opening when someone responds in such a way that you should no longer hire the person. Phew! Good to find out *before* you hire them rather than invest lots of time and resources into training them, only to discover issues down the line and then have to let them go.

When you find your perfect VA, agree on the set number of hours that your VA will work for you each week or each month (and their working hours, especially if they are in a different time zone to you).

Hiring a VA sits somewhere in-between an employee and a freelancer. You don't have the additional costs or commitments of employment, but you would hope to have more stability than a freelance arrangement.

Sometimes people offer certain benefits to their VAs too like an annual bonus, paid vacation days, and private healthcare insurance.

That said, pretty much all the points that I made regarding the downsides of hiring freelancers stand for VAs as well. The flexibility and freedom of a VA arrangement (albeit potentially less flexible than freelancing if you have a service agreement in place) still means that you could end up doing a lot of hiring and replacing of VAs, meaning a lot of recruiting and training.

Sadly, the 'disappearing VA' is a thing, just like a disappearing freelancers. It's often just really bad luck if it happens but I've known it happen to many people. In fact, it happened to a good friend of mine who had a long-term VA in the Philippines who had worked for him for about 18 months and was doing a good job. The relationship seemed pretty solid but then overnight she disappeared, never to be heard from again. Not an email, or a call. Nothing. This has happened to me twice with VAs who had worked with me for a few weeks, but not what you expect when the relationship is so established.

You pay a smaller fee to VAs in offshore locations like the Philippines and India because the cost of living and wages is that much lower in those countries, but you do open yourself up to more risks. That is not to say that a US or UK-based VA won't just disappear overnight too, but it seems more common with offshore VAs. I guess that's because of the distance. Onshore VAs seem more worried about references and their reputation. In my view, there are just more potential consequences for onshore VAs.

On the whole, if you manage to hire a great VA then this can be a wonderful working arrangement. It has worked well for me over the years. Always hire for the skill-set and don't expect to find someone who can do everything. VAs can become as firmly established members of your team as any full-time employee. They can be dependable, reliable and fully bought into your vision and values.

Hiring an employee

Often there comes a point where you realize that you want to have particular roles or tasks covered by an employee of your business as opposed to doing them yourself or working with freelancers and VAs.

I realized fairly early on in building my creative agency, Content 10x, that I needed to hire employees. There was no doubt in my mind at all that my business was not going to thrive unless I hired employees. I needed people who were committed to the business, bought into our long-term vision, and overall "why", were able to help foster the team culture that I strived for, and invested in developing a career with us.

Recruitment and training was time consuming and costly and something that I did not want to be continuously doing.

As a service-based business it was not possible to deliver a repeatable, fast-paced and extremely high-quality service to our clients if I was dependent on freelancers and VAs. The two did not go hand-in-hand. To succeed I needed a solid, dependable team who were fully bought into our core values and our long-term vision.

It really does depend on the nature of your business as to what is the right staffing model. It depends on whether your business is product-based or service-based, what skills you are hiring for (how niche?), if there is a lot of training required or not, and the time it takes to source and hire replacements.

Hiring an employee is a lot more complicated than working with freelancers or VAs. Truth be told, it can be a bit of a hassle, especially if you don't have an in-house HR team!

If you're bringing your first employee on then you have a whole host of administrative concerns. Of course, it completely varies by country and so you need to know exactly what the process and labor laws are in your country.

For example, in the UK you have employer insurance costs, setting up government tax payments (PAYE), National Insurance contributions, finding a payroll provider, setting up a pension scheme (this is the law) and various other administrative tasks. You need to have contracts of employment and policies in place.

The benefit is that you are investing in someone for the long term and it's a more solid, two-way commitment than freelancing. The employee is also investing in you.

Employees have benefits that they wouldn't have as a freelancer. For example, paid vacation, sickness and pension. You might even throw in other benefits like a bonus and private health insurance. They also have security and are more likely to be invested in your business, from a development of skills and knowledge perspective.

When it comes to attrition rates and people leaving, many of the downsides that I have mentioned for freelancers and VAs, even just the whole 'disappearing' thing, can still happen with employees. You're not exempt, that's just life, but you've got more protection from this happening.

In conclusion

When you are weighing up whether you should hire help or not, consider the alternatives. One alternative may be that the work doesn't get done so you need to know how happy you would be with that scenario. How important is it that the work gets completed and should that be within a particular time frame? If you did hire help, would you see a return on your investment?

Another alternative is that you do it yourself. In that case, work out the value of your time. Work out if it's more cost effective to do it yourself as opposed to hiring someone to do it for you. Consider what you will not be able to do if you are doing this work, because there is only one you and 24 hours in a day, so working on something means not working on something else.

As a final tip, remember that if you outsource some activities to a freelancer, VA or employee, it's important to remember (and this is often overlooked) that you'll need to build in time to manage that person, and review/quality control their outputs. Even if you dig deep into your pockets and hire a really experienced person you still need to set direction, manage and guide them.

The less experienced a person is, the less you're paying them, but then the more time you are likely going to need to put into managing them and their outputs. As such, hiring cheap is not usually the most cost effective option overall.

CHAPTER 20

Done for you

When you have a larger budget to hire help with your content marketing then, as with most things in life, options really open up for you. This is the point at which you can take your content repurposing to the next level. It's pretty darn exciting!

We all want to get as much value as possible from every piece of great content that we create. It's time to explore the many repurposing opportunities and the difference they can make for your business.

For example, let's say you have a weekly podcast episode and you want to repurpose it every week into a short blog post, a long-form blog post, an infographic, a YouTube video, a SlideShare presentation, social media videos, social media images, audiograms, a LinkedIn article, an email, lots of social media posts on all of the platforms, and a content upgrade.

To do that amount of content repurposing, every single week, I'm going to assume that you will hire help! When you have a bigger budget you have the option of outsourcing to a service provider or hiring your own in-house content team.

Let's look at that in more detail:

Use an agency/service provider - like Content 10x!

There are digital agencies/creative agencies that you can hire to help you with content repurposing. This is exactly what we do at my agency, Content 10x. What differentiates us is that we focus *only* on content repurposing. We've, quite literally, written the book on it!

Content repurposing is our specialism, or as we like to say, it's our superpower. We are experts in determining how you can get the most value from your content. In terms of what we do for clients, we offer a fully managed end-to-end service. My team is comprised of the different roles and skill sets needed to comprehensively repurpose content.

Our service is essentially an outsourced content team. Our clients pay a regular monthly fee and for that they have a team of experts in their respective fields who work on repurposing their content every week (or whatever the frequency is). We publish all of the content too if our clients want us to.

My team operates as an extension of the client's business. Everything that we create is very much as if we are part of their business. The style, tone, brand, voice, etc. Everything is developed from scratch for each client. The team assembled to work on each client are the same team, week in, week out, so the consistency is always there, but the client only has to liaise with one single point of contact, their Content Manager.

We complete all of the content repurposing, leaving our clients to focus on other aspects of their business. As long as our client creates their one form of original content each week (or in a batch) whether that's a podcast, video, livestream or blog, we take care of the rest.

For example, one of our amazing clients records a video every week, puts it into Dropbox, and we create and publish all content as follows:

- Edit the video from 'raw' cut to fully edited.
- Extract audio from the video and professionally edit it to produce a podcast episode.
- Write podcast/video show notes.
- Upload and schedule the podcast episode to her podcast host with the show notes.
- Upload the video to YouTube with the show notes.
- Write a longer form blog post.
- Create a blog post image and other artwork.
- Upload the blog post to her website and schedule it to publish, along with the podcast player, artwork and video.
- Create a collection of social media images for all platforms.
- Create a collection of short video teasers to post to all social media platforms.
- Write engaging copy to go with all social media content.
- Schedule all content on various social media platforms.
- Write and send an email to her email subscribers.
- Publish an article to an industry/professional website.
- Create a content upgrade for email list building.
- Create the Facebook and Instagram ads for the content upgrade.

This is just an example, but the key point to remember is that the only thing that our client needs to focus on is recording an awesome video! We create everything else based on watching her video and bringing our expertise to the table to create lots of new content every week.

The beauty of outsourcing is that it enables you to focus on what *you do best*. You let outsource providers do what *they do best* (for you!). It basically puts everyone in a position where they are working within their zone of genius!

But there are so many other benefits too:

- No recruitment responsibilities - no candidate sourcing, interviews, hiring.
- No HR responsibilities - no training and development, or performance management.
- Reduced cost of having employees and reduced administrative burden associated with employees. E.g. pension, tax, insurance contributions etc.
- No dependence on freelancers - removing the worry of them moving on (or even disappearing), finding replacements, training.
- No managerial responsibilities - team management plus review and quality control of outputs is no longer your responsibility, a huge time saver.
- Consistency - you have a consistent service provided to you each week (also, added bonus, this forces you to be consistent too).
- Expertise across skill sets - the multimedia skills required for high-end content repurposing can be vast - it's unlikely you could find one individual skilled in all areas.
- More innovation, creativity and continuous improvement - this is easier to foster when people work within their areas of expertise and passion.

It's funny because I started my career working in outsourcing as a management consultant, working for a big global consultancy firm. We provided outsourcing services, amongst many others, to some of the biggest organizations in the world, who relied on us to deliver IT, HR, procurement, and other key business functions to us. Sometimes it seemed very risky. My first client was the world's biggest bank and they outsourced their entire IT application development and support function to us. But you then came to realize that it meant everybody was operating within their zone of expertise.

Everyone was focused on what they do best, e.g. the bank focused on banking and not on trying to be an IT company. It enabled a high level of service to be maintained, plus innovation and continuous improvement. This is exactly what we strive for at Content 10x

If you want to really take repurposing your content to the next level and reach a bigger audience, outsourcing content repurposing to a 3rd party like Content 10x could be the answer. If you want to find out more about what we do, head to www.content10x.com.

Another option is to hire an in-house content team.

The in-house option

Instead of outsourcing your content repurposing to an agency/service provider, like Content 10x, you can always hire an in-house team to complete all of your content repurposing. The kind of help that you can hire basically builds on from all that I talked about in chapter 19, Small Budget & Hiring Help, but with more of a budget, you can hire more freelancers, VAs and/or employees, thus forming a team.

The pros and cons are pretty much the same, just on a larger scale. With freelancers and VAs you have flexibility but lack long-term stability. With an employee you have a more stable, long-term commitment but the whole process is more complex and costly. Both still require your managerial oversight.

If you decide to go for an in-house team versus outsourced, and you opt for a mix of employees vs freelancers, it's a good idea to do this in a strategic way. Consider the risks and consider where you could cope best should the risks materialize into issues. E.g. the roles that are easier to fill/the skill-sets that are easier to find, could be okay for a freelancer. The roles that are extremely hard to fill may be best for a long-term employee. Also, the roles that take a considerable amount of time to train someone on may be best for an employee.

Considerations are:

- Recruitment - you will need to recruit your team members. Whether that's freelancers or employees, there still needs to be recruitment processes in place.
- Attrition - when people resign, retire, get fired, go on maternity leave, or go on unplanned leave (e.g. sickness), you need to manage this situation and ensure business continuity (and in this case 'content continuity'!)
- Training - you are responsible for training everyone in the team.
- Cost of employment - as mentioned already in Part Three, there are additional costs associated with employees -, tax, pension, bonuses, benefits, health insurance, statutory obligations (e.g. sickness, redundancy, maternity pay) etc.
- Administration - there are a lot of administrative tasks involved in hiring and running a team, so bear this in mind.
- Consistency - consistency is really important when it comes to content creation and content repurposing, therefore it's important to build in consistent systems and processes. Team members will come and go, so you need to build and document good processes and ensure your outputs stay consistent.
- Managerial oversight - you must ensure that you have time to manage the team. Reviewing content, and providing guidance and direction are all very important and

time consuming tasks. There are always more 'people-related' issues that come up than you ever imagined.

- Control - you will have control over everything because everybody works for you.

It's really important that you hire for the skill-set, and the kind of skills that you may be looking for could include:

- Graphic designer
- Video editor
- Audio editor
- Copywriter
- Website/SEO expert
- Social media expert
- Content publisher
- Overall content/project/team manager

In conclusion

The benefits of having a content team working for you are considerable, whether you go for the service provider route or you hire an in-house team. It's very much a case of working out what's right for you. Know your budget. Understand what level of support you want. Understand how much time you personally have and want to put towards this work.

Making a move like this will raise your content game considerably, no more playing it small. Not only will you create more content and be more consistent, but the content will be of a high quality too. No more worrying that your competitors are doing more than you. No more feeling frustrated that you're not doing enough or the fear that you're not reaching enough of the right people and missing out on some key platforms.

If you were previously doing a lot of the work yourself then suddenly the weight is lifted, particularly if you go the outsourced route. Very importantly, your quality content is being repurposed into more and more quality content, maximizing the time and effort that you put into it for maximum results. All the while, you are able to focus on running and growing your business. When your epic content brings in leads, you are ready to turn those leads into customers.

PART 4

Making Content Repurposing Manageable With Systems & Processes

CHAPTER 21

Planning & creating content for repurposing

In Part One I covered what content repurposing is, why it's so important and the business benefits.

In Part Two I provided you with lots and lots of different ways to repurpose content.

In Part Three I shared mistakes to avoid and strategies to use when you are doing it all yourself, working with a small budget, and when you have a healthy budget and want to really raise you game.

Now, let's look at the systems and processes that sit behind effective content repurposing. Something that I talk about a lot, because I really do believe in it, is that you must create content with repurposing in mind.

Repurposing should not be an afterthought

How do you reverse engineer the content creation process so that you have content that is perfect for repurposing?

I truly believe that most content can be repurposed in some

way, shape or form. Even if repurposing was the last thing on your mind when you created it, even if you hadn't a clue what repurposing was when you created it, there are still repurposing opportunities to be explored. Trust me, I will always find them!

But if you create your content with repurposing in mind, you make the whole task of repurposing a lot easier.

If you step back and think about it, it seems obvious. For example, if you plan out what you are going to eat for the week, write out a shopping list with the ingredients you'll need, then head to the food shop to buy it all, you're more likely to be able to cook the meals that you want through the week. If you want to eat healthily then you're more likely to achieve your health goals with this kind of planning and preparation.

Alternatively, you could turn up at the grocery store with good intentions but no plan, buy anything at all, then every day wonder what you're going to make with your (potentially pretty random) collection of food. Both will work, in that you will eat food, but one is somewhat smoother than the other and more likely to move you towards your goals.

Coming back to content creation, if you create content with repurposing in mind, then the entire repurposing process will be smoother. Because you have planned your content in-line with your business goals, you are far more likely to achieve your goals. A haphazard approach risks not achieving your goals.

Here are some of the key things you should consider when creating content, so that it will repurpose like a dream:

Make your content timeless

Where possible, try and create content that is timeless, often referred to as 'evergreen'. I know this might not always be possible, sometimes we create topical content that is very much 'in the moment' and that's fine but if content can be evergreen it helps with repurposing.

Some minor tweaks to what you've written or said can help

make your content stand the test of time. For example, don't reference current affairs unless it's really relevant. Don't mention in your video the "news just in today regarding xyz...".

If you can avoid it, don't use terminology like 'today' or 'tomorrow' if it isn't required or if in doing so your content is no longer timeless. When planning and creating your content, ask yourself, does this topic stand the test of time? Can and should I make this piece of content timeless? What can I say or write to make this content evergreen?

Good examples of timeless content are 'how to' guides and the types of content that solve problems for your audience.

Focus, focus, focus!

Keep your content focused on one specific topic. Make one clear point and always address the 'so what', the 'because', and the 'who cares' of your point. Content that is really focused and doesn't go off on lots of different tangents is a lot easier to repurpose.

TOP TIP: Keep your key point at the front of your mind the whole way through creating your content. If you are recording a podcast or a video, have it written on a whiteboard or a post-it note. Don't allow yourself to forget and lose focus.

Structure

Does your content have a beginning, a middle and an end? Can your content be divided into sections? Can your content break down into stand-alone points/thoughts? This is something that can make content repurpose like a dream.

One blog post could form five mini blog posts or five LinkedIn posts. Or one twenty-minute video could become ten two-minute videos.

Bringing structure to your content can really help with repurposing.

For example, when we are repurposing Facebook Live

videos into podcast episodes or shorter videos suitable for YouTube and social media, we always ask our clients to try and structure them in such a way that the core topic is sandwiched in-between live audience interaction so that we can remove what we don't need and work with repurposing just the core topic.

Similarly, you may be recording a video where you answer FAQs. In that case it's a really good idea to have a structure whereby you introduce each question individually and clearly. You will then have lots of short videos that you can go onto repurpose, for example, into Instagram videos.

Keep your sentences short and punchy. Whether written (for a blog, article, or your website) or spoken (for a podcast or video) your sentences should be short, clear and concise.

Having a clear structure is a good habit to get into. Believe me, from working with many of our clients, I know that repurposing is a whole lot easier if you can do this. It's easier to create short videos, or quote graphics, or short teaser clips etc., if you are succinct in your communication style rather than rambling on!

Quotes, facts and statistics

Do you have powerful, impactful quotes that you would like to share? If you're creating a podcast or a video, have them to hand. They could be quotes of your own, and/or quotes made by others. Similarly, are there any facts or statistics that you want to share? They add credibility to your content and they always make good visual content.

Facts and statistics are perfect for infographics and slide or presentations. If you are aware of any facts or statistics that are relevant, and boost/back-up your content, include them!

Lists and step-by-step guides

Can you create a list or a step-by-step guide? Breaking content down in this way is perfect for repurposing. "10 Reasons

Why ... " "Five Ways To Do ... "

For example, your video entitled "10 Reasons Why You Should Repurpose Content "can be repurposed into 10 visuals, 10 short videos for social media, ten podcast episodes, a great infographic, and so much more. There is a lot that you can do.

Content stacking

A good friend of mine, Colin Gray, founder of ThePodcast-Host.com and the podcast editing app Alitu, was a guest on my podcast and he talked about a repurposing approach that he likes to follow called 'content stacking'. The term 'content stacking' makes perfect sense because, essentially, he 'stacks' podcast, video and blog content together.

Why?

Text in the form of a blog post is really important because it's how you reach the most people. It's the easiest way to get found thanks to good old SEO.

When people have found you, video is the content that really ups engagement. Your personality can shine through more on video and therefore it provides more of a chance to connect with people and gain trust.

Podcasts offer a more in-depth look at topics and are something that you can move people to when they are ready to consume your content in a more focused way. This is where you really get attention and you gain loyal fans and subscribers.

Colin explained that he's seen this happen time and time again. People find him via his blog posts, like what they see and start to watch his videos, then they become a podcast subscriber and many go on to become customers.

The method: it starts with the idea

It's really important to think through your idea, then plan it out. This is far better than making decisions on the fly. Colin's tip was to think about the most common questions that you get asked, then break that down even further into many more related and deeper questions. From that you may even have a whole season of content.

When you have your idea, create a bullet point outline. This is for the overall content idea, not specific to a blog post, podcast or video. It's the idea that will be communicated across all three.

Once you have your outline figured out, get both your camera and audio equipment ready and film yourself recording your podcast episode. The audio can be extracted from the video and used as a podcast. This was covered in detail in chapter six, video repurposing.

Break the video down into very discreet sections and take specific sections out to be shared on YouTube.

The philosophy behind this is that people are not as likely to watch a 30-minute video on YouTube as they are to listen to a 30-minute podcast episode. They are more likely to watch a 3 to 5 minute video on YouTube so whilst you have one podcast episode here, you may have anything from one to six short YouTube videos.

Once you've recorded your video and podcast, you can use your initial outline/plan to create a blog post.

TOP TIP: Write your blog post as soon as you have recorded your podcast and/or video, whilst everything is still fresh in your mind.

Colin advised that by creating podcasts, video and blog content, his business has seen much deeper engagement from their audience.

Not everyone follows the same route of blog, to video to podcast. Some people find them on YouTube, then they head to the blog post, then they listen to the podcast. Some people find the podcast first, then head to blog, then video. Everyone is different. The deeper engagement they have seen creates loyal fans, brand advocates and customers.

If you want to give this content stacking approach a go then don't overcomplicate things initially. Use a smartphone and a smartphone tripod to record the video. To make sure that you record good quality audio, if you don't have a microphone then consider getting a lapel microphone (like a Rode Smart Lav+) which plugs into your smartphone and records really good quality audio.

Repurposing starts at the planning phase

Whatever your approach and whichever type of content you create, always remember content repurposing starts at the content planning phase. Never forget this. Always consider what you would like to do with your content before you have created it. How are you going to repurpose it? What could you do when you create it to make it easier to repurpose?

If you'd like a checklist for creating content for repurposing then head to **www.Content10x.com/checklist**.

CHAPTER 22

What to repurpose?

We often talk about how to repurpose your most recent content as fast and as easily as possible - it's fantastic to get those procedures locked in as consistent habits. However, don't forget, your back catalogue is a treasure trove of repurposing potential. If you've been creating content for a while I can almost guarantee you have a ton of repurposing opportunities in your archives. But why repurpose your older material and how do you identify what to repurpose?

Why repurpose old material?

Repurposing older content provides two kinds of value to your audience:

1. A second chance to catch something they missed.

2. A fresh look at a concept they saw the first time but that bears repeating.

1. The second chance

You can't assume that even your most hardcore followers catch everything you publish. There are many reasons why someone might miss a piece of content that they'd still love to catch up on. Some will have missed it because they didn't follow you back then or maybe they didn't even know who you were!

Some will have been on a break from your content. No need to take this personally, perhaps they were on a break from consuming content in general. Or maybe they were on vacation or got too busy for a while, or any number of other reasons.

For some, your content simply wasn't relevant to them then, but it is now. For example, let's say you did a post a year ago about podcasting. A segment of your audience may have not had a podcast back then but have gone ahead and started a podcast since then, and they would love to listen to the information in your old post.

Or, some people may not ever consume the form of content that you created as the original piece. For example, you created a video and there are some people in your audience who just don't watch video content. As simple as that. But, you repurposed that video into a podcast episode and some of those people, who would never have seen your video, do in fact love your podcast and that's how they were able to consume that particular message.

2. The fresh look

It's not only people who missed your content the first time who will appreciate seeing old content repurposed. They may have seen it before, but how great is it when something you enjoyed is brought back to the forefront again?

The other day, while I was watching TV and an old film from my childhood popped up, The Flight of The Navigator. I was overjoyed! It's a great film and I haven't seen it for ages. I was so pleased the TV network decided to bring it back. I welcomed the repeat. I also really enjoy repeats of Friends, Frasier and Seinfeld!

The same can be true of your old content. Most of your audience will welcome a reminder of the great value you provided before, especially if you present it in a fresh, new way. You are not boring your audience or being repetitive. Have confidence that it's okay to share your message in lots of different places and in different formats. You can do this more than once.

How do you decide what content to repurpose?

Now you see the power of creating new value from your old content, the obvious question is, "Which pieces of content should I repurpose?" You *could* take a stab in the dark but why risk it?

Instead, you have a few things to consider when selecting your winners, including:

- Which were the most popular?
- Which were the most engaging?
- Which were the best at inspiring people to take action?
- Which are the most evergreen or can be updated to be relevant today?

Perhaps you've got hundreds of blog posts and many are just as relevant today as the day you wrote them?

Or maybe you've just given yourself a pat on the back for recording your 100th podcast episode, but you know your episodes deserve to reach many more people. You now know (thanks to reading this book!) that what they need is the power of repurposing.

Find your most popular content, i.e. the content that your audience has really responded to. Clearly you struck a nerve with people or managed to really connect with them with that particular post, video, podcast episode or livestream because it was so popular. This is the kind of content that you should consider repurposing so that it can reach more people.

How do you know if the content was popular? Don't worry, you don't have to guess.

Identify your most popular content by looking at your analytics

Instead of simply taking an educated guess, here's how to use solid data to decide *what* to repurpose:

Website analytics

Firstly, assuming your content is on your website, you can look at your website analytics. Most people use Google Analytics but there are other tools and apps that can be used for website data and analytics. If you don't currently use *any* analytics tools at all, it's time to start! Google Analytics is completely free.

Use your analytics to find the content on your site that had the most hits and the content people engaged with for the longest, presumably getting lots of value from it. This popular content is a great place to start with repurposing. If website visitors liked it, let's find more of the same people!

There's so much you can find out from your website analytics that can help you understand your audience's behavior. This in turn can help you make strategic decisions over what content to create and what content to repurpose.

For example, as well as the most viewed posts, you can find out:

- **The incoming traffic source** *Where* people came from when they landed on your site. Was it direct, search or referred from another site (including social media)?
- **Behavior on your sit**e If they liked a post, where did they go to next?
- **How long people stay on your site** and the **rate at which people leave** without taking any action, known commonly as the bounce rate.
- **Where in the world your audience are from?**

- **Are your visitors mainly new or returning visitors?**
- **What pages are people exiting your site from?**

When working out what your audience would like to see, always consider that some of the answers may lie in your website analytics. If those people who found your website liked that content, what about all the people who haven't found you yet?! Maybe they need your content to be repurposed into a format that they consume, and published on a platform they hang out on, in order to discover you.

Also check out Google Search Console for more on how your content is doing in search results. This includes click-through rates from certain search terms.

Social media analytics

Secondly, look at your social media analytics. You can get really good insight into the content that your audience loves the most by looking at your social media analytics.

For example, if you have a Facebook Page, look at Facebook Insights and you'll see all sorts of information about your most popular posts and much more. Facebook Insights is Facebook's built-in, free, analytics tool and it's very powerful.

Insights tracks likes, page views, shares, reach, and more. No matter what your goals are on Facebook - getting your long-form content in front of the right people, building brand awareness, communicating with customers, or getting followers to take action - Facebook Insights provides the analytics that will help you understand *who* your most engaged audience is and *how* they're interacting with your page.

You can see which post topics made your audience go wild with engagement and which post topics were 'blah' and saw them skipping on over to the next cat video. This is fantastic intel that you can use to work out what content to repurpose. If they loved that topic being discussed on Facebook, maybe they'd love to see you go deeper and create a podcast episode about the same topic, or a video, or more social content.

Similarly, Twitter has built-in analytics as well. When you are logged in to Twitter, head to analytics.twitter.com. You can find lots of useful information about what your Twitter audience love to hear you talk about. This is a huge green flag telling you to find content that you have previously created on those topics and look for opportunities to repurpose it.

Instagram provide post analytics. Similar to Facebook they are called Insights. You need a business account for Instagram Insights.

For all social media platforms you can get useful analytics and data from third-party tools as well as their built-in capabilities. In fact, many third-party tools provide considerably better analytics (these third-party tools allow you to schedule and publish content but also provide analytics as well). With Instagram in particular, if you want really decent analytics you're going to want to use a third-party tool. For example, Later.

Analytics and data allow you to see what topics your audience want to hear you talk about. This in turn can help you work out what to invest time and effort into repurposing.

Podcast and video data

If you have a podcast then of course don't forget to review the analytics provided by your podcast host so that you can identify your most popular episodes and topics. By doing this you can discover what your audience wants to learn about. Sometimes you'll see a sudden spike in interest on a particular topic. Grab that episode and get repurposing!

You can write a blog post from the episode. You can create social media graphics. You can use clips as teasers. You could create an infographic, a presentation, or a video on the same topic. And remember to review chapter five, podcast repurposing.

Similarly, if you create video content, look at your video analytics. For example, on YouTube you can look at video views and delve deeper into analytics to get a feel for exactly what your most popular videos were. It's really interesting to look at retention levels and find the videos that people watch from start to finish. Clearly the video and the topic were extremely interesting because maintaining attention for the length of an entire video can be very hard. Ask yourself, can you repurpose these videos?

Consider videos that have really high views, even if they don't have a high retention rate. It shows you that people were drawn to the video title and/or topic so it's still worth considering repurposing these videos. You've already done the hard work of creating the video, so to go on to create new content based on the video should be less work than creating content from a blank canvas. For this particular topic you may decide to repurpose the video into a blog post, only for it to become a top performing post! You may also find shorter clips of the video shared on social media go down a treat.

Email analytics

Data from your email list can be invaluable in finding what struck a deep chord with your audience.

Look at:

- Open rates on certain topics
- Clickthrough-rates on links related to certain topics, regardless of whether those links are pointed to your own content or someone else's.
- Which lead magnets and content upgrades brought in the most leads. Data on your lead magnets might be the most insightful data you have.
- If a topic inspired lots of people to not only consume your content, but to give you their email addresses, they probably have an on-going appetite for it.

Did people reach out to you privately?

Whenever someone reaches out to you privately about a topic, it's a huge sign that there's a hunger for it. Private contact includes email, your website contact form, or 'PM's and 'DM's on social media platforms.

Scan through as many of the private messages from your audience as you can. Make a note of the topics most of the messages were about. If there are any clear winning topics, go through your back catalogue and pick out all the content you've published about those topics.

Who knows? This tactic alone might keep you busy with guaranteed-popular repurposed content for months!

Ask people!

You can find out what content you should be repurposing using the art of good old-fashioned speaking to people! If you have a business where you interact with your clients and your target audience regularly, notice what they ask you about the most.

Do you keep getting asked the same questions? Have you written content, filmed a video or recorded a podcast episode that answers the questions people keep asking?

Directly ask your audience what they'd like to hear more about from you. In person, or on social media; do a poll. Facebook and Instagram Stories are good for running polls. Or, email your email subscribers and ask them. You could even create a survey and ask your social media followers/subscribers to complete it.

You will find a whole host of topics that people want to hear more about. Look through your content and identify where you have already created content on those topics. This is the kind of content that you want to add to your 'must repurpose' list!

Find your best, evergreen content

Your past content can fall into three rough categories:

- Totally evergreen content. E.g. How to be more productive.
- Timely content that you could update to make it relevant today. E.g. Best productivity tools on the market.
- Ultra-timely content that doesn't really have any relevance today. E.g. Breaking news in the productivity industry.

You could use ultra-timely content to help create new content. For example, if you posted about an update for a piece of software your audience loves, you could use that to help create a new post about the software's history. Unfortunately though, you can't just update it to be relevant today, no matter how popular it may have been.

As mentioned in the previous chapter, evergreen content can repurpose really well so when reviewing what to repurpose ask yourself, is it content that's still as relevant today as it was the day I wrote it or does it need a good refresh? Or was it totally related to a fixed point in time and not really repurpose-able at all? For example, that 5,000 word blog post on your predictions for the US elections! On the other hand, your post 'Three Reasons Why You Should Drink Red Wine' is likely to be timeless.

It may be that you just need to tweak some popular content to bring it to relevancy again.

When you've identified evergreen content, the next question is, is it really high quality? I'm not suggesting that anyone reading this would ever create terrible content. However, I think we all know that some of our content is good, some very good, and some so insanely brilliant that you should actually be awarded some sort of prize for its brilliance. Is there a Nobel Prize for online content?!

It's always a good idea to try and repurpose your popular, timeless, cornerstone content. If it's one of your epic pieces of content, it's likely to be full of repurposing gold!

In conclusion

Don't let all that potential go to waste! Content repurposing isn't just about new content. It's about maximizing the value of everything you create and making the most of the time and effort you put into it.

And remember, don't be afraid to bring back old content that people might have seen before. They won't mind. Imagine a world where we didn't have Friends reruns on TV all the time. There's a reason they do that. It's great content and many people still love it, time and time again.

Look at the data and other signs you have at hand. Find your past pieces that struck the biggest chord with your audience and repurpose those first. You don't need to take a stab in the dark. Make the most of what you already have. It's just sitting there, waiting for you to tap into it. It's time to bring your older content back to life.

CHAPTER 23

Consider the opposite angle

There's an approach I like to ask people to explore when it comes to content repurposing, and it's all about looking at how you can communicate your message from an entirely different angle.

Let's say you have a cooking blog and you write an article titled, *Five Ways to Cook the Perfect Steak.*

There'll be a certain type of person who will be drawn to that sort of article. Perhaps they just flunked an attempt to cook a great steak and want to get some ideas before they try again. Perhaps they've been cooking steak one way for years and want to get some more methods under their belt.

You could repurpose that piece into new formats, i.e. record a podcast episode or a video, etc. But there's another thing you can do to inject even more life into it - take all the research you did for that article, flip the angle, and write: *Five Biggest Mistake Most People Make When Cooking Steak (Are You Making One of Them?)*

It's more than merely rewriting the same thing in a different way. The opposite angle will actually attract a whole new segment of people.

Imagine someone who's been cooking steak for ages and thinks they've got the technique perfected. They see the *Five Ways to Cook the Perfect Steak* article. They're likely to scroll right past. They already know how to cook steak just the way they like it. Who cares?!

Later, they come across the "Five Mistakes" article, and a whole different part of their brain lights up. There's something magnetic for people about the possibility they're doing something wrong. They might also want to see if they agree with you.

Everybody's different in terms of what interests them and what view of the world they have. Some people respond to positive slants, some negative, and it's even deeper than that. Some want to correct their existing knowledge more than they want to learn new things. Some might naturally identify more with one part of a story than another, for example: "How a Salesperson Found a Mental Loophole that Shot Him to the Top of the Company Leaderboard" vs, "Why The Reciprocity Open-Loop is a Powerful Psychological Persuader".

Play with different formats & combos

When I talk about repurposing content, it's usually about how to turn content from one format into another. The great thing about this "different angle" method is you can use any format you like, even if it's the same one!

- You could repurpose one blog post into two shorter posts
- You could keep the original blog post on your site and syndicate the "flipped" version on LinkedIn, Medium, or as a guest post.
- You could add layers to your repurposing and turn an article into a video that takes the opposite angle. The possibilities are endless.

For example, from "How to eat healthy at Christmas" you can create "How to avoid piling on the pounds this Christmas".

One could be a podcast and one a video with a blog post to go along with each one. Why not?

You've already done the research. Why not make the most of all that hard work? You may as well repackage the information you've already gathered instead of coming up with an entirely new topic every time.

CHAPTER 24

How much time?

How much time should you spend on repurposing your content? I get asked this question all the time! My initial thoughts are that the question should be reframed because content repurposing is still a form of content creation. Content creation and content repurposing shouldn't really be seen as two separate things.

The question shouldn't be how much time should I spend repurposing content. Instead ask, how much time should I spend creating content overall?

I find that a lot of people view content repurposing as an entirely separate thing to content creation. I then hear people say that they simply don't have time to repurpose their content. They spend so much time writing for their blog, or creating videos, or podcasting, or live-streaming, that there simply aren't enough hours in the day to repurpose their content as well. They tell me that that would be literally impossible!

This is the wrong way to look at things.

In that situation, what you're doing is constantly putting out new content, but not necessarily doing enough to promote the content and drive traffic to it. You're also not investing time in achieving the maximum value from the content that you have already created by ensuring that it has the biggest impact that it can have.

Talking traffic generation alone, expecting people to just stumble across your content without making any attempts to drive traffic to it, is an unrealistic expectation. If you repurpose your content, you help drive traffic back to your website. In chapter one I shared many of the benefits of repurposing your content, traffic generation being just one.

Quality over quantity

I would also argue that constantly putting out new content is not the best approach. The focus should be on quality over quantity.

Years ago, when I first started learning about digital marketing and online business, I joined a digital marketing training academy. It was ran by some very old-school internet marketers who achieved success and fortune marketing online in 2006/2007. They mostly hadn't moved on from those times and would preach to their students to write a blog post every single day (and have it flooded with affiliate links to their landing pages because they ran a quite shady MLM scheme as it turned out!).

I soon found that this wasn't the most effective strategy. The blog posts were hardly the best quality and organic reach today is not what it was in 2006! Back in 2006, people who were blogging a lot were getting organic reach. Times have changed.

Spurting out high volumes of low quality content will not get you very far.

Even the search engines are more sophisticated today and are programmed to source and return quality content. You must focus on creating high quality content and then have a plan in place to repurpose your content. Do not neglect the repurposing aspect.

The beauty of this approach is that your repurposed content continues to be of a high quality because it feeds off the amazing first piece of content that you put time and effort into. It serves the purpose of driving more traffic to your content, reaching new audiences with your message.

The 80/20 rule

Although I've heard it many times since, it was from experienced internet marketer, Derek Halpern, that I first heard it said that you should spend 20% of your time creating your content and 80% of your time promoting your content. I think he makes a good point. After all, who wants to create content that no one sees?

Personally I would say 20-30% creating and a 70-80% mix of content repurposing and promoting. It's all about working out the time trade-off that's acceptable to you between creating new versus repurposed content.

I recommend first working out how much time you are going to spend creating content overall. Regardless of whether it's fresh content or repurposed content, remove that distinction initially and just work out how many hours per week you'll spend on content. You must be realistic. This will either be your own time or, if you have a team, it will be the overall time you can put your team on to content each week.

When you have that worked out, next consider how you'll allocate that time. Do this wisely. Think about how you'll allocate the time in such a way that you create content people will actually enjoy and benefit from (quality) and find (promote and repurpose).

Perhaps calling the content 'new' vs 'repurposed' is not the right terminology. Your repurposed content is new content as well. After all, you or your team have just created it! It's simply based on the research, concepts and ideas that you put into your original source content. Creating repurposed content will (hopefully) take less time because you have already put a lot of the hard work in. For example, creating a video from scratch as opposed to creating a video based directly off a blog post.

Let's look at the allocation of time, assuming you're a podcaster, doing it all yourself, with 10 hours per week available for content creation:

Option 1:

- Five podcast episodes - 2 hours each

Option 2:

- 2 hours on your podcast - prep, the episode recording itself, post interview work
- 8 hours on repurposing, consisting of ...
    - ☐ 2 hours writing an article
    - ☐ 1 hour on creating a video or number of small videos about the topic
    - ☐ 2 hours creating a download for your audience related to the topic
    - ☐ 1 hour creating social media graphics
    - ☐ 2 hours publishing content on social media, your blog, YouTube etc.

This approach means lots of multimedia content and lots of links directly back to your website. Your content is more focused on one topic. More people can be reached in different places. You also use different content formats to reach people. We all consume content differently and we don't all listen to podcasts. You are reaching people where they hang out and in their favorite format.

What is your allocation of time when it comes to content creation? Start with realistically working out the time commitment overall. Then assign the proportion of times to your core content and your repurposed content. Go!

CHAPTER 25

Tracking & measurement of your content

It's only to be expected that you would want to measure the effectiveness of your content repurposing. There's an age old saying, first credited to Peter Drucker (but the internet cites a number of people as being the first to say it so don't quote it!) "If you can't measure it, you can't improve it."

When I worked in 'big corporate' as a management consultant, terms like 'data-driven decision making' were frequently thrown about. In fact, I attended training courses on data-driven decision making and taught others on the topic too!

There's no doubt that when data and analytics are available you are in a good position to measure the effectiveness of something but I'm a firm believer that you shouldn't blindly put all your trust in the data. Data only tells one side of the story and just because something can't easily be measured does not mean that it's not worth pursuing.

In chapter 22, when I talked about what to repurpose, I encouraged you to identify your most popular content by looking at your analytics: website analytics, social media analytics, podcast downloads and available data, video analytics, e.g. YouTube, and email/CRM analytics, to name a few, but please note that I didn't *only* talk about data-driven methods.

When it comes to tracking and measuring your content repurposing efforts to find out if they are really working, much of the same data that I referred to in chapter 22 can be considered here too. Look at available metrics to review if there is an impact.

Ask yourself:

- What really matters to you?
- What do you want to achieve and, therefore, what do you want to measure?

Don't track everything. Track what matters to you and what will help you in pursuit of your goals.

For example, if all of your content repurposing efforts have two main goals, more website visitors and more email subscribers, then the obvious data to track and measure are your website analytics and your email subscribers. It can be difficult (but not impossible!) to directly work out what results are due to content repurposing versus something else.

Google Analytics & goals

Use Google Analytics to evaluate whether your repurposed content generated more organic traffic, leads, or social shares and engagement.

Website traffic is essential because we all want as many of the right people as possible to find our website. There's lots of action that we'd like them to take on our website, for example, sign-up to services, download free content, purchase a product, but it doesn't matter how good our website is if no one visits it!

Therefore, a lot of the time when we create repurposed content, our big goal is to drive traffic to our website. Use Google Analytics to find out how much traffic your website gets and *which* piece of content is bringing in the traffic.

Plus, pay attention to *where* your traffic is coming from. This is really important. For example, if you are spending a lot of time repurposing your content onto social media with the intention of driving people from social media back to your content on your website, then you want to review analytics and see if it's working. Are people coming to your website from social media? If they are not then you might want to review your social media strategy.

Bear in mind though that even if your content on social media is not driving a lot of traffic to your website, that does not mean you should consider it a waste of time. There may be benefits to your social media content other than generating website traffic.

For example, for me, social media is largely about building brand awareness, particularly my personal brand. Whilst my repurposed content on social media does not always directly link to website traffic, I do not consider the efforts to be a waste of time. I see a lot of benefits of social media when it comes to engaging with my audience. That engagement may not lead to them immediately going to my website but they may in time, the more they engage with me and the more they get to know me socially. This has happened to me many times.

Whilst generating website traffic is very important, when you get people to visit your website, your job is not over. You want them to stay on your website and take the action you want them to take. You want conversions and sales.

Other analytics that you need to look at are your bounce rate, the rate at which people leave your site. If you have a low bounce rate it means that people are liking your content and staying. A high bounce rate means they arrive on your site and leave without visiting another page on your site.

If you are a dab hand at Google Analytics, or if you have someone in your team who is, you can set up specific goals in order to see what content led to visitors taking certain actions.

Decide what the goal is, whether it's filling in a form, looking at a particular web page, staying on a page for a certain amount of time, signing up to your newsletter or whatever action you want visitors to take that you can define as a 'goal'.

With the goal specified, track the goal within Google Analytics. For example, you can see which pieces of content help you to achieve the goal. You can also understand what traffic sources are helping you achieve your goals.

There's no doubt you can find a lot out through your website analytics so it's really useful for considering whether your content repurposing is having an impact.

Search

When I talk about the benefits of content repurposing, something I often refer to is that creating more content, if done in the right way, will help with your SEO and lead to you being found by the search engines.

Therefore, when you are looking at whether your content repurposing efforts are having an impact, one thing you may want to measure is how well your content performs in search results. As I mentioned above, your website analytics provide you with a view of how people are finding you via search, but there is more that you can do to measure this.

Today, with our smartphones by our side pretty much every waking hour of the day, we no longer spend much time at all pondering the answers to our questions. We reach for our phones, 'Google' our question, and get the answer to pretty much anything we need to know (whether it's the right answer or even if there is a right or wrong answer, is a whole other matter that we won't go into right now!). We are in the information-age or perhaps the information-*overload*-age.

Given that people are constantly searching online and, given that most people click on the first result (or at least the results on the first page) it's important to try and ensure your content performs well in search.

To review how you perform against the keywords that you want to rank for, open an incognito window or private window in your browser and perform a search. Review whether you appear in the top three (amazing), first page (still very good), or other pages (you have some work to do!).

If you embark upon content repurposing with the goal of improving your SEO against particular keywords then this is something you could measure over time. Perform an initial review of your performance against those keywords. Then, when you are repurposing your content, for example, creating written content based on your videos or your podcast episodes, focus on optimizing against those keywords.

It will really help if you gain links to your content from respected sites as well. This will increase your website's authority online. Can you repurpose your content into guest articles and features on respected sites with links back to your site?

Review how you perform against your desired keyword searches over time. I suggest you review this every 30 days. It takes time to gain authority online and rank high against particular keywords, don't expect magic overnight, but if this is one of your key focuses for content repurposing, devise a plan to make it work and measure the results. Be patient.

Social media

When it comes to repurposing content, you may have a number of goals for the various social media platforms. As already discussed, if you repurpose your content onto social media with the intention of driving more traffic to your website, you can measure this in Google Analytics. You can directly see how many people are coming to your website via the social media platforms. In Google Analytics look at Acquisition > Social > Network Referrals.

Remember though that data only tells one side of the story so, whilst it's very important to know whether your content on social media is leading to website visitors, that may not always be truly reflected in Google Analytics. For example, someone discovers your content on social media, perhaps starts to follow you, but they don't immediately go from social media to your website. They might visit your website later. They might find you on social media on their mobile device but then go to their desktop computer to look at your website. There's all sorts of behavior that cannot be tracked.

There may be other goals that you have when it comes to content repurposing and social media that *are* measurable. For example, number of followers, number of likes and shares, the rate of engagement on your posts.

You can measure all of this within the social media platforms themselves via their built-in analytics but you can also measure your content marketing success on social media platforms via lots of different 3rd party tools. For example, if you post your social media content using tools like Buffer, SmarterQueue, CoSchedule, MeetEdgar or Agorapulse, to name a few, they all provide you with data and analytics on how your content performs.

When I started my podcast and, at the same time, started repurposing my podcast content, I went from being fairly unsure about what to post on my social media accounts, to having a firm plan every week. I created lots of repurposed podcast content for each platform. I found it to be really important to pay attention to what worked on each platform, and tailored content accordingly. This approach enabled me to stay consistent on the platforms that I wanted to focus on and grow an audience.

It's important to keep track of what is working and not working. What are people engaging with the most? Likes are great, and comments too, especially if you can enter into a conversation with someone. Shares are fantastic because if someone goes to the effort of sharing it with their network/audience, that means they loved your content.

Be dynamic with your content. Measure what is working then, if required, change your approach to do *more* of what is working and *less* of what is not.

On social media, it's not about having thousands and thousands of followers, especially if many of them don't engage with you (or could even be fake accounts and bots). It's about having an audience of people who care about what you say. A small but highly engaged audience is far better than a large, disengaged audience. Make sure that you bear that in mind when working out what metrics matter to you the most.

Podcast, video and email/CRM data

If you are repurposing content for the purposes of getting more podcast downloads, the analytics provided by your podcast host are going to give you the data you need to measure those downloads. You can review if all of your repurposing efforts are increasing your podcast downloads by comparing before repurposing and after.

Did you know that downloads are not the only metric you should look at though? It's one thing for people to download your podcast but did they actually listen to it? Did they listen to *all* of it? That's what really matters isn't it? It's a bit like social media. It's good to have lots of followers but do they actually care what you post and do they engage with you?

Apple Podcasts present a metric called "Average Consumption" in their analytics. This metric enables podcasters to measure how much time and attention listeners are giving to their podcasts. Spotify calls the same metric "Episode Performance" and Stitcher calls it "Average Completion Rate." "Average Consumption" percentages are great because they go beyond just the download and help you work out whether people consider your content to be good quality. Did they listen to it?!

Similarly, if you create video content and you are repurposing your content in order to get more video views, review your video analytics. Look at how many views you are getting but also pay attention to the audience retention statistics too.

If your ultimate goal with all of your repurposing efforts is growing your email subscribers, that's the metric that you need to be measuring.

Website analytics can be useful in helping you measure the effectiveness of content on whether people sign-up to your email list. You can set a goal whereby, for example, if someone lands on the 'Thank you' page for your email list (or whatever your lead magnet/freebie is) then that is the ultimate goal. You can track how many people achieve that goal and obtain more data on who they are, where they came from etc.

Your email service provider will also be able to provide you with data to track and measure. You'll be able to determine which lead magnets brought in the most leads. Also, review email open rates to determine if the leads that you have are engaged. All of this really matters.

Less quantifiable indicators

When it comes to measuring and tracking the effectiveness of your content repurposing efforts, it's not always in the analytics and data. As I mentioned previously, data-driven insights can be great, but data doesn't always tell the whole story. There will be many other benefits of content repurposing that simply cannot be measured by numbers, stats and analytics dashboards.

For example, by creating lots of repurposed content, you are reaching more people and connecting with them in different ways. You never know who is watching, reading or listening. Your content could lead to you being invited onto podcasts and video shows. This has happened to me many times and it's all due to the content I create.

You could be invited to speak at events. This may not be everyone's goal, but if it is, speaking at events can do wonders for your credibility and your personal brand. I have been invited to speak at events as a result of my content, e.g. organizers have reached out to me because they saw my content on LinkedIn or they listened to my podcast or read one of my blog posts.

Building your brand, getting in front of more people via your content and via the opportunities that can lead on from your content, like speaking at events and being a guest on other people's podcasts, all has business benefits. It all leads to more awareness of who you are and what you do, which in turn results in more leads, more conversions and more sales.

In conclusion

When it comes to tracking and measuring the effectiveness of your content repurposing efforts, it all comes down to working out what matters to you. To understand what really matters to you, you need to have goals that are clearly defined. Plus, your goals need to align with your overall business objectives.

Your goals may be quantifiable and therefore you can determine what data you can track and measure, and how you will do this. Some goals may be less quantifiable and more qualitative, in that case you'll need to work out other ways to determine your success factors. I've said it before - don't track everything. Track what matters to you and what will help you in pursuit of your goals.

CHAPTER 26

Setting up repeatable processes

Setting up systems and processes is so important in business. I'm a firm believer that for any business, your ability to weather any storm lies with your systems and processes. It's crucially important to hire great people to work in your team but inevitably people will come and go. Yep, even that star performer that you never, ever, want to leave will, more than likely, one day will leave. What will help you through this situation will be well documented systems and processes because, whilst people will come and go, systems and processes can stay the same, you simply have different people performing the work.

Even if you are not quite there yet with having a team or others to help you with your content, it's still really important to have documented systems and processes that you follow. This will help you no end when the day comes that you decide that you want to get help. Documenting systems and processes also helps you to build efficiency into the work that you do. Often, it's only when you take time to work out what your processes are, that you notice ways that you can be more productive.

It may not be you personally that spots inefficiencies in your processes, it could be someone entirely separate from the process that can review it with a critical eye and suggest improvements. All the more reason to get everything documented.

How do you set up systems and processes?

When we talk about having processes in place, what we mean is that we don't just make things up as we go along each time we do something. Instead, there is a method. Creating content involves multiple steps. If you are a podcaster, the process is not as straightforward as: switch the microphone on, hit record and speak (if only!).

There are processes prior to recording your podcast episode, the planning and preparation. If you interview guests there's a whole load of steps involved in diary management and booking time with them, confirming details, obtaining information from them and such like. If you record solo shows, as I regularly do, there's often a lot of work involved in research and storyboarding out your episode.

After you have recorded your podcast episode there are so many post production steps, as well as publishing. From editing your audio and uploading to your host, to thanking your guest for coming on the show, to writing show notes and creating social media content.

If you create video content for YouTube, or you livestream on Facebook, or you write blog posts ... whatever your core content is, there are regular steps involved in bringing it all together every time.

You should document all of these processes. There are lots of ways that you can do this. Let me share with you what we do at my agency, Content 10x.

1. Identify your processes

It might sound really obvious, but before you can *document* what your processes are, you need to *identify* what your processes are! It's useful to sit down, on your own or with your team if you have a team, and work out what processes you currently follow when creating content.

To do this, use Excel, Numbers, Google Sheets, whatever is best for you. It's useful to document what the process is, any related processes, if there is an SOP (Standard Operating Procedure) for the process and, if not, do you need one?

2. Write Standard Operating Procedures (SOPs)

At Content 10x we write out all of our processes. Again, you can do this in Word, Google Docs, Pages, whatever is right for you and your team. Once you have identified your processes, write out how to complete the process, step by step. How? Imagine you are training somebody and they only have your process document to help them.

If it helps, accompany your process notes with video tutorials/screen recordings. We like to do this because sometimes it's so much easier to simply show people what to do via video. You can use really simple tools to record your screen like Loom, Screencast or Movavi (Mac only) to name a few. Your SOP can provide links to the supporting videos. Likewise, if it helps explain the process, put images in the document too. E.g. screenshots of your computer.

If you are the only person working on content right now then maybe it seems like overkill to have video recordings and screen grabs or even a written SOP but believe me, you will be happy you did this if you ever want to bring in help.

3. Track the execution of your processes

It's really useful to use project management tools to track the status and execution of your processes. If you've been following along, by now you have documented what your processes are. I'm going to assume you are a weekly content creator and you've documented what you do each week to create and publish your content.

Now you simply need to follow these processes every week.

In order to track this I highly recommend using a project management tool like Trello, Asana, or Basecamp (there are others).

You can create task lists that show (at a task level) the processes within your SOP and you can repeat the list every single time you follow the process, meaning that they are followed correctly and nothing is missed.

4. Incorporating content repurposing into your processes

When you have your content creation processes all set-up you're in a really strong position as a business. Whilst creating content is a creative process and creativity is key, to succeed as a consistent content creator you need to blend creativity with process. There is an art *and* a science to it.

As you're reading this book you are learning about lots of different ways to repurpose your content. The steps involved in content repurposing can be added to your existing content creation processes. I've mentioned previously that whether you are repurposing content, or creating your core content, it's all content creation. Content repurposing is all part of the same process.

When you start to repurpose content, especially if it's you working alone without a team, I recommend taking it one new step at a time. A big mistake that people make is they think the world of content repurposing sounds fantastic, and they try and do too much at once. What often happens in that situation is you do a lot for a very short amount of time, lose the consistency, and eventually end up back at square one!

It's far better to start with adding one extra repurposing step to your current process and work on that for a while before adding more. I talk about this more in chapter 18, covering approaches to repurposing when you are following a DIY approach.

If you are *not* doing it all yourself, and you have someone or a team to help you, then it's still important to take things one step at a time. With resources available you can move and scale faster with your content repurposing approach than you would if you were going it alone.

When you are defining your processes and incorporating content repurposing into them, think about how you are going to measure and track your efforts too. Build in processes related to tracking and measurement. Refer to chapter 25 where I share lots of insight into what to measure and how.

Batching content and automation

As I've mentioned previously, there is definitely an art and a science to effectively repurposing content. You need to really understand your audience and be creative. You also need processes in place to ensure that you complete the tasks each week and measure results. When it comes to creating your content, it's a really good idea to batch produce if you can. I talk more about this in chapter 18 but essentially what I'm referring to is putting some time aside to create a whole batch of content that can be published over a longer period of time.

For example, setting aside a whole day or half-day to record four, five, six (or more!) podcast episodes or videos, that can then be published over the next month or two. This is a highly effective and productive way to work. It often takes a fair amount of planning, for example, writing out scripts for your videos and podcasts or pre-planning having all of your show guests on one day. However you like to do things, putting the time in to condense production efforts into one batch at a time really reaps rewards in the longer term.

When it comes to publishing your content and getting it in front of your audience, you can look for ways to automate the process and schedule tasks in advance in order to save time.

For example, your blog posts can be written and put onto your website, along with whatever else you post with your blog, e.g. video, podcast players, graphics etc, but you can schedule the date that the post is going to publish in advance.

Similarly, your podcast episodes can be scheduled for future release via your podcast host. Your videos can all be scheduled for future release on YouTube. If you can't do this, you likely need to convert your channel to a brand account.

All of your social media content can be scheduled for posting on a future date and time. On Facebook you can schedule your page posts from within the platform itself, which is great because you are still posting natively on the platform (getting as much reach as possible) but controlling the time that you post.

A more straightforward way to manage scheduling social media across multiple platforms (whilst also monitoring engagement) is to use a social media scheduling tool like Smarter Queue, Buffer, Meet Edgar, CoSchedule, Agorapulse or Hootsuite (and there are lots more!). I talk about this more in chapter 14 on repurposing social media.

A combination of batch producing your core content, and scheduling content where it's possible and where it makes sense, can really help you with time management and productivity.

Cross posting on social media

I often get asked the question, "should you automate posting content and, in particular, should you cross-post when it's on an option?"

Cross-posting is when you post your content from one social media platform to another, automatically. In particular, I get asked about Instagram a lot, specifically whether you should let Instagram also post to Facebook and Twitter. Is this a smart repurposing strategy or just plain lazy?!

Firstly, does it affect the reach of your post?

I did some research and found a really interesting study conducted by Agora Pulse. They were keen to find out if cross-posting from Instagram to Facebook affected your reach on Facebook. Their initial hypothesis was that it would have no effect at all. However, they were wrong with their hypothesis.

In fact, there was a noticeable negative effect on the reach of their Facebook post when posted directly from Instagram versus native on Facebook's platform. From the small study that they completed they found that native posts on Facebook got 72% higher reach than the same post, cross-posted from Instagram!

Their conclusion - don't cross-post from Instagram to Facebook if you don't want to see negative effects on your post reach within Facebook.

Admittedly things change on social media platforms all the time. The algorithms that decide how to treat content are constantly being updated as is the user interface, so this finding may not still be the case today. However, I found it really interesting that Instagram and Facebook are both owned by the same company yet they still far prefer you to post native content instead of cross-posting from one platform to the other.

This finding would not have surprised me at all if reach on Twitter posts was considerably lower when cross-posted from Instagram because they are entirely separate organizations. If there's one thing we know about social media platforms, it's that they all want to keep people on their own land! But regardless of whether it's Facebook or Twitter, if you auto-post from Instagram, prepare to see a potential negative impact on your post's audience reach.

Every platform has unique features

In chapter 17 I really went to town emphasizing that social media platforms are all different and you need to respect them. This is an important consideration when it comes to cross-posting from platform to platform.

Is it appropriate to be so blasé with what you're posting, such that you just assume it carries the same relevance across platforms? I would argue that it's often very obvious when someone has cross-posted and it can, dare I say it, be a little annoying because features do not carry over from platform to platform.

For example, links. On Instagram you can't have clickable links in your post captions so there's not a lot of point in putting a link that people cannot click. Instead, when we post to Instagram, we're more likely to have a call to action along the lines of 'link in bio'.

On Facebook and Twitter you *can* include a link and so what do you do if you are going to cross-post? Do you put a link in Instagram that people can't click? Or do you have no link at all to suit your Instagram audience, but then you lose the opportunity to include a link on Facebook and Twitter? Plus, you wouldn't want to have the 'link in bio' CTA carrying over to Facebook or Twitter because that makes no sense!

This is a classic example of when cross-posting simply doesn't look good.

There are also complications when it comes to the use of hashtags. For example, Instagram is all about hashtags, especially if you're trying to grow your audience whereas we don't really use hashtags on Facebook at all. There is some evidence that hashtags can even reduce your reach on a Facebook post.

There is a way around this if you want to cross-post from Instagram. My tip is to have no hashtags at all in the wording of your post/description and instead put the hashtags in your comments. Hashtags are picked up by Instagram whether they are in the post captions or in the first comments so you're all good with that approach. If you do this then at least when you click the cross-post to Twitter or Facebook buttons you won't have all those Instagram hashtags carrying over to those platforms.

Similar to hashtags, you need to think about terminology too. For example, terms like 'like', 'share', 'double tap', 'follow', 'retweet' aren't totally interchangeable across each platform. When you write your posts, if you are going to cross post, keep your description relevant to all platforms.

In my opinion the cross-posting from Instagram to Twitter is quite a funny experience for people on Twitter because they are provided with a short amount of text (which usually gets cut off) followed by a link. The link takes them to Instagram where they actually see the image posted. They don't see the image directly on Twitter at all. I guess this is great for Instagram because you post on Twitter but only in so much as to get people from Twitter straight over to Instagram. This explains why Instagram are perfectly content to allow you to cross-post to Twitter!

If you simply don't have time to go to Twitter and post there then it's not exactly the worst thing in the world to do to cross-post but I would argue that it's far from ideal.

Does cross-posting create a negative impression?

If people notice that you are cross-posting all the time, does this create a negative impression with your audience? It depends on what and how you are posting. It also depends on who your audience are, their sensitivities and expectations.

If you have the time to go to each platform and spend a moment making your post relevant to the platform instead of cross-posting I think it's worth it. I'm all about respecting the platform! Posting directly on a platform (native) is likely to provide your posts with more audience reach and you can ensure the post is tailored to that platform by using platform specific terminology, links, hashtags, dimensions of graphics etc.

If you don't have time to post everything natively within each platform, whilst cross-posting is an option, you could also consider using social media scheduling tools as mentioned previously. E.g. Smarter Queue, Buffer, Meet Edgar, CoSchedule and Hootsuite, to name just a few.

By using a scheduling/management tool, you can post to all platforms but you get the chance to adapt what you are posting and where. This still isn't considered native posting but it's more tailored and generally more strategically managed than cross-posting. You can respect every single platform and post content that is suitable to the platform and your audience on there.

If you do cross-post, think about where your post is going to be published and make sure you recognize that in your terminology/description.

Whether you post natively, cross-post, or post via a social media scheduling tool, you still need to ensure that you are there to engage with your audience on every platform that you post on. If you get comments, make sure that you engage with people. Be sociable because that's what social media is all about!

In conclusion

It's so important to set up systems and processes for your business. In particular, because it's what this book is about, you must set up systems and processes for your content marketing.

Identify what your existing processes are and then document them. When you have control of your processes you can work out where there is opportunity for change and improvement.

Remember, people will come and go in your business. You cannot be dependent on being as good as your people. You need to be as good as your systems and processes and hire great people to follow them!

Work out how you can incorporate content repurposing into your daily and weekly processes. Take it one step at a time. The most important thing is to be consistent. Batch producing content and scheduling your publishing can really help with time management and your overall productivity.

PART 5

Next Steps & Resources

CHAPTER 27

You've got this!

We've come to the end of our journey together. Congratulations and thank you for taking the time to read my book!

If you've taken one thing from this book, I hope it's that you're going to repurpose your content! Honestly though, I hope that you have taken a lot more than just one thing from this book. I hope that you feel equipped with lots of ideas, tactics and strategies for getting the most value from the content that you create.

Mastering the art and science of content repurposing can help transform you into a content machine. This in turn will help you to get in front of your target audience, converting content consumers to leads and leads to sales, growing your business.

I'm not saying it will always be easy. You'll need to work out where your strengths lie and what is possible within the constraints of your time and available resources. You'll also want to identify when it's time to invest in getting help.

The most important thing is to be consistent.

Consistency is key. It's not about publishing a video once in a while, occasionally blogging, and going live on Facebook when you're in the mood. Instead it's about consistently showing up for your audience.

Make sure that you incorporate systems and processes to help you execute your content repurposing tasks. After you have consistently created your content, your content repurposing machine needs to kick in to create more and more content.

Content repurposing is not a 'set and forget' approach.

You need to ensure that you respect the platforms that you publish to and you need to show up and engage with people. If you are getting likes, comments and shares, be there to interact with people. Be sociable. If you are not getting any likes, comments or shares, look at how you can change things up a little. Test, test and do more testing until you find what works for your audience on each platform.

Content repurposing requires a shift in mindset.

You need to be prepared to see the maximum potential in all that you create. Content repurposing actually starts at the initial idea and creation stage. Do not let content repurposing be an afterthought. Don't think after you have created your content, hmmm, what will I repurpose this into? Have a plan from the start and your content repurposing endeavors will go far more smoothly.

And remember, you do not have to do it alone!

Throughout this book you've heard mention of the tools and resources that my team and I have built to help you implement everything you've learned. Go to www.Content10x.com/toolkit to find out more about The Content 10x Toolkit. If you want a single resource to help you implement what you have read it this book, today, this is all that you need.

My podcast and blog, www.content10x.com/blog, are full of practical resources, tips and advice that will help you with every aspect of content repurposing (you'll also have the opportunity to see the power of content repurposing in action with almost every single post!)

If you are interested in my creative agency, Content 10x, and our done-for-you content repurposing service head to www.Content10x.com.

If you are a TED or TEDx speaker, or any kind of speaker, and you're keen to find out more about our one-time repurposing package for your talk (video and photographs) then please head to www.Content10x.com/ted10x

You can also reach out to me on Instagram, Twitter and Facebook. I'm @content10x on all of them.

Thank you for reading my book, I hope you have found it helpful and enjoyable. Good luck and happy content repurposing - aka content 10x-ing!

IMPLEMENT WHAT YOU LEARN IN THE BOOK TODAY!

The Content 10x Toolkit equips you with templates, tools, videos, processes, swipe files and more...so that you can repurpose your content, reach more people, and grow your business

Head to **www.content10x.com/toolkit** to find out more

CHAPTER 28

Resources

Throughout the book a number of resources have been mentioned. For a full clickable list of all of the resources organized by category, head to www.content10x.com/bookresources

Disclaimer: Some of these links are affiliate links meaning that if you click and then purchase, I'll get a small affiliate income. You do not pay any more than you would otherwise. If you really don't like the thought of buying me a cup of coffee, simply type the name of the resource into Google instead.

About the Author

Amy Woods is one of the world's leading authorities on content repurposing and helps content creators to maximize their reach and impact online.

She is the Founder of Content 10x, a creative agency that specializes in content repurposing. Amy and her team work with successful businesses and ambitious online influencers who want to connect with a large audience.

She's also an author, podcaster and speaker, having delivered talks about content repurposing on many coveted stages around the world.

Find out more at www.content10x.com

Printed in Great Britain
by Amazon